The
Secret of
Happiness
Locked in
Your Fears

The Foundation of Life Long Inner Peace,
Harmony, Health and Weight Loss.

Zsuzsanna Fajcsak-Simon

BALBOA.
PRESS

A DIVISION OF HAY HOUSE

Balboa Press books may be ordered through booksellers or by contacting:

Balboa Press
A Division of Hay House
1663 Liberty Drive
Bloomington, IN 47403
www.balboapress.com
1 (877) 407-4847

Print information available on the last page.

ISBN: 978-1-9822-2430-1 (sc)
ISBN: 978-1-9822-2432-5 (hc)
ISBN: 978-1-9822-2431-8 (e)

Library of Congress Control Number: 2019910104

Balboa Press rev. date: 08/06/2019

With lots of Love.

Recommendation

During my journey of growth, I have developed many questions, searched for many answers, came across many theories and faced many insecurities.

Today, when self-development programs are coming out of the faucet, it is difficult to choose, which way to go.

This book is unique because no one tells you what you did wrong or what you should do. You will come to this knowledge on your own. The experience is yours, when you stop putting energy into preventing yourself from seeing "who you are" and finally use it for your own good, to take these steps.

Start reading, and you will never be the same person you were up until now.

If you are ready, I wish you the best for entering into infinity.

If you are not sure about change, then put this book on your shelf and dust it off from time to time. Whatever you choose, that will be YOUR JOURNEY.

Jules Simon

As an editor, I set aside emotion while reading, to remain completely impartial. However, upon reading Dr. Zsu's book, that I can only describe as a guide for a personal journey into healing, I found myself deeply and profoundly affected in positive ways. I highly recommend this book to everyone in search of the age old answer, of how to improve the quality of their life.

Siobhan Godsell Hanes

Contents

Foreword

Dear Reader Friend,

Welcome to the *"Live your Life Alive"* program!

Congratulations for being brave enough to choose this book. I am immensely grateful and honored that you allowed me into your life!

I intend to bring you an experience filled reading, with moments you cherish for the rest of your life. Those who have read the book so far, confirmed they received life-impacting, positive instructions.

Before we proceed any further, I would like to ask your permission, to address you directly and openly in this book. This will make your communication and learning more comfortable and productive. Thank you!

How is this book structured?

This book is the first part of the complete *"Live your Life Alive"* program and comprises of two sections: *"The Past"* and *"The Future."* The second part of the program, *"The Now"* comes later in a separate edition.

The present book is the result of my 25 years of formal studies, professional and personal experience. The most impactful learning, however, came from unlocking my deepest fears and reaching my real inner power.

My studies have been extended by 20 years of yoga practice, 12 years of yoga master trainer practice, 10 years of NLP (Neuro-Linguistic Programming) Coach practice, and 9 years of Vipassana meditation[1] practice.

The first part of this book, *"The Past,"* contains the most powerful teachings in my life. This knowledge came as a Divine gift from God, as I call it. (All other resources are noted throughout.)

The channeling of these Divine gifts began in early 2011. I had no idea where these Divine voices came from. The voices came during meditations, workouts or running. The most powerful learning came in the middle of the night about 3 am. I had nights I was writing notes in bed on my phone. These voices were answers to specific life events and crystal clear instructions, which enlightened my soul and filled my heart with deep inner peace.

Wisdom had been coming to me unexpectedly after looking at difficulties objectively. The knowledge came with higher density when I saw something

---

[1]   Vipassana meditation is an introverted meditation, which was developed by Gautama the Buddha. This simple meditation process teaches us to look inside of us, and learn to see our thoughts, emotions and life objectively. The result is deep inner peace, gratitude, and living out of loving-kindness and good-will. www.dhamma.org. Vipassana sets a healthy lifestyle, independent of religion.

incorrect in life. I understood that incorrect things were mirrors of myself. I have done these incorrect things, hurting others and myself in my past. At that time I only had incorrect tools. The wisdom brought the correct tools, the precise, definite life instructions.

I started to write these Divine life instructions and statements on social media. The positive feedbacks to these posts have been growing ever since. More and more people experience change and find solutions to their problems via these messages. More and more people can make a change in their lives, to get what they have been seeking.

These crystal clear instructions bring solutions to life events. This wisdom makes you see the truth and shows you the kind and compassionate way to handle life. These pearls of wisdom cleaned my life out, made me grow to become a better human being, building a new life based on these principles.

As years have been passing, the practice of objective observation and compassion in my own life, extends into life in general. Seeing the truth in others, helps me to find the root cause of their problems and form step by step, easy to implement solutions. The solutions empower one to face fears and go forward bravely on a path of growth. The answer or knowledge within, comes up to the surface when specific questions are asked. I help my clients to see their problems and find the solution themselves.

Everyone has to see the truth themselves. One needs time to discover the root cause, the real root cause and the truth about the problem. The truth at first is bitter and painful. The truth about myself was very painful for me too. When the truth comes out, more likely, we actually "die" in the process. Who in us dies? Our old self dies and the new selfless person is born.

Subsequently, I found videos and books on gurus, who went through similar experiences by walking through different paths.

Many roads are leading to the top of the hill. One can experience change in different ways.

Writing and sharing one's experience of change, can motivate and inspire others to step onto the road too. The more detailed the change process, the less afraid people will be to take these steps.

One never knows when the so-called "aha moment" happens for others. I hope to inspire you to write about your experiences too.

Lastly, I realized, that wisdom is actually nothing more than being connected to your intuition. It resides IN you!

Once you unlock the ego-created-fears, your intuition path opens, and you will receive wisdom for your own life. Your intuition is the path to connect you to the Divine portal. Any information coming from the Divine portal, brings healing. Healing for you, your family and the world.

It happened to me! I healed myself, transformed my past! With the transformation of my fears, I changed my life. I finally live the life in inner peace and love that I have always dreamed of.

If I can do it, so can you! It can happen for you too!

The second part of the *"Live your Life Alive"* program, *"The Now,"* will contain lots of tools and useful, practical information for a long, healthy happy, and active life.

My last task, before unlocking the treasures in this book, is to humbly pass you light, strength, and love from my heart to yours.

I hope this book can make at least a small change in your life too. Any small change is significant! If small change continues to occur, you will multiply your results and reach a happier, healthier and more successful life.

I wish you a wonder-filled journey through your beautiful discoveries and experiences.

Dr. Zsu

Acknowledgment

My deepest gratitude for S. N. Goenka, who revived Vipassana meditation 50 years ago. Through establishing the Art of Living Trust, he made it possible for millions of people to learn this beautiful technique to heal and clean one's self. The regular practice of Vipassana meditation cleaned out the deep-seated emotional issues and allowed light into my body, my mind, my heart, and soul. I am devoted to growing every day.

I don't have enough words to express my gratitude to Tedi Ware, my Theta Healing mentor, who has been working with me very diligently. I am eternally thankful for our initial year, accomplishing nine impactful sessions, to reach the cellular level and speed up the cleaning process. She helped to transform blocks that I could not reach.

My affectionate gratitude for my husband Jules Simon, who brought the real light into my life. Being with him I am able to grow in the light and practice acceptance, patience, understanding, compassion, emotional support, honesty, humility, humbleness, while living with good-will and loving kindness. I am very thankful for our two dogs Rocco and Albert who taught me compassion on the highest level.

I am very thankful to all my clients that I worked with and grew close together, to further develop my focus, objective observation, acceptance, and compassion. Learning to apply the special blend of strength and gentleness is the key to help them to grow effectively.

I am very grateful to Dr. Terezia Fauszt, who taught me the ageless living and the maximization on the Universal energies via Feng Shui. She is a living example, how devoted work can build society while giving warm loving care for all. She is an example of pure unconditional love.

I am very thankful for my family and friends around the world for their acceptance, understanding, and support, which made it possible to share the foundation of how to *"Live your Life Alive"*, beginning with this book: *"The Secret of Happiness locked in your fears."*

A special thank you for my editor Siobhan Godsell Hanes, for her time, talent and for "removing the Hungarian accent" as she calls it, from my writing. Smoothing it all out while maintaining the originality of the book.

I have tears in my eyes to express my gratitude to those Friends, who contributed and raised the funds to make this book physically come true worldwide.

I hope every one of you that helped, can feel your own share in the book. Be proud of yourself for taking part in such a cause, which will help the world to heal its fear.

Thank you ALL for believing in me! Thank you for all your support, which is helping millions now.

Introduction

Fear and Secret. Two words, which are married to each other. Even though we don't talk about these words openly, they are in a relationship.

Let's take a closer look and see what the word fear means?

Fear, commonly known as a feeling, shows up as anxiety and restlessness. There are unrealistic things behind this fear feeling. Fear is blocking and limiting our life, our happiness, our relationships and our development on any level. Fears are holding us back to live a complete and fulfilled life. These fears are harmful and destructive.

Fear appearing as an inner warning, comes from our intuition and can be positive in our lives. This is a signal telling you to pay attention to something for your own good.

The difference between the two different kinds of fear, is the body sensations that come to the surface. The first fear is based on something irrational, something that doesn't exist and something which is unknown. Therefore, it causes anxiety and restlessness. The second type of fear, is a signal from your intuition, a real warning sign. This warning sign is about a specific actual event or circumstance. Paying attention to this warning sign can prevent mishaps. If we act upon these intuitive signs, we prevent unnecessary things from happening. If we don't act upon them, we create resentment, hatred, anger and more stress.

There are three reasons why we don't act upon our intuition. The first is the lack of trust in ourselves and the second is fear of our intuition. The third reason is that we believe that we don't deserve to have such an inbuilt signaling system.

How does the word secret, get married to the word fear?

Our deepest fears hide within secrets. Secrets protect our fears from being found out. These secrets prevent us from looking at our deepest fears. The secret keeps the fear non-existent too.

Fear is one common taboo. Fears make you apply many different protective behaviors. Keeping our fears secret, is the way the ego creates an incredible victory over us and keeps us in fright mode.

Some people will openly talk about their fears. These are superficial fears, like the fear of fire or fear of driving. However, deep down this is not what they are afraid of. The subject of the deep fear is something else, and of course, it is hiding in deep secret as well. We will talk about these deep fears later.

Another specialty of fears, is that they mask themselves and can keep multiple locks on each other.

The first part of this book works with the past. *"The Past"* part of the book contains tools to identify your fears, then transform and resolve them.

Fears are complex and have many different shapes and forms to control our lives. This section of the books gives a gentle hand to guide you through the process to face your fears and unlock the knowledge hidden in them.

Let us discover:

- Why are our fears so secretive?
- Why does it feel like an impossible task to face your fears and unlock them?

Please know, that you are not alone with your fears. Millions of people live in fear. However, those who unlocked and transformed their fears, discovered the gift inside them, which made a change in their lives. They transformed their fears into positive life instructions. Putting these specific life instructions to work, they created a new and happy life.

The second part of this book is *"The Future."* This part contains planning tools to set up new achievable goals. This section is about building short and long-term goals for your entire lifespan. You will learn to dream big and also to plan step by step, taking life at bite-size pieces.

This part of the book includes an effective evaluation tool for your value and belief system. This evaluation helps you identify very deep-seated blocks, which may be still holding you back from reaching your potential. This evaluation exposes more fears and then prompts you to transform them. Once you transform all your blocks, you become unstoppable!

The second part of the *"Live your Life Alive"* program is *"The Now."* (Due to its volume, it comes in a separate book.) The Now contains tools and practical information to live our life healthy and in high quality. This book provides useful and practical information on exercise, nutrition, nutritional supplements and hydration and meditation practices.

The *"Live your Life Alive"* program sets the foundation for total health. The program completely changes your lifestyle. The foundation is to establish happiness and deep inner peace. The implementation of the information and tools presented are highly individual. You can start anywhere and complete the program in the order it suits you. This is how we walk step by step and cover all aspects of health, from mind, soul, and body.

Each chapter gives understanding and experience. Read it from the beginning or pick any section randomly. It doesn't matter where you open the book, you will find a personalized message for yourself.

Open the locks on your secrets, to expose your fears. Treat your fears with love and break through them gently. Transform your fears to love, kindness, happiness, health, abundance, and success forever!

THE PAST

THE PAST

Realizing the "Creator Within"

> **In this Chapter, you find the answers to:**
>
> - How do I see the relationship between my external environment and my inner emotional life?
> - How did my life become so miserable?
> - How do I understand why my thoughts create my feelings?
> - Do I have an inner voice, which I can always listen to for guidance?
> - How do I create my happiness using free will?

There are many different cultures and conditioning. Therefore, one can understand the title in many different ways.

I am wondering, what would, *"The Creator within"* mean to you?

Webster's says the following about the meaning of the verb, to create:

> To Create (Webster)
>
> To make or produce (something)
>
> To cause (something new) to exist.
>
> To cause (a particular situation) to exist.
>
> To produce (something new, such as a work of art)
>
> by using your talents and imagination.

I can't see into your head. I can only hear and feel the energies from some of you when I say the "Creator" word. Now, the only thing I can do, is to show you, and explain what the word means to me. I would also like to share with you, why I gave "The Creator Within" title, to one of my signature sessions.

First, I would like to make it as clear as a bell, what I don't mean about the word "Creator." I'm not talking about creation in the sense of our existence. Nor am I talking about the creator as God, who made the circumstances for our parents to meet, for our conception.

The creation I'm speaking of is:

- We create our feelings and emotions or, how we feel.
- We create our thoughts, and what we think about.
- We create our words through our communication.

- We create our actions, reactions, behaviors, and addictions.
- We create our life circumstances.

It is also possible that my words are pressing different buttons in you. You may feel upset, feel a dislike or feel a slight opposition. If you feel upset by any of the above, it's completely normal. I still ask you to please stay with me and read on. Let's find out what you're upset feelings mean.

Being upset is a reaction to something you experienced. In this case, you read something here, and the meaning of my words made you upset. It is not the book or the words, but their meaning to you was upsetting. Based on your chosen meaning, you decided to get upset. Consciously or unconsciously, you created the feeling, hence became upset. Similarly, to an angry feeling, we create a whole nine yards of negative feelings. Surprising, isn't it? Can we create our own misery? Please read on, as we uncover this creation, you will understand the entire process.

How is it possible to create our own misery?

- How is it possible that something can make us upset?
- Can anyone or anything possibly make us upset?
- Are we making ourselves upset?
- Are we crazy to give power to anything and anyone to upset us?
- How is it possible that something that happens outside of us, can cause such an emotional reaction within us? One that we don't even know about?

How is it possible that you realize the upset feeling, only when
you are already in pain and misery from being upset?

Excellent questions, aren't they? Have you thought about the answers?

What are the reasons we don't see that we are creating misery?

We don't see it, because our conditioned, automatic behavior patterns are running in us. These automatic behaviors make us blind to see, make us deaf to hear and insensitive to feel.

Where did we lose our sensations?

The loss of our sensations is the result of our conditioning, which happened between 0-7 years of our lives. During this time we received the software, which has been acting like a filter. Whatever comes through the filter, we see, hear or feel. Most of the things, however, go through the filter unknowingly. By the time we grow up, these filters become automatic behavior patterns. These filters control us and define us as adults. These filters attract in certain circumstances to make sure we have enough pain.

These filters in our conditioned mind, create certain protective emotions, feelings, and behaviors to compensate for those feelings we don't want to feel. These filters will delete things, distort things and generalize things. The mind will do everything, and anything to keep you in an illusion and make you believe everything to protect itself. I will explain this in detail later.

How do you know that your mind is conditioned and you live in compensation?

Take a look at your day. The entire day is a series of compensations. In the compensation process, we use different emotions. We use anxiety and stress so we don't have to feel those unwanted emotions, which certain people and circumstances would make us feel. The anger feeling, will keep us away from people who pin-point the truth about us, and that truth is painful.

Covering up the truth needs a compensating behavior. The process of compensation makes us lose time and space. We begin living in our heads. We make all our interpretations and emotions into undeniable beliefs. The conditioned mind-created-illusions become the truth, only because they justify our anger.

In the second phase of the compensation, we actually start looking for circumstances where we can practice our anger, resentment, guilt, fear, blame and feeling like a victim.

These automatic behaviors control us subconsciously so we can hide our deep-seated emotions. This way we cover up all those feelings that we would need to face and work with.

In the third phase of the compensation, the conditioned mind can't handle the feelings anymore. Lastly, the conditioned mind chooses the most comfortable way out, which is numbness.

Being numb is the ultimate protection of the conditioned mind. The mind makes you believe that not feeling anything is the best way to compensate.

When we live numb and can't feel anything, we ensure ourselves about not caring and not feeling anything in life. Living in numbness, we have no clue about where we are and what happens to us. We are never where we physically are. Regardless of the physical disorientation, we still get bored staying in one place for too long.

Another example of the disorientation is when we are not well and are stuck at home. Our head is everywhere but at home.

We continue the illusionary process by building our lives around creating circumstances and events to practice anger, complaining, hatred, and being in pain. We create events to practice rejection, blaming, cheating or humiliation. We attract the circumstances to punish and belittle others, create injustice, sadness, fear, depression and make ourselves a victim. We arrive at living our lives in numbness, yet in constant suffering.

How long do we suffer, before we can change?

There are individual differences in pain tolerance. The length of your suffering depends on when you feel, you have had enough, and say *"Anything is better than this."* I found that the lower the pain tolerance is, the sooner one becomes fed-up with the pain and will do something to change.

Similarly, the higher the pain-tolerance, the longer the suffering lasts. I am not talking about the amount of complaining, but the deep seeded belief about the level of pain one deserves. Some people put their pain in words and some people just swallow it down.

If we look back on our childhood, it becomes visible, that we have been trained for pain. We developed a belief system that "we only deserve suffering" and "something is only valuable if it is painful." We learn to use these painful beliefs as protections. The mind makes you believe that the little pain is your protection from bigger pain. These protections ensure the belief that "life is suffering, and nothing else exists but misery." This suffering belief makes one complain and be dissatisfied all day long. If anyone with this suffering belief wants to change, he or she most likely needs to reach the "death-door." The "death-door" is where one feels so much pain and suffering, that they feel the real threat of death. This is the point for them to really do something and change.

The length of your suffering will be as long as the reaching point: "Anything is better than this."

This is supposed to be the pivot point where change occurs.

Change occurs in a split second.

The road leading to change takes time. It takes time to accumulate enough self-created suffering, so you give up creating more pain.

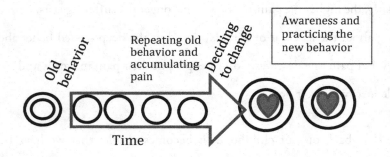

Change happens in a split second when we realize our own suffering. It takes time however, until we reach the point to admit and accept, that what we feel right now is suffering. We also need to recognize, we are the creator of our own suffering. We also accept suffering and are no longer afraid of feeling pain. That is the point when we let go of creating more pain!

The road to the point of change can be a tricky journey. The conditioned mind continually tries to convince you that there is no life, beyond the mind. It is trying to convince you further that life is equal to pain and this is what you deserve.

The conditioned mind also wants to keep you in this pain and tries to pull you back from change. You must be aware of this mind-made program when it arises in you.

Change comes from giving up on being controlled by the mind.

Giving up on the mind comes with being aware that you are so tired of everything. First, you grow tired of the pain. Then you accept pain as pain. You no longer want to change to feel anything else. This is the first time you are brave enough to take pain face to face. You no longer wish to run away from pain. This is the time you begin to realize that your suffering is self-created.

The pivotal point in change, comes when we realize that we can create pain and are also aware that we are capable of creating feelings other than pain!

Realizing our creator status, brings the responsibility to create consciously. Creating consciously, however, takes awareness of the now. If we can live in the now, in the present moment, we find the way out.

The way out of suffering leads through awareness!

The power of awareness

Change begins with awareness. The consequence of awareness is developing the ability to behave and act differently than those behaviors, which created suffering. The changed behavior builds into practice when we become aware. Awareness means mindful. The more aware one becomes, the more change can be put into practice.

First, we have to be aware that we have such a thing as awareness. We get to awaken to our awareness, through training our concentration. When you train your concentration, your awareness or mindfulness becomes sharper and sharper. The more aware you are, the more possibilities will show up in life. Awareness gives room for new, clearer decisions and refined behaviors.

Awareness will help the change process to become temporary and sustained on many different levels.

Now, let us see, the importance of awareness or mindfulness.

How does awareness serve us?

Awareness serves the process of our change, in many ways.

The first gift of awareness is the present moment. Awareness keeps you in the now and keeps you present. If you are aware, the mind can't wander to the past or the future. Awareness keeps you precisely in the now. When you are aware, your body and mind will be in the same geographical place. Doing your chores with awareness makes you conserve your energy. Whatever you do during the day, you will be less tired. Awareness keeps you strong and healthy!

The second gift of awareness is the control over your mind. As long as you are aware, you will see your mind creating illusionary, provoking thoughts and interpretations. Awareness catches the little voice talking in your head, creating labels and making negative criticisms. Awareness will sort your thoughts. Which ones serve you positively and which ones don't. Awareness brings change by stopping the first negative, provoking, thought. Before it becomes a whole thought avalanche and you lose control.

The third gift of awareness is to keep you in touch with your emotions and feelings. Awareness helps to sort through your emotions and feelings, which ones serve you and which ones don't. Awareness gives a signal when a certain non-serving feeling arises, and you need to apply patience and objective observation. Similarly, awareness helps to observe pleasant feelings, to prevent excess and craving more. Any feeling or emotion, pleasant or non-pleasant, will pass. This way the power of awareness helps to stop ourselves from doing something that we will resent later.

The fourth gift of awareness is prompting us to engage only in proactive actions. Awareness tells us what to do. By staying aware, we realize the appropriate solution. Awareness keeps you in the mindset of rising above and finding solutions, which serve everyone.

Awareness allows us to observe the current destructive thoughts and emotions. Awareness gives us strength to remain patient and gives us time to wait, breathe and do nothing. Awareness gives us the power of stillness and Zen calls it "the power of doing, by not doing." Our breathing is the only doing. Breathe and practice existing. With this, we create time and space to decide what else we would like to do, instead of those actions led by destructive thoughts and emotions.

How do we use the mind to serve us?

Let us learn about the conditioned mind in more detail.

When we increase our awareness, we use our mind to think only when we need a solution. When a problem arises, we turn the mind on. We either have an answer or we don't. We may conclude that currently there is no solution and we let go to think further. After the conclusion, we turn the mind off and go into observation mode.

The observation mode is compelling to bring a solution. The so-called "Doing, by not doing" is actually doing something. While in observation, non-searching mode, we rest our minds. Only a relaxed mind can become creative to bring a solution. So as magical as it is, by non-thinking we suddenly get an answer or solution. The key is staying aware of our mind.

Awareness is outside of your mind, and not in your mind. Awareness carries so many benefits that we can call it the game changer of your life.

How does awareness make our life better?

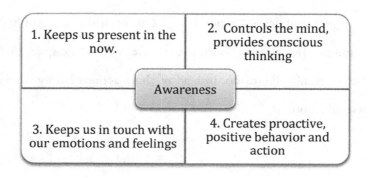

The first step in training your awareness, is understanding the battle in your mind.

Everyone has awareness. Some people are also convinced about its benefits. Most people, however will say that awareness is too hard. Did you think about who in you, is really saying *that awareness is too hard?*

The conditioned mind wants you to believe that awareness is too hard. This is how the conditioned mind wants to prevent you from changing. It ignites a fight in you, so you don't change. Let's take a closer look at this battle, so you have a clear understanding of it.

Change is difficult for the conditioned mind as it refers to a process or journey. A journey takes time and effort. It takes you to a place you haven't been to and don't know about.

Wouldn't it be nice to have a pill or a shortcut for awareness? There are pills for many things, but unfortunately not for awareness.

> *Reaching awareness is a process, a journey and it takes time. You must accept this. This process or journey has to be experienced to gain benefits.*

The level of your awareness shows the effort you put into the practice.

Training your awareness is a life-long process. Accept it.

If you don't train your awareness, you simply can't see your old behaviors to make the change you want. You can promise and say convincingly, "I will change." However, if you don't put effort into training your awareness, you can only practice your old behaviors. It is as simple as that.

Practice takes time. Anything, which takes time and requires effort is referred to as a journey. The conditioned mind doesn't know what journey means and is afraid of the effort. The effort means a struggle for the conditioned mind because it lacks the prerequisites: Self-discipline, diligence, and perseverance. If you already practiced these behaviors, your conditioned mind couldn't convince you about the struggle. You will struggle your entire life though, if you don't apply self-discipline, diligence, and endurance in your life.

You must accept that training takes effort and focus. So what? If you focus, you avoid struggle and make things easier. If your focus is off, your mind makes you struggle.

Only when you put effort into training your focus,
can you begin practicing your new behavior.

You must accept awareness-training to be part of your life. Training your awareness is another task like taking a shower or eating lunch. You have to learn to enjoy your awareness-training just like you enjoy a tasty meal.

The conditioned mind knows only to crave for something that you don't have. The conditioned mind craves further and demands to get things done, when you are in the midst of something. The conditioned mind can't stand anything that takes time. It wants it right away.

The hardest part is going through the initial "battle" phase, while you realize, accept and feel grateful to do what it takes to train your awareness. You do the daily training happily, as you realize this is the only way out of misery.

Training your awareness is the prerequisite to
practicing new and genuine behavior.

There is excellent news.
By training your awareness, you, just
like everyone else, can change!

The key is to be aware and able to rise above, when your mind says: "*You are lazy, undisciplined, have no endurance and change is impossible.*"

The more training you invest into your awareness,
the more opportunity you have to change.

What happens when the conditioned mind is in control?

Have you asked yourself and wondered about the question: "Do I know what else I want to create?"

Stop here and think for a moment. Now answer this question, please.

Interestingly the answer to this question shows a lot about the level of conditioning your mind received, while growing up. The answer to this question also reflects where you stand in life due to this conditioning.

If you want to make lasting change, you must answer this question appropriately.

Do you know what else you want instead of what you have?

You don't? The "I don't know" is a common answer. Having no answer is entirely reasonable and totally understandable. Let me explain further. Most of us are conditioned to complain, criticize, be humiliated and get upset. Why? Because, we have been criticized, humiliated, heard only complaining and seen angry, manipulating people. When our mind is conditioned for reactive behavior programs, we have no clue that other programs exist, outside of what we practice.

Conditioned behaviors and emotions

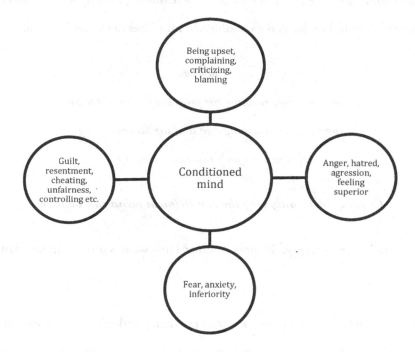

Let me share something else. As strange as it sounds, when the conditioning, criticizing and complaining program is running in us, the mind controls us. Furthermore, we feel awkward in peace, harmony, and love. We start to feel restless and uncomfortable in any other environment than criticizing, complaining, being humiliated or humiliating others and of course being in fear. Inevitably, we start to look for chances to insert a criticism or provoke it. We will attract a situation to blame and generate resentment and abandon others or ourselves. The most exciting thing, is that we all practice the negative behaviors out of good-will and good intentions. We "think" we are helping ourselves. We also justify ourselves about, why we did this and why it was right. Another interesting thing, that we will interfere in situations and make justice for others. We can also have positive reasoning for why we gave others a lesson. We all do this, as the conditioned mind has to always be right!

Did you know?
If you are simply running the program of dissatisfaction,
complaining, blaming and wishing for something
else, you are only practicing craving.

Craving is the only way the conditioned mind can behave.

Let us talk about craving. What is craving? How we recognize it in our daily lives?

Craving is, when you shop obsessively, even when you don't need clothes, cars, cosmetics jewelry or other things. I am sure none of you reading this book can recognize this in yourself...Smiling. Furthermore, craving is when one lives an obsessive sexual life, smoking or drinking out of compulsion. Craving can make one live in financial dependence, stock up on unnecessary gadgets and become obsessed with making money. All behavioral addictions such as fear, anger, criticizing, blaming, being a victim, etc. come from craving. One feels only useful when they can practice these behaviors.

All these addictive behaviors are based on a general subconscious
rejection of the present and craving for something else.

These addictive behaviors become the ruler of our lives. They control and define us.

Craving make us join specific groups, where we feel accepted precisely for the way we are. It is much easier for the conditioned mind to seek out these groups, than to face our rejection issues and learn acceptance. It is also more comfortable for the conditioned mind to use compulsion and addiction to compensate for not daring to face the root of our inner rejection.

Fear is also a compulsion. We also create fear out of addiction. We allow fear to hold our hands and make decisions, which road we should take. Walking along with our fear is the only known and therefore easy way. We will continue to dissect fear a bit later, however, let's stop at the addiction.

Smoking is another addiction. Let us see how smoking serves you. Smoking buys you time, the "me" time. While one smokes, one takes time out exclusively for oneself. Smoking buys time, which is free from worry. While one smokes all seems well, and the whole world is round. There are no problems that exist in this space. We allow ourselves to feel important and valuable as long as the cigarette lasts.

What do we really crave?

Is it the cigarette or the feeling that we are actually buying, by smoking?

We don't crave the cigarette, but rather the feeling of being important and deserving. We crave to feel special and valuable.

We can continue the analysis of all addictions. However, the foundation for all dependencies is the feeling of craving.

The bottom line is that we crave the feeling of craving.

Craving addiction

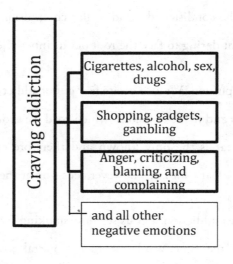

When craving becomes an addiction, we only know one feeling, the feeling of craving. Craving addiction shows up in every part of our lives. We know only wanting, desiring, needing, hoping, dreaming and not reaching.

If we reached a goal, we would have to stop craving. Without craving, there is no life for the conditioned mind.

Addiction is independent of its object. It doesn't matter what we are addicted to, but the fact that we

have an underlying mental program running, which is CRAVING. We are addicted to the feeling of craving and not to alcohol, drugs, sex, anger, etc....

Understanding the craving addiction, you can see now how people who crave, can't reach any goals in their lives. They are addicted to craving or wishing. If they reached a particular goal, their wishing would stop. Regardless of the magnitude of their possessions, wanting and not having is their only comfort zone. They simply don't know what to do with the feeling of "I have." They only know the "I don't have" feeling. They have never seen or experienced how to live with the feeling of "I have."

A person who doesn't "have" generally criticizes everyone and everything. Nothing is ever good enough for him or her. If you ask them what shall be done differently, they will say: "Why are you asking me, you should know that as it is not my task to know!"

Another awakening moment is, when we realize that we don't know what we want, because we only know how to crave.

We don't know what we want because we haven't really seen any other behavior in our lives, other than what we practice. We haven't seen relationships based on acceptance, love or patience. We haven't seen people communicating with understanding compassion and respect. We haven't seen a personal and business relationship based on honesty and fairness where everyone is a winner. However, this is not the end of our life, because we can always learn. Thankfully, with practice, we can discover new behaviors too.

If we haven't seen and experienced acceptance, love, patience, respect, compassion, and fairness, it is time to learn them now. If we don't learn the new behavior tools, the mind doesn't have any other option, but to practice what it knows. We only know the old habitual programs.

Changing old un-serving behaviors, assumes the practice of awareness and putting the mind through the transformational exercise. The beautiful thing about the transformational exercise, is that the mind will realize by itself what to do.

Through the transformation process, we get the new software, which includes new behavioral tools.

How do we create lasting change and new software?

> *The new software is the collection of new behavioral tools,*
> *which replace the old destructive and addictive behaviors.*

The first step in building new software, is training your awareness. Awareness is the foundation for the new software to be downloaded. The more aware we are, the more conscious we become. The more conscious we are, the more we can stay aware of our behavior. We can then sort out and clearly distinguish between serving and non-serving behaviors. Real change takes place when we can choose our new response consciously, put it into practice and experience the changed result.

A change in behavior can come from two places, intellectualization or compassion.

For change to last, the change in behavior has to come from compassion, from inside our heart. Change has to come from every cell of the heart and the body.

Change is lasting when the changed behavior
comes from the cellular level.
Only cells (atoms) vibrating with loving kindness
can produce genuine loving behavior.

Characters of a person with genuine love

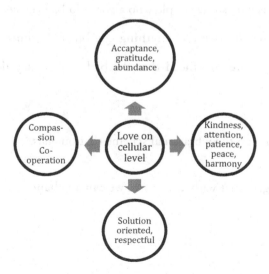

Genuinely good behavior begins inside our cells. Genuinely good behavior needs no circumstance or condition. If you want to behave positively, then teach your body to vibrate positively.

How do you know if your body cells vibrate positively or negatively?

The answer is straightforward. When you are not aware, you don't know your vibrations. When you don't know or remember your vibrations, the mind takes over. When the mind takes over you end up doing things to make you feel upset, stressed or angry. The loss of awareness about your behavior is the result of your unconscious negative inner vibrations.

Your positively vibrating cells however, fuel awareness.

A behavior, bad or good, is genuine and matches the underlying inner vibrations. Imagine the cellular vibration of an unconscious destructive behavior! This is why some people who always do bad things are called bad to the bone. They don't know anything else but pain, hurting others and themselves. They are convinced that the bad things they do are actually good.

One can act only on the vibrational scheme that one has.

The good thing, is that with awareness, we can all change this!

What happens when the behavior comes from an intellectual level?

What is pretending?

As you see now, a behavior, positive or negative, conscious or unconscious, can come from the intellectual or cellular level. A positive, intentional intellectually rooted behavior has expectations. A positive unconscious, heart originated behavior is free giving and has no expectations.

Pretending is an intellectual originated behavior. There are 2 types of pretending. One is unconscious, the other, conscious. Regardless of the conscious or unconscious behavior, pretending behavior is always well intended.

Unconscious pretending is a behavior we use when an external condition forces us to be kind or helpful. We genuinely believe that the circumstance caused our behavior. We also pretend when there is something at stake, the truth is about to be found out about us.

We pretend something didn't happen, that we didn't want to fulfill, as we couldn't say no to it. We pretend out of fear, so the truth remains covered. We are so afraid of the truth that we unconsciously pretend or lie.

Conscious pretending takes place when we must save our rear ends so we create a lie. We pretend to be kind and manipulate others, to gain a good impression or something else from them.

We must pretend to divert attention from the truth.

Conscious pretending however is an effective tool in the process of change, when we don't know a specific positive behavior. Conscious pretending is when we copy someone else, who is genuinely behaving kindly and gratefully. We mimic until it becomes a part of us. During the learning period of our new behavior, conscious pretending comes to our service. We consciously pretend and act with kindness and gratitude, when we are learning to live with compassion and gratitude.

Wouldn't it be amazing to behave kindly
all the time, without much effort?
Can you imagine living your life in peace and acceptance?

The first way to teach our body cells to vibrate with acceptance and gratitude is through recall. Recall works when you have experienced accepting something, not wanting to change something, or being grateful for something in your life. Now go back to that time and recall this feeling. Now use these reference feelings consciously. Now vibrate the feeling of acceptance and gratitude throughout your body, then express acceptance and gratitude in your behavior or action.

If you haven't been grateful or haven't seen anyone who is grateful, look for people who are accepting and express gratitude. Observe how they say "Thank you." Observe their tone of voice and their timing. Observe the circumstances in which they say it. Now copy them. This is a very, very good start! I personally learned to live with gratitude this way when I was in my mid-twenties. I copied those very dear genuine people in my life that

I felt great to be with. I felt great to be with them as they accepted me and were grateful for what I had done for them. I practiced and practiced until it became more comfortable and easier. Living with genuine acceptance and gratitude was the result of cleaning my emotional life out.

The journey to reach genuine kindness may begin with conscious pretending of kindness and gratitude. Conscious pretending will make you familiar with the new behavior and then new vibration. So go ahead and copy others behaving out of genuine compassion and gratitude. This exercise is an essential step to teach your body to vibrate kindly and lovingly.

The third powerful technique is Theta healing, which teaches our body to vibrate genuinely positive.

I respect Theta healing for this knowledge and my eternal gratitude for my coach Tedi Ware who helped me through my journey to change my negative, unconscious, vibrations, to those which are really serving me.

Without making the vibrational change in yourself,
you will only make attempts to change.

You will be able to do the changed behavior out of control a few times, then revert back to the original behavior, guided by your conditioned vibrations.

Many of us have to experience many different techniques and practice different kinds of meditations until we reach the work on our cellular level. The work on our cellular level will make it possible to establish and build relationships based on genuine loving kindness. When your cells vibrate with kindness, you are kind to everyone and in any situation. Kindness coupled with firmness will get everything done without craving as well.

Your "Conscious Creator" within, is based on teaching your body cells to vibrate with loving kindness. With these generously loving and kind vibrations, you will create genuinely favorable circumstances to practice loving kindness there.

The process of learning a new behavior

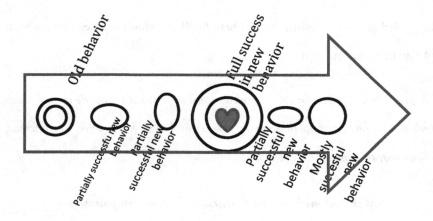

Learning is a process of practice, no matter what you learn. The more aware you are, the faster you learn. Awareness is vital, especially when you are learning a new behavior.

Learning a new behavior needs you to stay aware of
your testing, triggering events or circumstances.

The learning process of a new behavior has its own steps. Steps of knowing how the behavior looks like and also feels like. It is another step to know when to apply the new behavior. Therefore, we will still attract the old kinds of situations so we can practice the new behavior. This is the natural process of growing and making long term change. If you stay aware 1 or 2 times out of the 10 and choose positive behavior consciously, you are winning! If the level of your anger and frustration remains lower than before, it is also progress. The more you practice awareness, the more you will progress toward changing the new behavior into a habit.

The critical step is observing the thought or feeling that leads to the old behavior. Observing the first thought or feeling, requires your sharp focus to work on your awareness.

Accept that the learning process takes time. Forgive yourself when you see yourself falling into your old, negative behaviors. This circumstance happened so you can practice forgiveness.

The negative attraction will fade out when you no longer need your old un-serving behaviors.

You no longer need to and want to practice your old behaviors, to hurt others and yourself. Pain is no longer serving you. You finally realized that the old behaviors are harmful to everyone and you. The only thing that serves you is the loving-kindness, compassion, and goodwill for all.

Traveling into another culture where these new behaviors are habitual, can be very helpful in your own practice. Being with naturally kind people, speeds up your personal growth. Visiting some countries of Arabia, East-Asia or the Far East can be very useful for this purpose. The positive vibrations of the people in these countries, make it very easy and non-threatening to practice the new positive, loving, kind, behaviors. Being with these loving people, sets your new positive behavioral patterns faster and smoother. I lived in Asia for 11 years and received an incredible opportunity to grow.

What is the meaning of the Law of Attraction?

Working on the cellular level is the prerequisite to realize and experience "The Law of Attraction."

If the underlying vibrations of the new behaviors are genuine, with time and practice, they will become habitual. The practiced new habits then become your new you.

> *The growing process takes time and commitment from you. The commitment to practice diligently, attentively and with endurance.* ***It takes time until the vibrations of the old negative habits fade out, and the new positive vibrations take their place.***

This is when the change takes place on the cellular level. This is when we become so aware that we will be able to feel all of our vibrations. We can recognize and differentiate our vibrations. We can observe them and let only those vibrations come to the surface, which serve us.

Observing vibrations on the cellular level doesn't mean you suppress the un-serving feelings. Observing objectively means accepting feelings, without any reaction. When this vibration is negative it is time to excuse ourselves, quiet down and just observe our feelings objectively without any expectation. Objective observation of those feelings arising in you, is not their suppression. It is their acceptance. We talk about the process of observation later.

When you are committed to change, you only allow loving kindness vibrations to come to the surface as words and actions. Love and respect yourself enough to make a vow to yourself that you allow only positive vibrations to actualize in thought, word or action.

The more we vibrate positively, the more

positive things will happen in our lives.

Our positive cellular vibrations will ensure success in everything, what happens to us! Everything will serve us!

Now we come to the realization or meaning of "The Law of Attraction." If you can genuinely create the positive vibrations and let them become automatic, habitual programs, your old conditioned behaviors, will have no space or way to vibrate in you.

You have two choices in life: Learn to be conscious or continue to be unconscious.

Conscious vibration will build you and serve your growth. Unconscious vibrations will control you, take over your life and destroy you.

As your awareness, mindfulness sharpens, you will be able to observe the spark of the old behaviors. You will be able to catch the very first thought or feeling, which differs from the positive ones.

Use your circumstances as a mirror of your inner self. If things don't work out the way you wanted, look at yourself deep inside. See how you vibrated earlier and what possibly triggered the event. Recognizing life events, based on the vibrations running in you, is the next step. Your vibrations such as dislike and anger, create events so you can express your dislike and anger even more. These are true for all negative and positive vibrations.

Understanding your dislikes, is a significant step in making change last.

Don't dislike and wish for your negative habits to go away. Don't hate them, don't desire anything in place of them, just accept them. This way you start practicing the acceptance vibrations, which will be the bottom line to stop your inner fight against your own self.

Change comes without wanting or craving for a change!

What is our life all about?

Our life is about learning to manage ourselves on the cellular level, independent of what happens in our lives.

Life continuously brings tests, so whatever happens, we can keep our positive vibration, attitude, behavior, and action.

This is the process of conscious change. Take care and stay aware of your vibrations and continuously sort them to see which ones serve you and which ones don't.

When you are aware of your vibration driven emotions, you have a choice over them. You can observe them objectively, accept them without any reactions, and let them fade out. Then you are in the position to choose positive vibrations like gratitude, which will bring you desired, positive results.

Awaken to the "Creator" as a higher power, the Universe or God, which resides in you!

The Universe, God in you, will keep generating the adverse circumstances to make you realize that you need to change!

If you stay open and observe your feelings, vibrations, eventually you will start feeling the divine guidance, your intuition, which tells you the right thing to do.

The answers to all questions are in you! The questions arise because you need the answer. If you didn't need a specific answer, the question wouldn't arise.

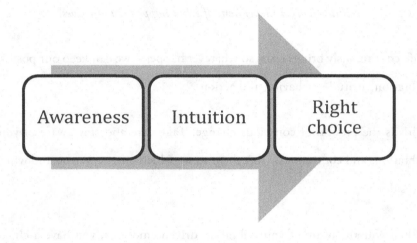

The "CREATOR" LIVES IN EVERY ONE OF US. The creator works through every one of us. We are part of God, therefore, we are all ONE.

It is time however to realize, understand and experience that the only way to survive this life, is via the path of loving kindness.

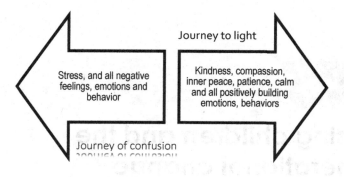

Journey to light

Stress, and all negative feelings, emotions and behavior

Kindness, compassion, inner peace, patience, calm and all positively building emotions, behaviors

Journey of confusion

If you are interested in experiencing the life Transforming Training events, to make this shift of change in you, register for our next "Recharge your life" Retreat. This program can be booked for particular groups in your location, or you are welcome to our site. The program also runs individually online. Inquire in email drzsu@drzsu.com

I send you all my love, strength and health for this amazing journey to discover the magical inner "Creator" within yourself.

Dr. Zsu

Now, let's step into this journey together. Turn the page and let's discover your past.

Understand your past so you can make sense of your present state in life. Then open the gifts locked up in your fears so you can build an empowering future.

Raising children and the generational change

In this Chapter, you find the answer to:

- Why did we become the type of adults we are?

- What if I was not alone in my loveless childhood? Are there others who had the same difficult parenting?

- Where did I learn my parenting style?

- What if we can learn something precious from our past, regardless of how difficult it was?

- What is the solution to resolve our painful past?

- How can we fix and repair the relationship with our kids or parents?

"Where did I come from and where am I heading?" –asked by most of us who reached the point of change.

In this chapter, I will bring you random stories of different children. Through the stories, I want to show you what childhood emotional pain causes, once reaching adulthood. There are many stories, and yours may be another one, which belongs here.

My intention with the stories:

1. To help you realize the importance of your past.
2. To show your history from the angle of objectivity.
3. To show you the personal wisdom locked in those painful memories.
4. To motivate and empower you to step on the road to transform your past.
5. To show you how healing yourself can change your life for the better.
6. To show you the value of change.

Story 1.

Once upon a time, there was a little girl. She was about five years old. She had an older brother who used to pick her up from kindergarten, babysit her in the afternoon, while the parents came home from work. The boy spent most afternoons on the playground with the other kids from the block. The little girl, therefore, joined her brother on the playground. The boys played a lot of football (soccer), and the little girl often joined them. Spending so much time with boys, she felt like one of them. She also wanted to prove that she could keep up. When the boys teased her, she teased them back by kicking the boy's shins. Kicking the boy's shin, was her way of proving her strength.

One afternoon she was the goalie. In one heated moment, a boy standing a few yards away kicked the ball to the goal, but the ball hit straight into the girl's tummy. The pain was unbearable for the girl, she could hardly breathe. The most painful thing for her, was that the boy kicked the ball out of anger. The anger took over the boy, and he had no idea for his action. The little girl didn't understand, how can anyone lose control and do anything hurtful to others.

By the next morning, the pain had escalated and her parents took her to the hospital. The doctors assumed appendicitis and kept her in the hospital. This was the first time the little girl had been to the hospital since birth. She didn't know where she was and what would happen. The pediatric unit at the hospital had strict visitation rules. Visitations were allowed only on the weekend.

The little girl spent the first two days in immense fear. The doctors were coming and going by her bed asking: "Shall we have surgery on her or not?" She had no idea what would happen to her. She saw the other children in the same room who came out of surgery with all sorts of pipes coming out of them. She did not want this.

Luckily, the therapy was successful, and she didn't need surgery.

The little girl looked forward to visitation day on the weekend, which was only two more days away. She was shocked and disappointed that the visitors were not allowed in the hospital room. They were on the balcony on the other side of a glass wall. These glass walls were the windows for every room. She could only see her parents through a window. The balcony was full of parents who were visiting their children. The kids could see their parents through the window. Speaking to them was only possible through a telephone. The children had to wait for their turn to talk to their parents, who were also anxiously waiting on the balcony.

The little girl was very anxious to talk to her parents. She was in tears waiting for her turn. Her impatience grew as did the size of her tears. She wanted to feel the hugs and kisses from her parents. She needed that hug to reassure her that everything was ok and she was safe. She cried and cried and repeatedly said "Take me home!"

When her mom saw the girl crying asking to go home, she turned and ran away. The mom could not take the pain of seeing her daughter in tears, asking to go home. The mom was powerless. However, the little girl had no clue what the mom went through. The little girl only saw her mom leave her and felt hurt. "Mom didn't even listen to me, she just rejected my request." The painful thought went through the little girl. The little girl stayed there with her father and continued to cry. The dad's heart was also broken, seeing his little girl in such emotional pain. Despite his wife leaving, he stayed with an aching heart and talked to his daughter. He did the best he could to make his little girl comfortable. He repeatedly assured her that all would be ok and soon she could come home.

In spite of the dad's efforts, the little girl's heart was broken, seeing her mom leave. She had no idea why her mom, her "everything" and most important life-line, had left her. She could not imagine what had happened. She kept asking herself "Why can't mom stay and talk with me?" The little girl only understood, that someone she loved so much didn't love her back. She didn't understand how her mother could hurt her so much.

Growing up and not understanding this whole situation made the grown woman, enter into many painful relationships. In these relationships, she either pushed men away or got left out in the cold. She was attracted to relationships, where she continuously lived through the "I love you so much why you don't love me back?" story.

Dear parents and parents to be,

The story of the little girl was only the first. I am sure you are beginning to grasp the concept of emotional wounds. I am bringing you more stories to show you how the emotional wounds develop and what they cause by adulthood. I will show you how vital the role is, to be a parent. How important it is to become an emotionally balanced parent, to raise emotionally stable children.

A small thing for an adult can cause a life-changing emotional wound for a child!

(The transformation chapter of this book deals with this painful childhood event and brings tools for resolution.)

Now it is time to look at the same story from different angles. Let us see the point of view from little girl, then the mom and finally a view from objectivity.

At the time of this event, the little girl was five years old. She had no idea that this event was painful for her mom. The little girl didn't understand her mom's inability to manage her problem. The little girl believed her mom, an adult, was supposed to know how to solve problems. Running away from a challenge seemed childish to the little girl. The little girl believed that adults should be stable and secure. Adults don't run away from problems. Adults know all the solutions. The little girl could believed that she did something wrong and this is why her mom left. She could not understand this whole scenario and kept asking "What did I do for you to leave. Where are you going? Why did you leave me here?" She wanted only her mom's consolation.

Lets look at the story from the mom's point of view and objectivity. The mom was hurting inside and was also looking for someone to console and hug her. The mom also couldn't get any consolation.

When someone craves for consolation, they
are unable to give consolation!

To understand the situation further, let us look at the childhood of the mom. The mom grew up in a broken family and without love. Her mom (the grandma of the little girl) always kept a distance to her daughter, thinking her daughter is only here to serve the family and boys. Her sons were the center of her world. The mom didn't receive much love, caring, emotional support and consolation from her mom, only distance. She learned that having a gap between mom and daughter is healthy. Keeping distance is not love. She never experienced a close mother-daughter relationship with love and sharing. Therefore, she could only give the kind of love that she had received.

You can only give what you have received!

The story of the little girl continued when she came home from the hospital. Her mom yelled at her for playing soccer with the boys. She said "See all of this happened because you played football with the boys! Why can't you play with dolls as girls should?"

This story demonstrates how children learn their parenting style. The only way to stop this cycle is rising above and applying forgiveness.

Mom came from the same criticizing and blaming mother, who raised her children alone. Hugging children was not in fashion at that time either. So the mom of the current story's mom, had never received hugs or physical and emotional support, so she could not give these to her daughter either. Can you see, how the lack of emotional support ran through generations?

The mom, having only brothers, grew to be a tom-boy. As a young adult, she also played with boys and ran into all kinds of relationships with guys.

See, how different this story is when we look at the big picture and when we look at the story of compassion? Generational tools for raising children trickle down. Parents repeat parenting precisely the way it happened to them unless they awaken.

Please realize and cry out loud:
It's not your fault if you can't give!
Not knowing what love is, also not your fault.
None of your past conditioning is your fault!

It doesn't matter when you realize this and how old you are. Realizing that "it is not your fault"- one big step in liberating yourself from your past. It is the first step, which helps to eliminate the fear of the past and see the stories there more objectively.

The past offers a tremendous learning opportunity!

Many years later, the little girl, now as an adult, talked through all things honestly and resolved all issues and genuine forgiveness took place.

If you read this book as a child, please talk to your parents. If you are a parent, please speak to your child and initiate the conversation. Initiate the conversation with love, understanding, and kindness and close the issue with love, kindness, respect, and compassion.

It is incredible to realize, just how fragile children are! From the parent's point of view, a seemingly small event can make scars in children. That scar will create a belief in the child, that "I am not good enough and I only deserve to be abandoned and rejected."

Having children is an enormous responsibility! I didn't take on this responsibility because of the level of my inner healing and the lack of a father prospect while I could physically have children.

I chose to put all my efforts into my passion to teach, build the society and become an example of living with loving kindness. I devoted my life to a life long practice and growth.

A healthy and harmonious relationship begins with resolving relationships with our parents. I am grateful for having the chance to clear things out with my parents, while they are on this Earth. Both my parents are happy and fulfilled in their second marriage for almost 30 years now. I am very grateful for them giving me life and the experiences as a child. They did the best they could, so I stay very respectful of them.

> *If you have love, acceptance, and gratitude running in*
> *you, people will love you back freely, out of their free will.*
> *Those who love you unconditionally will be part of your*
> *life. Those who don't learn to love you will fade out.*

It is necessary to clear out things in yourself and with your parents, even If they are no longer in this world.

It is life changing to transform your past history, then apply forgiveness and let the hurt go. Replace your memory about your past with the teachings. Change will finally become lasting, when you put those teachings into practice.

If you are a parent and your parents are alive, then you can make a difference for three generations. The first is your own, then your parents and your children.

You must learn to love yourself and work out all
your past hurts and emotional pains.

Transform! Transform! Transform! Transform until
you only have love and compassion inside you!

What to do when your parents carry so much pain from their past? The answer is the same: apply objectivity, acceptance and more compassion.

Seeing things objectively and out of compassion will give you enough strength and tools to be with painful parents and people.

I call people "painful" who are not aware of their pain. Your parents may be one of these people. Feeling sorry for "painful" people adds to their feeling that they are victims. Blaming them for their pain rejects them even more. Excusing yourself for not being able to rise above and see things objectively is not a solution either. Only acceptance and seeing the story from the other person's point of view is the solution.

Story 2.

The next story is about a little boy and his path to believe: "I am not good enough."

Once upon a time, there was a little boy. Despite the frequent arguments between his parents, he loved them dearly. He loved his mom for being his protector and looked up his dad for all the big things he did. He wanted to be like his dad. He kept on doing things to prove himself to his dad. The boy would do anything to get his dad's appreciation. Getting his dad's recognition would have made him feel valuable and important. The dad didn't see this in the boy, therefore seldom gave appreciation. The dad's child raising tools were criticizing and threatening. He expected things to be perfect. Why did the dad become such a hard parent? Let us see his upbringing.

The dad learned to be a perfectionist from his parents and was only accepted at home if he did things correctly. So he learned that being a perfectionist gave him value, power, and importance. He lived a hard life and to practice his power, he manipulated or threatened others to get everything he wanted. It was his way or no way.

The conflict began to rise came when the boy became school age. The little boy didn't like to go to school. He was the kind of child, who didn't do well in the standard education system. The little boy had no interest in going to school and learning useless things. He barely passed tests and exams. Since he couldn't do things perfectly, he got turned off from studying. He was not perfect, to his dad's measure, but he still wanted to be appreciated. He did things to get attention and ended up receiving a lot of criticism and punishment.

The little boy also didn't understand why his dad loved his sister better. Could one reason be that she was a straight A student, therefore perfect?

This conflict divided the parents and the children too. The mom protected her son from the dad's criticizing and made all naughty things that the boy did, disappear. The dad however, always found a way to express his dissatisfaction with the boy.

A few things about Father and Son relationships: A father's acceptance and acknowledgment of his son, is the most vital emotional support for a boy. Through acceptance, recognition, and acknowledgment, boys learn to be valuable and important. Genuine and stable, self-value makes boys become givers, to fulfill their biological role as being a male. Only a boy, who feels genuinely valuable can share and give. When a self-valued man gives to others, they also give to themselves. The process of giving makes him feel important. While giving to others, a stable self-valued man expresses self-importance to himself.

The lack of acceptance and the constant fight for proving themselves is one cause children to overeat. Kids eat, eat and eat to feel loved. Eating and more eating to feel loved and important was the case with the little boy in our story.

As time passed, the differences in character and value showed up between the parents even more. The lack of understanding and communication, pushed the mom and dad miles apart. By now the teenage boy realized that he is never going to be "good enough" for his Dad. The boy learned to hate his father, as an encounter with him made him feel like a failure. Nothing was ever good enough for his dad. Through constant criticizing, the boy learned to criticize. He became very critical with others and always compared himself to prove his value. The boy believed his dad criticized him for being worthless. As self-protection he started to criticize himself.

The boy grew into an adult who talked himself out of doing things. He believed that he wouldn't succeed in anything and said: "I won't succeed, so why should I start anything?" He believed that he was a failure.

The boy craved acceptance, recognition and love. He only felt valuable when others expressed their approval and love for him. There was not enough love and caring for him. He learned to crave. He lived his life craving and not having. Growing up to be a man, he soon discovered sex to be the source of love. If girls slept with him, he felt recognized, acknowledged, important, influential and loved. He had many, many relationships. And none of them worked. When he lived with those girls, he realized that sex was not enough to make a relationship. When the grayness of daily life began, and his imperfections and lack of motivation to do things were found out, acknowledgments ceased. He needed affirmation and idolizing to feel loved. He needed to feel wanted and valued and influential again so hunting for a new prospect began. So this was the story for his adult life — evil circuits of affairs. Let us see where did the boy accept the option for an affair?

If two people can't accept themselves, they wont be able to accept each other either. Their life is full of criticizing and rejecting. They can't communicate patiently and with compassion, because if they did, they couldn't practice rejection. If two people are addicted to criticizing, they will practice it regularly, just like a smoker would smokes a cigarette. A smoker lights up a cigarette; a person addicted to criticism "lights up" a critique.

The boy copied precisely what he saw at home from his parents. As an adult now, he learned to yell and discuss things loudly, only to demand his righteousness. The boy however, ran away from all communication, which addressed the real issue.

Since the parent's marriage didn't work, his father looked for other ladies and in time the boy found out. He was shocked to catch his dad once, in the act of having sex. After this, the boy learned that it was ok to use girls for sex and then throw them away.

The boy as a young adult left home early, got married and divorced many times but never found a home anywhere in life.

If you have never felt accepted, you will
never find a home in this world.
If you don't accept yourself, you feel "homeless."

We feel home where we feel accepted!

How do we know a relationship will work? We have to examine the value system, the level of compatibility and communication.

The difference in the value system and being under the unconscious control of the conditioned mind, will make any relationship short-lived. To succeed in a relationship, one must succeed first building a relationship within himself or herself. One must clean out the old beliefs and values, establish new ones and learn to communicate.

The reason, why people don't have relationships, is because they have no connection with themselves either.

Not wanting to connect with yourself is the sign of self-rejection. If you believed as a child: "I am not lovable," you will multiply your addictions to make yourself feel loved.

Dear parents and parents to be,

Many relationships turn into marriages due to an expected pregnancy. A marriage out of necessity provides a poor emotional environment for a child to grow up. When one of the parent's says "yes" out of this necessity, then the child who is on the way is already hurt. Those who gave in and said "yes," will generate colossal resentment and hatred later. The resentments on the long run, turn into a blame game. This unhealthy environment trickles down to the child.

The parent's pain toward each other, overflows to the children. If there is a second child, all the pain,- parent's and sibling pain, will be passed to him or her. In a home filled with pain, siblings fight and compete all the time, to create more pain.

Imagine the life of a second child, who carries all the pain in the family! What kind of adult will he or she be?

Do you have a better understanding now of your parents and the experience you received from them?

Love the person you marry. I am not talking about the Hollywood type of love you see on the movies, but real true love. True love has the foundation in unconditional acceptance, gratitude, and mutual respect.

Who do you think can give unconditional acceptance, gratitude and respect for his or her spouse?

What kind of human characters, does one have to develop to love someone else the same way?

Take your time to have children. A newly married couple, where both parties are coming from painful childhoods, have some work to do on themselves first before even thinking about having children. The personal growth has to increase to such a level, that they practice acceptance and gratitude for months and preferably for two years. Why for two years? Because it takes time to clean and retrain the mind. It also takes time to practice the new behavior until it becomes automatic.

It is worth the wait to have children until loving kindness is practiced easily at home. Imagine how different a child's life will be, if he or she is conceived and born in a loving and caring environment?

A child has to be born in a genuine loving relationship to become a healthy adult. A child expects to arrive in a loving family.

If the pregnancy came "accidentally," the parents have to make a responsible and conscious decision for the interest of the child. They have to make the best possible adjustment for the child to grow up in love and receive optimal emotion support. Keep in mind that the child will learn through the parent's example. The chosen path for parting and divorcing is also an example. Its good to be aware of the model parents make.

Children copy parents. Children copy parents
for expressing their love too.

Parting can happen for many reasons. There are times that parting serves the child's health. Explaining what happened without blaming is the first step managing the child's fear occurring during a divorce. Second is, to ensure the child will receive continuous emotional support, safety, and love after the parting. Parents then must keep their word on this, to decrease the harm caused by the divorce. Technology and internet communication via video helps to compensate for the lack of physical attendance. Parents and children can stay in each other's life to a greater extent.

Keeping regular communication, listening to the child's issues and respecting the child's point of view, will be critical in ensuring their healthy emotional growth.

Giving love via money or gifts is different than being accepting with the child and considering their feelings.

If we didn't come from a loving, accepting and supporting family environment, then we must re-parent ourselves. Reparenting means to learn to be caring and supportive to ourselves. Reparenting means, to create enough love for ourselves, that we have a surplus to give to our children too.

Don't think that running into a relationship and having a child will change your emotional issues.

We have to fix ourselves first before attracting
a healthy loving relationship.
A child will fix neither our relationship nor our personal,
emotional issues. We have to be brave and fix our problems alone.

If we don't love ourselves, there is not enough love and
money to make up for the lack of love for ourselves.

We have to believe that we are made of love as our life is a gift, which comes from Divine love!

We are made of love. Divine Love created us.
And we were born to love!

Story 3.

Once upon a time, there was a little boy, who was the middle child. He had an older and a younger sister. Let's look at their parents. The mom ran away from home at the age of 16. She couldn't stand living at home with her parents.

Therefore, she quickly fell in love and got married. The frustration and the anger of her husband came out early in the new marriage. The husband was regularly beating his wife. She went back home and told the story to her parents. Her mother said, "If you chose to run into the arms of this man, then take the responsibility yourself. Go back to him!"

This was the misery-filled start of the parent's life together. Sex was compulsory for the girl. The girl didn't want children, but she had no choice. She was pregnant against her own will, one after the other. She was turning more frustrated and angry. Getting married and having children right away was the usual thing back then.

There were now three unwanted children from a father she hated to be with. She had no choice but to stay there and bare the beating. Once the children were born, they became the subject for the mother to take out her frustration. Her husband beat her, so she beat the kids. The kids received all the anger from the mother, which she felt for her husband.

Let's see what happened when the boy was born.

After the mother delivered the child, her breasts got inflamed, and she couldn't nurse the boy. The little boy was hungry all the time. He experienced that he is not loved because his mother doesn't feed him. He believed that he is not loved. Therefore they starved him. He screamed all the time. By his adulthood, he learned to feed himself to feel love. Food meant love to him.

He continued to crave for food and became obese as an adult. There was not enough food to make up for the lack of love he felt.

Being hungry for love moved over to other subjects. He was hungry for women and sex. He wanted to get every woman he cast his eye on. Then the craving went into owning things. He wanted to have expensive cars, motorcycles, houses, and clothes.

Craving made him win every business deal. There was no way he could lose money.

Let's look at the little boy again and understand how he developed this level of craving.

Children are easily susceptible to feel abandoned or neglected by their parents. The emotional absence of mom for boys and the emotional absence of mom for girls can awaken the abandonment feeling in kids. Any small thing can happen, and the child can feel abandoned. It is not always physical abandonment, but more emotional. Emotional abandonment can come in the form of disapproval, lack of acknowledgment or harsh criticism. Emotional abandonment makes kids feel alone with no self-esteem and undeserving of love. Abandonment builds a protective shield, which is emotional dependence. Being dependent on feeling loved. Men become dependent on women, and vice versa.

The craving for the opposite gender becomes so strong that "hunting" becomes a lifestyle. Whomever they cast an eye upon, they desire for sex.

Heated sexual relationships bring excitement as they begin to feel like they own their "prey." The "having" feeling awakens their emotional pain for the parent who abandoned them. They begin to sabotage their partner and give them pain. It has nothing to do with the partner. This is actually a pain they feel towards the parent who abandoned them. The craving for punishment awakens. They punish the partner because he or she is there. They punish the partner like they were the parents. The hatred grows until they destroy the relationship and the partner runs away. Just like the parent ran away in childhood. They are unable to hold onto or have a relationship.

The "having" feeling awakens boredom. When the hunt is over, they lose interest. The "having" feeling fulfills a craving, so no more craving is possible for the conditioned mind. No more hunt would mean an end to the craving. The mind demands its comfort zone and goes back to the "I don't have" feeling, so the craving and hunt can begin again.

The foundation of this adulthood craving is abandonment, which is a deep emotional wound, that children experience between 2-3 years of age. The subject of this craving is love and emotional support. Not feeling loved and craving love, creates an immense pain in children, which produces dysfunctional relationships in adulthood.

In such a dysfunctional relationship, the boys look for the mother figure in women, and the girls look for the father-figure in men. Do you understand now couples who have an age gap of 15-25 years?

Coming back to our little boy. He is an adult now. He ate, bought women, things, cars, and bikes and sold them in a few months. Changed them for newer ones. The sex was not really an enjoyment, but an outlet for punishment. "I had this woman, and I succeeded to punish her too. By punishing her, I punished my mother" – was the subconscious story.

Punishing the opposite gender occurs in both men and women. You can often see this phenomenon with women, who have been abandoned by their father. Their initiative is to punish the guy. But whom do they want to punish? Just think for a moment.

When an abandoned girl gets her prey, her pain and hatred will awaken for her father. After the sweet words and "honey soaked" experiences, the "I have him" feeling is realized and the punishment begins. Women will have a sudden change in their relationship with their guy. Guys often say: "She became a witch! She makes empty promises, and then blames me for the mistakes she did!" These are the symptoms of a person, who was abandoned as a child, shall that be a boy or a girl. Note the behavior pattern, and you will understand the emotional wound the person went through as a child.

If you have a partner with a massive craving like this, please rise above and see that the punishment your partner is trying to do against you, is actually for their parent, who left them. You have to help them with your love to heal. More often relationships break due to the accumulated pain. It takes a healed person to deal with a spouse who was abandoned and became very painful as an adult.

Let us see further the little boy's story and talk about this father. The marriage was also not easy for him. He was older and had a hard life making money and providing for the family. He used alcohol to ease his pain.

Interestingly, alcohol is universally accepted "medicine" for frustration, stress, anger, and heartache. When the boy was born the drunken father switched the subject of his beating from the mom to the boy. Since the little boy was the only male in the family, he received a daily beating, which his mom used to get. It doesn't matter if he did something or not, he got beaten up.

Since the little boy was thin, the father sent him to take boxing lessons. He said: "Learn to fight, so you don't get beaten up in school!" The boy progressed very well with boxing. Boxing and fighting became a way to prove his strength and demand his importance. When the boy grew up, he looked for fights. He looked for circumstances where he could show off his power, where he could prove his strength. This is why he got into all sorts of fights. He looked for events to provide justice with his fist. He punished all who did wrong. He punished everyone for the punishment he received at home from his father.

The girls in the family received their own shares. The youngest girl ran into a relationship, got pregnant as her mom did at age 16.

Broken lives and all sorts of tragedies!

Children brought up in a lack of love, will continue
to pass on the pain to their children. Ensuring
the hurtful and painful generations.

*We must stop and break the cycle of pain. Somebody in
the family must wake up and start the healing process!*

Thankfully, more and more people awaken and heal themselves from their
childhood emotional wounds. This healing brings healing to their families
and to the world too.

Story 4.

The next story is about what happens, when parents are missing from their
children's lives and substitute their presence with money.

Once upon a time, there was a family. The husband and wife got married
due to family pressure. Being only 18, the wife was very ambitious. She didn't
accept the expectation of her family, to become a housewife. She wanted to
have financial independence, so she planned to study to make money. She
was accepted in a business program at the local university. In the 3rd year of
her bachelor's studies, she became pregnant and gave birth to her son. She
continued her studies in the MBA program as well. Upon finishing the MBA
the second boy was born. The mom had an excellent business plan and began
to work on it immediately. Throughout the years, she built her idea into a
million dollar business. She reached her goal, built a successful business and
lived in complete financial independence.

While the first son was born the wife, spent her daytime at the university and
went home in the evening. The second boy was three years old and the first
born seven years old when the mom started to travel for business.

What happened with the family during this time? The wife spent long hours in her office. The husband was a businessman, who didn't spend much time at home either. What happened to the kids, while the parents were busy building a business and making money? Who raised the kids?

The first-born son had his mom at home on a daily bases until he was seven. This boy developed into an emotionally balanced child. The son paid attention in school and knew what he wanted to be in business. After his university studies, he joined his mom's company, at the age of 20.

The second boy was four years younger than his brother. He saw mom on a daily bases until he was three. Then the mom started to travel for business. The children had babysitters at home who raised them. The boys had all the money they wished for, so cars and things had no motivational value for them. They had a new car every year. They lived a high life: traveled, partied, and studied abroad.

What kind of problems started to show up in their lives? The first problem was a lack of motivation to do things in life. None of the boys were motivated for anything other than having fun. The first boy who joined his mom in business worked in the company but with not much motivation. The second boy however just drifted, not knowing what to do.

How can you motivate children who grow up without learning the value of things they have?

Providing a life for kids where money is not an object can backfire later. Spoiling kids with money without teaching the value of things, can be harmful to their adult life. These children have no goals in life. Most of them end up spending the family fortune. And that is all their life about.

The most emotionally balanced kids come from families living in smaller homes and like living in the middle class, shown by a study conducted in the USA. The study showed that children brought up in a modest financial background, living in smaller houses, spend more time with the family. The smaller space allows for closer relationships between parents and kids. The kids also spend more time with the kids in the community. These kids have more space and time to socialize with other children on the playground too. The kids in these communities communicate better in real life, as they learn from each other. They have the freedom to experience life as little people. These children become more accepting, helpful and co-operative. They are more creative and open to new solutions.

Back to our story. What other problems had arisen due to the lack of parenting? The younger boy finished a bachelors program but had a hard life. He was in trouble left and right from cigarettes, alcohol, and girls.

How is it possible that two boys, having the same financial background have a big difference in their growing up? How did the younger boy get so lost?

Let us see what happened objectively and apply compassion.

The big difference in the upbringing of the two boys is the time they spent with the mother. The first boy was already seven years old, but the younger one was only three. Mom leaving for business had not much effect on the older boy but left a deep scar in the younger one. The younger boy wanted his mom to stay and opposed every trip with his loud crying. The young boy learned to resist and fight, hoping to make the mom stay. He first opposed everything his mom said, then his opposition and rejection extended to everyone.

The young boy missing his mom, developed a craving for women, love, and closeness. By the time he was a young adult, he had defined love by physical proximity. Love meant to be the closest possible way to women, to have sex. He replaced love with sex.

He had a constant craving for being close to women. Subconsciously he craved the closeness of the mother that he didn't have when he was three.

The craving was so great that women were coming and going in his life. He could not hold onto any relationship. He got bored with the girls, cheated on them and left every one of them. After the "hunt" was over, and had his "prey" he lost interest.

A person who craves, can't have or maintain anything.
The moment they sense they "have" something, they don't
need it anymore. Having something would take away
their craving, which is the essence of their lives.

As soon as the boy had the girls, he began to sabotage the relationships. He also provoked and insulted the girls to leave him. He was subconsciously re-creating his mom leaving him as a baby all over again.

How did he provoke the girls? As soon as he had the girls, he became a real "a.hole" with them. He played with them and took advantage of them. He hurt them physically during sex. He used sex to give pain or punishment to the girls. His motto was "Sex is only good when it hurts." The empty promises meant more pain or humiliation, that he created for himself.

Painful, punishing behavior is rooted in a deep seeded hatred towards the parent of the opposite gender. In this case the boy's mother.

He punished women due to the lack of love he received from his mom. Every time he gave pain to a woman, that pain was intended for his mother. To further oppose his mother, he didn't take part in the family business either.

Let us see what the mom's story represents to her?

A lot of women go back to work after giving birth. They either have to go back due to financial reasons, or they chose to build a career and don't want to stay at home to raise the kids. There is a very painful consequence to the children when their mom goes back to work too soon and creates an emotional gap in the child's life. The same emotional gap raises up in the kid's life when parents get divorced.

What does the parent's presence represent for the growing child?

For healthy emotional development, children need both of their parents. Why does the quality presence of the parent of the opposite gender become so vital for the children? For a girl, this is the father figure, and for a boy, this is the mother.

We have seen on the above example what the absence of the mother does to young boys. What happens when the father figure is missing for girls. The father is the first man in the girl's life. Girls learn the concept of receiving love from Dad. They learn to be deserving, valuable and important to receive love. Girls learn to be receptive and to accept what they receive with gratitude. Girls learn to receive in general by having a healthy father and daughter relationship. Girls learn that the love and pampering they get, they deserve.

If there is no father figure in the girl's life, she learns from mom. Girls copy and duplicate their mom's role to be a giver. Growing up with mom, girls miss learning the concept of receiving love.

Look at single mom raising her daugther. The family unit of the two girls has no one to receive love from. The girls witness how mom dates and became a giver to men. (I believe to be a blessing if the mother finds a new guy, who is emotionally balanced and able to fulfill the father figure which represents the giver role, in the life of both the daughter and the mom).

Girls growing up with single moms, learn to give but not to receive or accept love. The deserving love feeling is completely missing for these girls. When they grow into adults, they become dominators and want to give to prove they are worthy to receive love. They are unable to accept love and everything else. They have to earn love and everything else. They also jump from one relationship to another in search of their father figure. This is why they prefer to go out with an older man.

Girls who grow up without a father, learn to fight for love and acceptance. They use every portal to prove themselves, to deserve attention and love from men.

Girls growing up without fathers become fighters. They lose touch with their femininity and become tough girls. It is a real tough task for them, to accept that being "gentle" is a female character, and they deserve to receive without doing anything to prove themselves. These tough girls need to learn to be brave to receive and trust that by receiving they are still worth it.

Having a "gentle" character may be misunderstood. A gentle word for the conditioned mind, means someone soft, who doesn't work hard, can't stand up for herself and lives as a dependent.

In real meaning, a woman is gentle, who handles things with softness, elegance yet with inner power. They call this woman a lady. A neck who moves the head of her man. A woman who knows gentleness, can allow herself to receive. Being gentle makes it possible to create space for a woman to receive soft, gentle love from a man. This softness makes it possible that love comes freely from the man. By learning to be gentle and kind, girls can give up fighting and to demand. Accepting our female role to be gentle gives a lot of peace, calm and patience. I personally received a lot of relief when I gave up fighting and demanding and allowed life to happen for me. I could finally breathe freely. I no longer needed to stay alert and see when I had to prove myself. The stress came off, and I finally relaxed.

When a woman is geared up to fight, she believes that she has to be tough. Toughness and strength give value. Strong women usually attract strong, but "bully" types of men. "Strong" couples will fight all the time.

The stronger the shell outside, the softer the person is inside.

The real softness of "strong" women is hidden under their steel outer shell. They are women who are "hard as a rock." It is challenging for men to hunt them down. This is why men who are motivated by the hunt love these tough girls. However, when men break these girls in, these girls have the most fragile heart. Women with a broken heart, come from a harsh childhood of not having their father around.

We shall think seriously, what happens with a child when they lose one or both parents. This is not always the physical absence but an emotional absence, the feeling of "absence." The absence and "not having" feeling, develop when children miss feeling the parent's loving emotional support.

Story 5.

Our next story is about children growing up in a large family. I personally admire parents who plan for a large family and have the management skills to raise emotionally balanced children. More often, however, children just happen to be born without any planning. Some parents think they have the skills, face the issues too late and grow a sincere regret. It takes an enormous amount of self-love to put yourself behind while raising a large family. No matter how hard parents try, to pay proper attention to run the family successfully, the emotional need of the different children is a challenge. It is because there is one mom and one dad for many children. Each child wants the same mom and dad at the same time. Sharing that attention and love, is an enormous challenge for children. I have observed many large families and dealt with clients coming from large families. I like to share the following with you. How a large family (more than 3 kids) affects the emotional development of children?

Our story is about a family with five children. The first-born who will become the oldest may possibly become the most painful adult when he or she grows up. The first-born child in this story was a boy. When he was a toddler, he got used to having the "exclusive right" to his parents. When the second, then third then the fourth baby was born, he felt that he lost his parents. The boy began to develop bad feelings. It was unfair that the other children took his parents away.

The second issue was the lack of understanding of what was happening:

- No one prepared him for the arrival of the other children.
- No one told him that he had to share his parents with the other kids.
- No one asked him if it was ok with him.
- No one said to him that he is still valuable even though there were other kids.

The above needed to be cleared out, but wasn't. As a result the boy developed multiples of emotional pain.

Understand the oldest boy's feelings:

- His childhood was cut short.
- He had to grow up fast and take care of the other babies. He had to become a responsible little adult.
- He always had to show an example.
- He felt that he lost his childhood.
- Developed confusion and inner conflicts about himself. He was continuously asking "how is it possible that I have to behave like an adult, while I am still a child? Why can't I be a child?"
- He lost his self-worth, self-importance, and self-value. He was disappointed and said: "I used to be the only one whom my parents loved. They don't love me anymore. Now I have to prove myself to get my parents attention. I have to keep competing and fighting to prove that I am lovable."

This child learned that essential things in life came through a fight. He learned to fight for love, attention, and everything. He felt rejected at home, so he learned to reject everything and everyone. He felt alone and undeserving of being loved. He learned to crave love. He punished his siblings and the whole world because they got what he was supposed to have. He felt lonely and misunderstood.

When the parents were busy, they asked the oldest child to watch over the other children. In this case, the emotional wound or painful conditioning also came from the older sibling. The lack of physical presence of the parents and then being passed over to a sibling, further increased the emotional pain in the kids. Taking care of the other four children, the oldest son was in heaven to practice his criticizing, rejecting and punishing behavior on the other kids. In our story, this was the case between the oldest and the second born child. This boy receiving the undeserving beating from his brother became an adult who spread justice whereever he went. Since it was unjust to get beaten, he learned to beat up others first to protect himself from getting beaten up. Since so much unfairness was done to him, he learned to be unfair and cheat others to defend himself.

Any child who feels rejected,- just like the eldest son in our story, after a while rejects the entire family. He leaves the family because he doesn't feel loved, valued and important. The family for him is the source of feeling worthless.

Proving himself becomes a way of life for his adulthood. He is continuously looking for improving himself, to look better and to be higher than the masses. He is obsessed about becoming special, to earn love and attention. "I will prove that I am better than you" becomes his life motto.

The youngest in the family, usually has it the best of all. The youngest gets used to other siblings being ahead of him. The youngest child gets the most attention too because he or she is the little one.

The youngest child has a lot more chance to learn from the example set by his siblings. He can become the most observant of the people surrounding him. He has the opportunity to develop the most wisdom.

Youngest children may become the most sensitive ones in the family. Being the most observant, they can take up a lot of pain from the family. When they become adults, they have to learn to let go of carrying other people's pain.

When we look at the chronological ranking of the family, the middle child is the next to talk about. They say, being the middle child is the least favorable position among the children. Middle-children float and drift in life to find their identity. They have not found their status in the family as they are neither old nor young. "Who am I and where do I belong" they often ask. "Everyone seems to have an identity, but me. Everyone is more important than me."

Middle children growing into adults, battle with undeserving emotions the most. They work hard, but the money flows out from their hands. They learn that they are undeserving of having anything. They only deserve to crave.

Story 6.

In the next story, I like to talk about a serious subject. The story is about little girls, who are physically, sexually and emotionally abused by their father, uncle or their older brother.

Imagine the kind of normalcy an abused little girl learns to accept in her life about a man. For emotionally, physically and sexually abused girls, beating and abuse is normal. They don't know anything else. It's no wonder what kind of man they attract when they grow up. These girls will accept men who beat them and abuse them. Only a physically, emotionally and sexually abusive man is "man" for them.

Since these girls never experienced loving, healthy emotional support from their father, these feelings are non-existent for them. They jump from one abusive man to another. Sadly, this is a prevalent story among women.

Lots of healing needs to take place in sexually abused girls. The bottom line is for them to learn what love really is. The second task is to apply love and care to themselves. Self-love, self-esteem and self-value will create all the necessary changes to turn their lives around. Only then will their attraction change towards men too.

Unfortunately, little boys are also the victim of physical abuse. They also learn abuse to be normal. Imagine abused young men and women living together and have a "hell of a life."

Recently and fortunately, I have been meeting men, who transformed their abusive childhoods and raised their children in the kind of love and care that they never received.

I hope that we all reach enough awareness to recognize these situations and help those in need. This is one big social responsibility for a healthier world.

Story 7.

Another familiar story when parents fell out of love, yet stay together due to financial reasons. They share a house like roommates and start dating.

Let us see an example, the husband meets another woman, starts an affair. The husband, who is the father in our story, finds a date to be good reasons to take the child along. He takes the daughter to visit the girlfriend.

Now let us see, what does the little girl understand from this? What kind of questions does she have?

She may be asking: *"Why dad is taking me to visit another lady? Why don't we visit mom?"*

The daughter gets spoiled by the girlfriend during the visits. When the daughter goes home, she tells the story to her mom. The little girl is raving about the good time she had with this new lady.

Now let's see, what happens emotionally in the mom.

"Why is my husband doing this to humiliate me in front of my daughter? Why is my husband doing all the things with this new girlfriend, which we used to do?"

What kind of emotional environment does this create at home?

What happens to the relationship when two people stop loving each other and stay together for financial reasons?

What happens to them when they are just too afraid to face their issues and fears?

What happens when they are scared to look for solutions?

The result is the "apparent family."

What kind of emotional environment can an "apparent family" provide for the child? Do you have experience living in an "apparent family?"

If yes, you know that an "apparent family" provides an ample amount of hatred, ignorance, and uncertainty. What do you think happens with the child growing up in an "apparent family?"

An "apparent family" brings a lot of unanswered questions to the child. The child doesn't understand what is happening. The child starts to blame him/herself for the parent's fights. The child doesn't understand why parents fight and asks:

- *"Why do mom and dad hate each other?"*
- *"Why do they blame each other?"*
- *"Why don't my parents love each other?"*
- *"If they don't love each other why did they give me life?"*

The fight between parents is one of the most painful events for the child. If parents don't talk to the child and don't clear out, that the fight is not about the child, the child will blame him or herself. Self-blame creates a deep emotional wound in children.

Self-blame hurts the kid's self-value right at the core.

The children can't understand why the parents fight. They come to the conclusion that they are at fault. They blame themselves for the parent's fights. Saying: "For sure I did something wrong. This is why mom and dad are fighting."

Where is the warm home environment, which is the only place for the child to feel safe?

The lack of safety and the lack of warmth builds the foundation for confusion, instability in the child. When the child grows up, he or she will look for uncertainty, confusion, and instability as a healthy way of life.

Children as infants learn safety, security, contentment, and orderliness when they receive enough food from their mom on regular bases.

Imagine what happens when the infant doesn't receive enough mother's milk and nourishment? The child learns to cry in hunger and develops craving to be the way of life.

What happens when the mom opts to bottle feed the child to protect her breast's cosmetic appearance? What happens to the child when his or her special emotional connection to mom, is lost?

Do you understand now why the world is full of "hungry" and craving people?

I can imagine you have many more stories like this from your childhood. Everyone has a story. It doesn't matter what your story is, what matters, how this event made you feel back then and what did you become as an adult because of this childhood feeling.

Parenting as a new subject in education

In my opinion, parenting shall be another subject in education. Good parenting is an essential subject to those children coming from a broken family, abusive or emotionally unstable parents. First, the damage in the character of these children needs to be healed. Therefore, it is imperative to teach personal development and self-management tools in kindergarten. Teaching breath observation meditation and along with compassion for children at a very young age is a very efficient preparation to fix the character damage in these children.

Offering self-development and healthy parenting courses for the parents whose children attend kindergarten and in elementary school can be very useful to promote change.

Secure and stable personal values, make it easier to introduce healthy, responsible sexual life and family planning for teenagers. Technology and the internet have expedited growth and the sexual life of teenagers. Kids with emotional imbalance would run into a relationship, rather than going home to hostility.

It is essential for children to know the consequences of an active sexual life. They have to be aware of their responsibilities, which comes with bringing a baby to this world. Youngsters need to get ready to become a parent before it happens.

Children don't know that you as parents, have personal issues because of your difficult childhoods. Your children don't understand why you ran into a sexual relationship to feel valuable. Your kids don't know why you feel so sad when they are present. Your kids don't understand why you have to argue and can't fix things peacefully.

If children are born in an unsettled relationship, they become unsettled adults. When parents don't know what to do, hesitate and run away, the kids will become the same kind of hesitant adults.

The first role of parenting is to build character
for children to become empowered.

Dear Parents,

You have been doing the best you could. Accept it and have an open mind to read further.

Next, I would like to introduce and bring specific child raising issues.

I will show you the disadvantages and the negative consequences, that the lack of family planning causes.

I would also like to show you, what family planning can do for you and your children. I intend to make sense of the benefits of thinking ahead when it concerns your children, to live a happy fulfilled life. Your planning will contribute to the health and wealth of the next generation as well.

Parenting, just like everything else, is based on trust!

Parenting begins with understanding and applying trust in ourselves, in others and in our children.

Your kids believe everything you say or do. Your kids honestly, unquestionably believe what you say about them is the truth. Take excellent care and think about what you like your children to think about themselves. Think twice on criticizing your kids and calling them stupid!

We also know now that criticizing is all about yourself. You are criticizing the child for those characters you don't like in yourself. So fixing yourself in this aspect can save your child from going through what you did as a child.

Your personal development now can prevent your
child from growing into a painful adult, who
feels lonely for the rest of his or her life.

Therefore, I repeat: "Take more time and think before you have children!" Decide in advance what kind of adults you want your kids to grow up to be. Then find the appropriate parenting style to match and support the end result you would like to see in your children.

Trust is very fragile. A child's trust is even more delicate.

> *Take care of a child's trust. Use the child's confidence for helping him or her to develop into a valuable, self-managing and loving human being who lives a meaningful life. Assist your child to grow into an adult who is capable of building his own wealth and health while contributing to society.*

Would you like your child:

- **to think,**
- **to ask a question,**
- **to make a decision,**
- **to carry out an action,**
- **to perform and work on his or her own,**
- **and to take responsibility?**

Then you need to give tasks to your child, through which he or she learns and practices thinking, asking questions, making decisions and taking actions, initiating help, working alone, and taking responsibility.

What do you have to have as a parent to be able to teach the above characters to your children?

You need patience, understanding, a clear head, forward-thinking and communication to coach your child.

You need to be patient to give gentle advice and explain to them how things work.

You will also need to be accepting and rise above when things don't work out.

You need to be emotionally supportive of your child. Emotional support comes in the form of acknowledgment and appraisal for the things the kids did correctly.

You need to be attentive and watch your kids doing things well! When the result is less successful, motivate and encourage your kids to do it again.

Even if he or she makes a less favorable decision, be there to assist. Let it be the child's decision and let the child learn the lesson. Of course anything life-threatening needs to be explained with kindness. Make sense to your kids and bring valid reasons for pointing out the hazard.

You need to see clearly if your child wants to do something to prove himself to you. When you recognise your child's self proving efforts, start working on more acknowledgment until the child feels valuable regardless of what he or she does.

The child will trust you, even more, when you trust them first.

A child who is empowered with your trust will have the strength to come back to you when things happen less favorably and say: "Mom or dad you were right, I should have listened to you." This is a prominent moment in building your child's character.

How do you handle when your child admits, that you were right? Will you criticize him or have the patience to use this moment to build him further with your acknowledgment?

Another critical factor is to have patience leading your child to his or her conclusion, kindly and lovingly. Your children will greatly appreciate that you didn't yell at them and call them all sorts of names for their less favorable action.

The child has to feel safe with you to tell you the truth. If the child feels safe, they will be honest with you as they trust you will help them sort it out. Through this process the child will learn that there is a peaceful way to work things out. The child will learn that a friendly and peaceful way is the only human way.

> *Trust is developed through you trusting yourself that*
> *you prepared your child, then you let him or her go.*
> *Now you have to trust that they will do well.*

A critical moment to recognize, when your child can say "You were right dad or mom." Give them high praise immediately! Imagine, how big of a deal for you to say these words! So celebrate your child for standing tall on the truth! If you tell your child "See I told you so, clean up your mess alone," he or she will just turn off and withdraw even more from listening to you in the future.

The child learns through criticism, that he or she is only good when things work out and they are alone and helpless when things don't work out. They feel valuable to receive support only when they do the "right things." As a next step, due to fear of failure, kids stop doing anything new.

The first role of parenting is to build character
for children to become empowered.

The origin of the painful generation and the way out

I am sure you see now, just how big the responsibility is, to fix yourselves before getting married and having children. You must fix yourself to have patience, acceptance, gratitude and to live honestly. You must learn to rise above, think, plan and communicate clearly. You must built your character to be ready to raise another human being.

Without fixing yourself, you will teach your painful subconscious behavior (anger, frustrations, hatred) to your children.

Children know and feel everything, just like
you did when you were a child!

Don't think that the child is deaf, stupid, blind or insensitive! Kids have good hearing, good vision, correct sensation and they are smart. Just like you were a susceptible child and felt all that your parents did. Why would you think your child is different from you? You also felt very hurt by your parent's insensitive behavior. Didn't you?

The pain grows into hatred at any age.

Unhandled pain destroys lives at any age.

Pain makes one live a lifeless, insensitive life.

An unwanted pregnancy is the first deep seeded pain for the child. Imagine how painful parents look at their unwanted child and see nothing else but their mistake in them, every single day!

For a painful mind, the unwanted child is responsible for the parent's mistake. Therefore the child must take the physical beating from the parents, for their own weakness. Parents beat the child out of frustration that they feel for themselves and their spouse. They blame the child for their own misfortune of being stuck in a marriage!

Imagine, what kind of adult will this innocent child grow into if he or she senses that he or she was unwanted?

You can see kindergartens and streets filled with children who come from painful families. They learn that pain is the only thing that exists and the only thing they deserve. Growing up, they think and act from the accumulated pain. The pain inside them is so great that they must dump it onto others. The pain automatically "overflows" when it's density reaches maximum saturation.

Pain makes one believe that the only way to decrease pain, is to give it to someone else. When one can't hold pain any longer, he or she will automatically download it.

How do you recognize people with overflowing pain?

These are the people, who must complain, must blame, must punish, must hate, must break things and others too. The pain must come out of them, so they survive or at least make the pain lighter.

Kids who grow up with painful parents, learn that pain is the only way. These kids may be broken for life just like their parents were. Very sad! Painful people living painful lives, raising painful children is the reason, I believe the world is filled with pain today.

However, there is a light at the end of the tunnel! The light is awareness. The light comes from all of the people who have woken up already and live in awareness.

If we raise the level of our awareness, the change will come all by itself!

When the emotional wounds truly open, acceptance, understanding, compassion and forgiveness flow into the wound space. The key to opening yourself, will be to go through the transformation exercise.

Most of us will get to do the transformation exercise as adults. Twenty years ago people in their sixties and the past decade people in their forties on the road of change. By 2018 young adults in their twenties awaken to face and transform their emotional wounds. We all need to let our pain go and continue to live with loving kindness.

Time is too short to live in pain and pass
the opportunity to let the pain go.

Many children are born today different. They are the rainbow children. This is the result of the reincarnations of those, who healed their minds. These healed minds are being reborn into children today. These children are born with all the Divine wisdom, and they live out of loving kindness already. These are the children, who laugh at their parents for yelling and fighting with each other. The level of loving kindness in them makes it impossible to hurt them with emotional wounds. These children usually help their parents to heal, to love themselves and each other.

Meditation coupled with the transformation exercises, gives the key to unlock yourself safely, awaken your inner wisdom and your calling in this life.

The first awakening is that we must put our emotional load down and let our fears and hatred go.

The second awakening is, to apply the soothing, fragrant balm of love, acceptance, forgiveness to our emotional wounds. Most importantly take the initiative and responsibility to heal the emotional wounds by ourselves.

The third awakening is that we must continue the application of our love until complete healing takes place and we can genuinely love ourselves and others.

The transformation exercise makes it possible to recall and remember the event the way we feel grateful for the learning. After the transformation is done, you only remember what the event taught you. You will remember only for those you are thankful to know now.

Deep wounds require more love for their healing.

Love transforms us back to the new-born state of a loving individual. Healing our wounds allows the outer shell of negative behavior to drop off and a caring individual to emerge to the surface. This is our second birth or rebirth. This is our second chance to live with loving kindness and happiness, which is our birth-right.

How exciting that this love has been inside us all these painful years!

How interesting, that all painful life events had to happen to teach us, how to live our lives!

We must reach the point where we only live by our new life instructions, new behaviors. These new behaviors come from the fragrant kindness, which healed our wounds and will be visible as soft words, listening with patience, compassionate and being objective.

With diligent practice, one day you realize that you became a genuinely loving person and the healing is complete.

Imagine how differently you can raise your children
when you have undone all of your life's pains.

Giving advice and raising honest children

In the previous section we discussed trust in building the new generation. In is section we will learn a new key, which is the art of giving advice to raise honest children.

Honesty is the next character, which is born out of trust.

So apologies if in this section, I repeat a few things. Repetition is the base of learning. By mentioning the same in different aspects, helps to create a more in-depth understanding.

Giving advice is one sensitive area where our growth can make a huge difference in raising the new generation. Unsolicited advice and criticizing are the work of the conditioned mind and damage all your relationships.

Competent advice, must:

- Be well-timed.
- Be based on understanding and compassionate communication.
- Land on the person's skin, like a snowflake.
- Be spoken softly.
- Be motivating and building the other person.

Giving advice is not about you! It is not about you showing off, how brilliant, bright and valuable you are! Giving advice is also not about making the other person feel inferior to you. Giving advice is also not about pressuring others especially children to look up to you, so you feel powerful.

Giving advice is about the other person!

Giving advice is the most sensitive area when it comes to raising children. Why? Because most of the emotional pain is installed in kids through "well-intentioned" advice. Therefore, children growing up with unsolicited advice, turn into adults who get upset frequently.

It takes a lot of maturity, wisdom, and compassion to give advice, which serves its purpose and makes your child grow.

Answering the following questions helps in the formulation of a piece of advice.

- How can you give well-intentioned advice without ordering and pressuring?
- How can you advise without negative criticism?
- How can you provide positive guidance to assure and acknowledge your child and state the possible improvements?
- How can you rise above a mishap, so kids stay empowered to do it again?
- How can you advise, so your kids remain honest?
- How can you inform kids, so they continue to trust you?
- How can you advise your kids, so they will ask you for more advice?

- How can you advise your children, so they feel motivated and empowered?

- How can you advise your kids to reach agreement and approval with them?

Your advising style will define how balanced your
child leads his or her life and solves problems.

Your advising style is another key to raise empowered children.

Does it make sense now, why loving kindness and objective observation are new tools for raising children?

What do you have to let go of to become an empowering parent?

To become an emotionally stable parent, you have to let go of all painful pressure and harshness. All painful experiences stop growth. Your children don't need your harshness. In case you are not familiar with harshness, this is how it sounds like: "I will show how it is done!" or "Shut up as I know better, and I tell you what to do."

Kids don't need physical disciplining! They need love!

If you beat your kids because your parents beat you, then what life are you projecting forward for your kids? You hated the beating back then. Did beating motivate you for anything useful?

Beating never brings positive results. So why would you think your child likes it and it would work for him or her?

Why do you think you don't know a loving way of raising children? Because beating and physical disciplining have been the only tools you experienced and know today.

If you think back to what you wanted to receive instead of the beating and harshness, you will realize that you wanted your parents to do. You wanted them:

- To talk with you understandingly, to feel your problems, and help you solve your problems.
- To ask questions about what happened and not believe the neighbor.
- To listen to you and trust you for the truth.
- To take your side and even if you were wrong, discuss it in person.
- To take you seriously and not to make fun of you in front of others.
- To make you feel safe to tell the truth, and ask questions.
- To be honest with you, so you learn to stay calm and not build doubt and self-blame.

The less doubt we leave in children:

- The more valuable they will feel.
- The more correct and objective their self-evaluation will become.
- The more stable their inner power will be to stand up for themselves.

The more inner power children have, the more patience and humbleness they will develop. Strong inner power is the core of a child becoming accepting, forgiving, who enjoys living out of gratitude.

Remember, your children were born to solve the problem of the next generation, not yours!

Would you like your children to really have a different life than you had? Do you want your children to live in a loving environment?

Then why is it necessary to use harsh and destructive behavior? Do you realize that you need these new parenting tools now?

Would you like your children to be honest, to say sorry and forgive you for your mistakes?

Then you need to show them what saying sorry and forgiving looks like. You must practice saying sorry to your kids and to others. Similarly, you must practice forgiving them and others.

If you don't teach your kids how to apologize and forgive, they will develop a multiple of fears. One of the debilitating and most destructive fears, is being afraid of the truth.

Being afraid of the truth teaches kids to lie.

Would you like your children to learn to lie to you? If you continue criticizing, blaming and rejecting them for everything they do, they will learn to hide what they did. They will **be afraid of the truth** as your reactive criticism is so painful, so lying is the way out.

The second step of being afraid of the truth is to delete the event. **The mind will delete all events, which would be very painful to admit and talk about.** The mind renders this painful event non-existent. They will learn to say "What are you talking about? It wasn't me, I wasn't even there!"

When kids learn to use lying as self-protection, they will carry it to their adulthood. Deleting something from the mind for them becomes frequent self-protection. They can also convince anyone about their lies. They will convince anyone in such a way that they start questioning their memory. This convincing is the protective mechanism of being afraid of the truth.

The power of saying sorry and applying forgiveness

Learning to trust the truth builds the foundation of honesty. Sincere apology and forgiveness builds honesty.

Apology and forgiveness need to be practiced in front of the children and with the children regularly.

If you want your child to become honest, you have to take him or her seriously as an equal partner! Children are little adults. You can't just hurt them because you are the parent. You can't just move on without cleaning up the mess you caused in your child.

If you want your children to take you seriously and be honest with you, you have to be honest with them first. You have to honestly admit, that your action hurt them and apologize for it. You have to ask for their forgiveness too. You have to become then receptive of what you will be hearing. One of the most trying times is to hear your child telling you, that you hurt him/her. You have to handle what you hear with acceptance, understanding, and compassion. You need to keep calm and patient with your tone of voice too. You have to make your child feel your support and caring. You need to learn to ask questions to find about the truth deep down. Let me show an example here.

What happens when you don't want your child to go to a hard rock concert or a late night party?

If you reject your child regularly, he or she won't even tell you where he or she goes. You may never find out where he or she went. Is this what you want though?

You are lucky when your child comes to you with trust and ask you honestly, where he or she wants to go. If and you reject the request, without any discussion, the child begins to build a wall of opposition. They will lock themselves in their room and start hating you. Next time they just lie and go to the party.

Is there a middle way?

Yes. The middle way goes through communication. If you talk to your child, discussing both of your points of view the child feels an equal party with you. The discussion shall be supportive and solution oriented. During the debate, responsibilities need to be laid out.

The most important task is to find out what does your child get; what is her or his benefit for attending the concert or the party. Find out the real reason. Most of the time teenagers just don't want to be home, as it is so painful or annoying to be there. So if this is the case, you must look into yourself and become a more switched-on-parent, who shows interest in the life of their teenager.

You must apologize that you have been overlooking your child's need to be with his or her friends. If you find the concert or the party too dangerous for your child, that has to be talked about also. Your child has to realize what is at stake. Now offer solutions. Ask for forgiveness if the solution doesn't match the unsafe choice. Ask the kids to look into the fun this event can bring.

Why not going to the concert together? Why not make a party at home?

Attending the concert yourself, can show your child that aspect, you have raised concern for. Teach them how to take care of themselves against negative influences.

Communication is the best way to support your child.

Not the one-way communication when you preach to your child. Effective communication has two ways. This conversation includes asking questions and listening to the answer attentively. This communication will make the truth visible. Then the task is to handle the truth kindly with compassion.

If the child doesn't answer you, you must look into yourself and examine your tone of voice and actions. Your child may not answer you, because he or she doesn't trust you. Your child doesn't feel safe to tell you the truth, because you will explode and criticize.

> *If you want your child to talk to you, you have*
> *to become a person they enjoy talking to.*

If children want to do something, support them. Sit down, talk out the details so the responsibilities will be clear. Prepare them well. All this needs to be done calmly and kindly before the event. After you prepared them well, you must let them go and trust them that they are smart to follow the soft advice.

Through this exercise, some kids will talk themselves out of going to the hard rock concert or attending an unsafe party. They realize, there is too much at stake.

- Isn't it better to allow the kids to realize themselves, so you don't have to force them?
- Isn't it great that your child realized it by her or himself, so you didn't break rapport with them?

- Isn't it great that you could avoid fighting, and building opposition and resentment in them?

- Isn't it great that what you wanted to happen, your kids want it too? Since they said it, they take ownership of the decision. Since it was their idea, they remain peaceful.

- Isn't it great that you didn't have to hear: "I always have to do what you say, mom or dad!"

- Isn't it great that the kids want the same things as you?

- Was the time worth the investment in communication, so you all stay in agreement?

- Isn't it great that with this exercise you strengthen your trust and relationship in each other further?

This above example was only one scenario. If you look back on your relationship with your child, you will find many, many events when you hurt them with your "good intention." Having a great detoxifying conversation with your child is a massive step in your healing and growth.

Dear Parents,

I wish you have the strength to say sorry and ask for forgiveness from your children, for all the pain you have given them. Don't worry, the child always forgives you! I wish you experience the liberation and the overwhelming joy through this process.

Imagine how would you feel, when you hear this:

"Oh dad or mom, it's ok, we all make mistakes, and we will do better next time!"

The amount of weight leaving your shoulders and the size of the rock dropping down from your hearts are indescribable, along with the self-liberating feeling.

The next step in forgiveness is forgiving yourself for hurting your child. You couldn't do any better then, but today you can! Forgive yourself for hurting yourself through hurting your child!

Having the strength to say sorry and asking for forgiveness is an enormous growing experience in becoming humble.

Asking for forgiveness teaches you and your kids to be humble.

Through the forgiveness process, we learn that we are not perfect and it's ok to make a mistake. Mistakes are positive learning experiences and not a way we devaluate ourselves.

We must accept everyone for our different capabilities.

We also must trust that every event in our
lives is a llearning possibility.

Everybody has the right to make mistakes.
It's everyone's responsibility to learn from it.

Generational change comes when we transform what happened to us and pay forward only a loving way of handling things.

Parenting has to build a child's character, so he/she becomes empowered.

What are the consequences of not saying sorry?

Not saying sorry and remaining with the pricks of unforgiveness, guilt and resentment, build incapacitating emotional pain. The pain from guilt and resentment makes the physical load unbearable on one's back and shoulder.

Guilt piles up from knowing the pain we caused, but we feel too weak to take responsibility. Therefore, blaming it on someone else is the only solution. Blaming is diverting our attention from our mistakes to someone else. Blaming is a sign of weakness and represents tremendous underlying fear. The fear of responsibility and the fear of being not good enough.

How does the blaming game look like between parents and kids? Parents living in emotional pain will find shortcomings in their kids. This way parents blame the kids for those things they should be saying sorry for. They even beat on the kids and force them to say sorry for something the kids haven't done. Imagine these children growing up! These children will be the next generation of people who have "sclerosis" of the heart. These people will be insensitive as their heart turns into a rock. They will become sad and weak adults, who play the superior at home and ensure the next generation, to grow into painful adults and parents.

You are never too old to forgive!

When is the right time to forgive?

There is no such thing as the right time to forgive. The right time is now!

Regardless of what happened, becoming conscious and aware of your parenting can bring change and healing at any age. You can never be too old to clear out things with your kids. It is never too late to look at your parents and see the truth about them. When you see what was done to them by their parents, you will have understanding. Your parents paid forward to you whatever they received.

Forgive right now and let go of your pain!

Make an effort and clear things out with your parents. If your parents are in a golden age or they passed away, your only solution is to look at them out of compassion. Forgive them and move on.

You need to accept, that there are people who will
go from this world without learning a thing. Your
*parents may be them. **Forgive them anyway!***

Forgiveness stops your energy leaking out and generating negative feelings for yourself. You need to accept that you are the one who learned from your childhood. Most importantly, you are still here, and the learning is yours to use it! So use it and be grateful!

Forgiveness is the only way out, from being stuck in the past!

Happiness and success

> **In this Chapter, you find the answer to:**
>
> - What does happiness and success mean for me?
>
> - What are the emotional blocks?
>
> - What are the specific emotions blocking my happiness?
>
> - How did my emotions determine my life?
>
> - What can we do with our emotional blocks?

Everyone wants to be happy and successful.

Do you want to be happy and successful?

What is happiness and success?

Success is measured by money, at least this is what we were made to believe as children. By this belief, the more money you have, the more successful you are.

We were also told that successful people are happy too. Let us examine this common belief now.

Have you ever wondered:

- *What does one has to reach in life, so one believes that he or she is successful?*
- *What do you have to reach personally to put the label on yourself: I am successful?*
- *How much money or things do you have to own to feel successful?*
- *What is happiness?*
- *What is happiness for you?*
- *How much happiness can money buy?*
- *How much do you pay for your happiness?*
- *What kind of happiness can money buy?*
- *How long does money-bought happiness last?*
- *Why do we crave for more money, when we already have enough?*
- *Why do we still want for more, bigger, better, shinier and different, than what we have?*
- *Why can't we sleep at night from our problems, stress, and anxiety regardless of how much money we have?*
- *Why does our back, neck or head hurts, and our muscles are in spasm, irrespective of the money we have?*
- *Why are we afraid to lose what we have, regardless of how much we have?*
- *Why do we resent those, who have more than us?*

- *Why do we over-feed ourselves with food and sweets, like there is no tomorrow?*

- *Why do we overcommit and use our busy life as an excuse for not facing our emotional issues?*

- *If you were able to think about the above questions, then please think about the following:*

  Are you sure that success and happiness are what you learned from your parents? Or is there a chance we have to look elsewhere for the answer?

- *What if the definition of success and happiness, does not depend on money?*

- *Do you have to use your health as a currency to pay for your success and happiness?*

Intellectual awakening: fears are blocks

I hope the previous chapter and the questions here have stirred up enough curiosity in you, to seek the answers.

The way of self-discovery includes taking concrete steps. Each step is an essential part of your journey. Read on and see where are you now so far in your journey of discovering yourself.

The first giant step in our self-discovery is to realize our creator status. We must recognize that we create all of our behaviors.

You create all your positive and negative behaviors!

The second step of our discovery is that all negative behavior results in destruction. Adverse reaction destroys our relationships, our health, our lives and holds us back from reaching goals.

The lies about our own behaviors and the life these lies create, cause the highest destructions in our lives.

The third step is to name each negative behavior.

Every behavior, which has the power to destroy, we call it a block. Imagine these blocks to be different sizes and shapes of plugs. These plugs build on the top of each other and plug in our hidden potential, our talent and our ability to love.

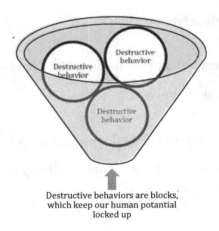

Destructive behaviors are blocks, which keep our human potential locked up

How do you recognize a person who is full of blocks?

Recognizing your own blocks is the fourth step in your self-discovery.

How do you recognize your blocks?

By looking at others first. Our blocks are reflected back at us from the mirror, what others put in front of us. Look at the lives of other people and look at their behavior. Is any of it make you upset and angry?

Your blocks scream out loud from the other person's upsetting behavior. Let us see few examples for blocks.

The **first type of block-filled person** is:

- Quiet,
- withdrawn,
- highly self-destructive via their criticism and rejections.
- Has random anger outbursts. These outbursts come in a seemingly irrelevant situation.
- Believes to have no use to live in this world, because he or she is not worth it. They continuously ask: "Why was I born if this world is so bad?"

The **second type of block-filled person**:

- Speaks loud and has to be always in the center of attention.
- Shows off by criticizing out of fear.
- Is full of anger hatred.
- Blames others and keeps others in physical and emotional terror. Threatening is the justified way to manipulate others, to get what he or she wants.

- Believes to be superior and everyone has to serve him or her.

- Plays God and believes to "know it all." Others must follow his or her way.

- Uses negative behaviors as protective shields so others won't discover his or her weakness.

- Uses negative behavior to express care. Uses destructive and hurtful behavior to teach a lesson, thinking that this lesson should positively build a person.

- Gives advice via a hurtful criticism.

- Gets very upset, when he or she realizes that his or her opinion is not welcomed and therefore he or she is not appreciated.

- He or she has short-lived relationships, consequently always alone and lonely.

The **third person who is full of blocks**:

- Pretends that all is well. Everything is in order, even when the extra kilos are coming on one by one.

- Tells that his or her life is just fine the way it is. He or she is happy and doesn't need any change.

- He or she has difficulty with change, as change always means a loss.

These were some examples of how blocks show up on the surface.

Did you recognize any of these characters in yourself? A little bit, maybe? If no, it is very reasonable. The conditioned mind keeps our behaviors hidden, so what we do is unconscious. This way we can live blind, deaf and insensitive.

Do you get upset by others doing the above behaviors to you? If yes, this is also normal. This is the mirror effect, I mentioned earlier.

We recognize our behavior in others.
If you recognize positive in others, you have
those positive characters in you.

If you recognize negative characters and behaviors
in others, you have those in you.

If the behavior weren't in us, we wouldn't recognize it in others.

Make a list of upsetting behaviors how others make you feel upset?

Recognizing and accepting our blocks in ourselves is the fifth step in our self-discovery. We might not do this upsetting behavior to others, but we do it for ourselves. Accepting these characters running in us is the foundation for change.

All negative emotions are blocks:

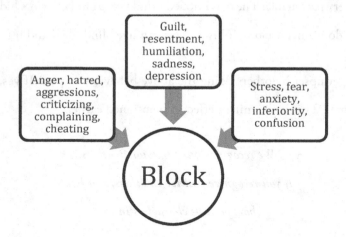

Accepting your blocks means you understand that your blocks are not you. Your blocks are your behaviors, your habits you have taken on during your childhood, which was the conditioning phase of your life. The seventh step of your self-discovery is to become aware of your behaviors and yourself, to be two different things.

In the following, we discuss the steps, how to manage the conditioning. Managing your conditioning means the process of change. This is the eight step in your self-discovery. If you completed the eight steps and managed your blocks, your true self will be visible. Let see the entire managing process.

What do we need to do with the blocks?

- Recognizing, accepting and admitting the blocks.
- Look in the root cause of the blocks.
- Transform the root cause.

- Put transformed behaviors into practice.
- Find a higher purpose and goal in life, so your new behaviors fulfill a meaning.

My intention in chapter III. and IV. to help you with the recognizing, the admitting process, and finding the root cause. Chapter V. Desrcibeds the specifics way out of your blocks and fears.

Chapter VI. will be the transformation, which unlocks the positive power hidden in your fears and blocks. This chapter shows you how a future can look like after the transformations. Chapter VII. discusses those specific locks you need to address in yourself to reach complete freedom from your conditioning.

The second part of the book,- The Future-, will make the new behaviors to become part of a meaningful mission in your life.

Why is it not enough to recognize the blocks?

Recognizing the blocks and not going more in-depth, is also the doing of underlying fears.

Recognizing the behaviors means staying on the surface. Staying on the surface will not bring deep and sustained change. Most popular motivational and spiritual teachings are designed for staying on the surface. They are popular as they only talk about the convenient part of the change. Most people will only take surface work. This way they convince themselves that they took steps on the journey of change, but it didn't work.

What is the work we do on the surface? Chant the mantras, repeat the affirmations, listen to certain music, or meditation, visualize things and look at candlelight. After a while, however, these rituals stop working. I personally had done this type of surface work. At that time I was only ready to work on the surface. Later on, I realized, these steps are illusionary but were necessary steps as well.

The work on the surface diverts our attention from the real root cause. These diversions help us to back-away from real change. By doing the rituals we can acknowledge that we did something, but it really didn't work. If we remained to have the same anger issues (to the exact same intensity and frequency), then nothing changed. Recognizing a block will justify us to continue to live by the block. We further convince ourselves that we are angry people, so it's ok to use anger. And that's about it as far change concerned.

Why is it not enough to accept your blocks?

If you recognize a block and accepted it without looking more in-depth, you will make more labels for yourself. "I am aggressive, I am depressed, I am sad, I am always hungry, I have to beat up everyone as I need to give justice." Etc...

What labels do you put on yourself?

Why do we need to find the root cause and transform it?

Lasting change occurs when the root cause is transformed. If we don't look deep within and find and transform the root cause, the change will be temporary. The change will be only on the surface of the mind. This means, if we are in a controlled environment we can use the new behavior. A controlled environment means we must stay aware. The moment we lose awareness, the old behavior slips back. So, if you want to go all the way and have lasting change, you need to transform the root cause.

Your success in making a real change depends on the depth, where you can make the transformation.

The transformation process is also a journey. It requires a lot of patience. As the layers of the onion come off, you are allowed to progress deeper and make the transformation there. The most important, however, is that you are the one making this journey to discover all that wisdom by yourself.

What does transformation do?

Transformation opens up your fears, and your positive life instructions become visible. The new life instructions are the sum of those positive behaviors, which you have to live by. This is changing old non-serving behaviors, for new ones and keeping them long-term. This new behaviour must be practiced universally with everyone and anytime. So be brave!

Every transformation process takes you only as deep as you can handle. Every transformation gives you new strength and more clarity to go deeper. So relax, stop your worries, for here we only learn about the blocks and their root causes.

The blocks and their root causes

Previously we talked about the blocks and three different personality types. As you can see, blocks show up on the surface in complex behaviors. The blocks make you believe that they are giant inextricable and entangled knots.

All of these deep-seated beliefs are fears. Fears then do their job to keep you in confusion and illusion.

A fear will simply confuse you. Fears create a belief that they are very complex, untouchable and can't be removed.

Fear creates beliefs.
Fear creates a belief about ourselves. Fear
makes us believe something to be true about
ourselves, whithout a factual base.

To resolve fears effectively, consider the following four points.

1. The first key point is that **the object of fear is not essential.** It doesn't matter what you are afraid of. What **matters is that you have the fear as an emotion, or vibration running in you.**
2. Therefore, the second key point that **fear is a feeling.**
3. The third point is that fear is a result of experience. Fear, just like every other emotion, is a result of learning. **Fear is a neurological process.** Therefore, **you can unlearn the process and substitute it with another feeling, which serves you.**

4. To make the change in the neurological process, one needs to **find the first event when the fear-feeling was established**.

When you want to resolve your fear, you must deal with this very first event. When we transform the first event, the fear feeling falls apart.

The transformation chapter provides all the tools to work with this first fearful event gently, efficiently and effectively.

What happened at the first event? Why is the first event so crucial? The first event, when we experienced fear, we established the roots of uncertainty, unknowing, confusion, tension and the feeling of "being nothing." The being nothing feeling equals to "not good enough."

When you experienced fear the first time, you had no idea that it was fear. Only when the same event happened two more times, you realized fear to be a distinct feeling. This is the point you learned to believe "I am not good enough" and life means living in fear. The "I am not good enough" feeling, is the most disempowering feeling for a child. None one on this world likes to feel the "I am not good enough" feeling. Do you?

Feeling not good enough on a regular bases, makes us dislike and not want to feel this feeling. The pain of "I am not good enough" is so great we learn to be afraid of it. The fear keeps us away from feeling the "not good enough" feeling. The mind chooses to feel the fear with its tension and anxiety, rather than to experience the sense of "I am not good enough."

To eradicate and rewrite the "I am not good enough" feeling and belief, at the root, we need to go back to the first event where fear was experienced. We have to take ourselves back there in a very unique way (this is the art of the transformations process) and rewrite the story there. We need to tell what story should have happened there. You will get to do this later.

What type of fears can block your success?

We have been discussing fears in general. Now let us learn about specific fears. Let us discover how these fears look like and show up in our lives.

> *Complaining, being regretful and resenting are*
> *three significant blocks in our success.*

When I mention this, most people react: "I don't resent anything!" Then they continue demanding: "You must help me because life is so bad and people do so much injustice to me. Why can others succeed and why do I always lose out. I work so hard, but I have such bad luck! I always meet the wrong people who use me!"

Dear Ladies and Gentlemen,

The first screaming sign of being resentful is complaining. The second is comparing ourselves to others.

Why don't we realize that the words we are saying are complaining?

When you grew up with people talking around you in a certain way, you will copy that. If they spoke to you gratefully, you would be talking today with gratitude. If you grew up listening to complaining, you learn to complain. The conditioned mind convinces you that complaining equals communication. Once under the influence of the conditioned mind, you don't even know what you are saying, as you are only stating the facts.

Complaining is the starting point of resentment.

Practicing complaining diligently fills up our lives with resentment. There are a few exceptions where we take good care and control our complaining. We manage our complaining at work when communicating with our boss or clients. We keep reasonable control over our complaining when we are with our in-laws. We control ourselves when our livelihood, our money or our good reputation depends on it. We manage our complaining out of fear of losing something.

Complaining becomes a way of life, and wherever we are, we find reasons to complain. We continuously talk about our losses and those events we regret or resent. If anyone else in our presence would complain, we make sure to stop them and voice our loss. We have to make sure to earn bigger sorrow. It sounds like: "This is nothing, listen to my story!"

Resentment is a very harmful, destructive emotion,
which keeps you in grief. Resentment chains you down
to your past pain, pettiness and victim feeling.

Resentment and regret are the foundations
of physical and spiritual poverty.

As long as resentment feelings run in you, you can't succeed.

How do we recognize regret and resentment?

Regret and resent are automated programs of the conditioned mind, you can't recognize them in yourself unless you become aware.

Complaining, regretting and resenting are protective mechanisms, to cover up our emotional wounds. We are unable to recognize our thoughts, our words and our actions, which are done out of regret or resentment. The conditioned mind keeps regretting, resenting, and grief is hidden, so you don't change.

Your first hint about your own complaining resenting behaviors can be found in the mirror. You will first recognize others for their regretting and resenting behavior.

If you want to recognize your own complaining, regretting and resenting behavior, you need to train your awareness. Awareness is your key to catch your resentment and regret programs. Training your awareness sharpens your ability to recognize all negative behavior in you.

Before you begin to train your awareness, let us see a few examples of complaining, regretting and resenting in real life.

"The neighbor has more than me."

PUPPETEER

CHÉRUNE CLEWLEY

BALBOA.
PRESS

A DIVISION OF HAY HOUSE

Balboa Press books may be ordered through booksellers or by contacting:

Balboa Press
A Division of Hay House
1663 Liberty Drive
Bloomington, IN 47403
www.balboapress.com
1 (877) 407-4847

Because of the dynamic nature of the Internet, any web addresses or links contained in this book may have changed since publication and may no longer be valid. The views expressed in this work are solely those of the author and do not necessarily reflect the views of the publisher, and the publisher hereby disclaims any responsibility for them.

The author of this book does not dispense medical advice or prescribe the use of any technique as a form of treatment for physical, emotional, or medical problems without the advice of a physician, either directly or indirectly. The intent of the author is only to offer information of a general nature to help you in your quest for emotional and spiritual well-being. In the event you use any of the information in this book for yourself, which is your constitutional right, the author and the publisher assume no responsibility for your actions.

Any people depicted in stock imagery provided by Getty Images are models, and such images are being used for illustrative purposes only.
Certain stock imagery © Getty Images.

Print information available on the last page.

ISBN: 978-1-9822-1562-0 (sc)
ISBN: 978-1-9822-1563-7 (e)

Balboa Press rev. date: 01/16/2019

The building was silent. Dim light spilled out from behind drawn drapes on the second floor, a sure sign that someone was up, probably working. But by two a.m. the most important man in America had dozed off at his desk.

Near the rear portico below, a dark figure jumped into the waiting limousine and was whisked away down the drive. The officer at the gate gave the occupant a smart salute and the car turned onto a deserted Pennsylvania Avenue. Minutes later its tail light flashed to signal another turn before it merged onto the beltway toward Maryland.

The man seated in the back took off his cap, revealing a military haircut, just beginning to gray, shrugged out of his jacket, medals gleamed in the bright light of a highway gas station then disappeared onto the dark seat. His hand reached down on the floor to pick up a small carryon bag, manicured fingers tugged at the zipper. He pulled out a fresh shirt, tie, jacket, and proceeded to complete his change. Since he entered the car he had not spoken to the driver until now.

"How long?" His voice was thin, strained.

"An hour." Came the terse response.

This was the twelfth time he had taken this run and each time his nerves were stretched tighter than piano wire. By lunch his head had begun to pound in anticipation of the nighttime excursion. He took his usual migraine medicine, but he'd had to take a second pill several hours early so he could continue to work. Now here he was, still in pain and all he could do was wait and hope that with his arrival the headache would dissipate like it usually did.

He understood the reason for the migraine. They never sent the same driver or the same car. He never knew when he got in the limousine where he was going. The last drive had taken well over two hours. He picked up the brown leather briefcase his wife had given him over three years ago when he was assigned to the White House. Evelyn hadn't a clue as to what his job was. She was simply proud of the fact that he was allowed inside the seat of power. If she knew what he really did for work, she would be frightened and there would be no pride at all. Most likely divorce would have been her reaction.

He opened the briefcase and pulled out a small penlight and a sealed red folder. This would tell him the agenda of the night's meeting. Each morning that folder appeared on his desk in the basement of the White House, a cold hand crept up against his heart and played strange games with his stomach. Despite his best efforts, he had been unable to discover who the silent messenger was. His right index finger slid inside the side opening of the folder and moved to the edge, effectively severing the invisible tape.

In the narrow light he could see the round black seal enclosing the white pyramid of the letterhead. Under the word 'Agenda' was the simple phrase, 'Plan of Action'. He knew what that meant. They'd decided. No more waffling. No more delaying tactics. He would have to report to the commander in chief in the morning, before breakfast, but, only if they gave him permission to do so.

Five years ago at forty-two, he'd been prepared to retire from the military. His desk job in intelligence had become boring, and he'd had some strong feelers from people in the private sector who were always looking for someone with his background in the Army. His ability to converse in several languages, knowledge of both the Middle East and Asia and an obvious committment to the intelligence community, made him a prime candidate for any industry with holdings in volatile countries.

Then General 'Bud' Anders, a three star general second in command at the joint chiefs' office in the Pentagon, approached him.

"Saw your retirement papers on my secretary's desk, Ed. I had you figured for more than a twenty-year man. What happened?"

"I'm looking for a little change, Bud. You know how it goes," he answered nonchalantly, "been riding this desk for the last couple of years. It's time to get out in the world. See what the other side has to offer."

"You don't mean a civilian job I hope. That's not for you. Tell you what. Some people I know are looking for someone with your qualifications. I'm going out there this weekend, why don't you come along. See if this is something for you, before you make a final decision." With that he pulled a folded paper out of his inside breast pocket, tossed it on the desk and left the office.

Ed opened up the paper and saw that it was his resignation with a 'rejected' stamped in red on top. Bud had effectively made the decision for him. He wasn't going to be allowed to resign. He had to go with the general that weekend.

"We're here, Sir." The voice of the driver cut through his thoughts.

They had pulled up to the front of an enormous log home he'd never been to before. Its' expansive porch was lit by lanterns spaced out on each of eight posts. Light poured from the windows of the home, upstairs and down. Cars and limousines were jammed in at every angle of the wide drive and parking area.

Colonel Ed Gately left the car and walked up the steps to the front door, which was opened for him before he even raised his hand to knock.

"Just in time, Colonel." General Anders said as he closed the door behind him. "We're in the back, it's more comfortable there." He said as he led the way down a long hallway.

"Gentlemen, ladies, the final member has arrived." The General announced as he opened the door onto what might be described as a "war room."

Men and women were seated around a long table. Red folders in front of each signified their presence was legitimate. At the far end of the room, in the shadow was another table set up to form the cross of a T. Six people sat there.

"We've saved your seat right here, Ed." The General said quietly as pointed out a chair at the bottom of the 'T' arrangement and sat down himself further up the right side of the table.

One of the men in the shadows began to speak.

"Now that we are all here, we will begin to inform you of our decisions." He paused, raised a water glass, took a sip and quietly returned it to the table. "It has long been known that the governments of the world have many ways of communicating other than what is seen in the media. It is also known that certain members of our larger corporations communicate with these same governments on an ongoing basis in the same manner."

Ed was waiting for the man, whose strong commanding voice he had heard before in each of these clandestine meetings, to get to the point. His mind was open and ready to receive his instructions, for no laptops, pens or paper were ever allowed at these meetings. Each person here was chosen for their incredible memories, high intelligence and their background of work within their particular countries.

"It has been decided that the governments represented here, in concert with all corporations with whom they already have a dialogue will immediately begin to form the worldwide government that will encompass all resources and areas, including natural, industrial, educational, military, healthcare, pharmaceutical, scientific, etc.

"Further," the man rose from his seat as if for emphasis, "drastic steps will be taken, to ensure complete compliance with this decision and the formation of this world government. Those steps will include actions, which, might be perceived by some, as terrorist actions, in order to bring the populace and leaders of each of our countries into full compliance and unity with our decisions. When this meeting has ended the timeline for reaching completion of the new government will begin." The man resumed his seat.

"How come I use to have everything back then and now nothing?"

"Why can XY make more money than me?"

"Why can this simple person be so smart to work his things out, and why can't I?"

"Oh, I thought you have already done that ..."

"You forgot again to take the garbage out!"

"How come I never succeed in anything? Why am I second in everything I do?"

"Why do I always lose out? Why do I pay more for everything?"

"You don't love me because you don't cook my favorite food!"

"You don't love me, because you bought new shoes for yourself!"

"I should have chosen the other company to work for, now I am stuck for a year."

"I should have gone with you, I missed out again!"

"I should have made money also to buy a house if I worked abroad."

"Why have did I go to meet that guy, it was such a waste of time and money!"

Resentment has two other forms: Envy and jealousy.

Jealousy shows up not only in personal relationships, but in every part of our lives. What does jealousy look like?

When we feel that others have, what we should have. When we are protective of our possessions, so no one can take them from us. When we are unable to share. This is also jealousy.

Where do jealousy and envy come from?

Both of these characteristics and feelings come from the "I don't have, but I want to have" feeling. Furthermore, they come from. "If I want to feel the –"I have" feeling, I need to possess and own more things than others do." Jealousy sets in when we believe that others have something, that we do not have. We think they are somebody because they have something what we don't have. They are making us feel insignificant because we lack the object they possess.

When we get any of the things we crave, we no longer want it. Can you see how much time people spend on getting rid of something that they wanted earlier?

We don't want to keep things, because having it would take our craving away. Having it would have to make us be content.

Realize, that "not wanting" is also a "wanting."

All wantings and not wantings are considered craving. All complaining, regrets, and resentments have an underlying desire. They are all rooted in rejecting what the present moment gives. Rejecting the present moment means, not liking what the present moment has for you. You reject the present when you don't like what happens there and you express it too. We don't like what the present moment gives, because we want something else. We don't even look into the possibility of liking something the present moment brings. We automatically reject it. Practicing rejection means practicing not wanting. This is really crazy! Isn't it?

Either way, if we don't do anything to make a change, we only create more events to practice complaining. (We will discuss craving in detail, in the next chapter.)

What is the reason for resenting and how can it be resolved?

One reason for keeping ourselves in resentment is to stay stuck. Being stuck makes a perfect comfort zone. Awaken now!

If you don't stop regretting and resenting, you won't be able to come out of your past and change your future and your destiny!

If you are waiting for a life event to happen, so you stop resenting, then your death will be the only life event. Do you really need something to happen in your life, so you end regretting and resenting? Circumstances and events are attracted into your life due to the resentment and regret vibrations in you. If you want to stop your resentment, you need to start on your journey to discover the root causes of your regrets and resentments. Once you have transformed the root cause, you will have a new road in front of you. Practicing your new behavior will show that you live in abundance and feel "good enough."

Digging down to the root of resentment and regret can reveal precious gift. The gift opens up when we look at those situations in the past and list what should have happened there, so all parties walk away feeling loved. "The what else should have happened there," gives you wisdom, for your new life. The wisdom contains all your life instructions to build your new life! If we use the new life instructions, we won't be able to regret and resent. If we apply contentment, the antidote of regret and resentments, then we no longer can regret and dislike anything. This entire process will be evident with the transformation exercise in chapter VI.

The antidote for resentment is contentment.

To eradicate resentment and regret from our lives forever, we must work on our feelings.

Resentment and regret are behaviors, which come from an emotional or vibrational root cause.

> *We can only produce a resenting behavior if we have*
> *the vibration of resentment in our body cells.*

Can you make sense of your life and the circumstances you have been attracting?

- Why is your life full of resentment?
- Why do those things happen that you will regret?

- Why do you react with resentment to anything that happens?
- Why don't you know any other behavior other than resentment?

The answer is that your body cells vibrate with resentment because they don't know any other vibrations.

Do you understand now, why you resent and regret?

We resent and regret because our cells vibrate with resentment and regret. We don't know any other vibrations. Therefore, we also don't know any other behavior. We resent and regret because we don't know what else we can choose to do instead!

The bottom line is that we resent because we don't know contentment.

Contentment comes from the belief "I am good enough and I have enough."

Genuine contentment is not an intellectual understanding about what you have. Contentment must be a feeling in every single cell of your body.

Contentment has to be an unconditional, genuine and general feeling. Absolute contentment doesn't depend on any object or personal relationship. Absolute contentment has no conditions. It originates in gratitude for one single thing, that is your life. Therefore, contentment doesn't depend on the size of your bank account. Contentment comes from your heart, feeling genuine gratitude for every breath you take. Contentment is a vibration on the cellular level.

If we don't learn acceptance and gratitude as children, we will grow up as resentful adults. Why? Because we have never seen acceptance, gratitude, and contentment at home. We have never felt accepted, being appreciated in school either. We have never been able to give enough at home and in our environment to earn acceptance and gratitude.

> *The key to your success is, learning the vibrations*
> *of acceptance, and contentment.*

What is success? Obviously, the definition is not what society has made you beleive. Success is a feeling. A feeling of celebration for being alive. Success means to create acceptance, gratitude and contentment and all positive vibrations, at free will.

- Do you now know why you don't consider yourself successful?
- Do you understand why you are not able to feel the feeling of success?

Look into your life and your emotions. What emotions and behaviors do you practice daily? If you are unable to feel successful, it is because you are lacking the contentment feeling. We lack contentment because we don't have a gratitude feeling.

So what happens when we keep trying to learn contentment and the feeling of gratitude, but we can't succeed?

The answer is straightforward. We don't have contentment because we don't have gratitude. And we don't have gratitude, because we are lacking forgiveness, letting go and deserving.

Forgiveness and letting go, breaks the chain of
your past regrets, pains, and grudges.

Deserving is a fundamental belief, to build strength to dissolve all negative blocks.

Guilt is another negative feeling, which is commonly instilled in children and blocks one's future. Guilt is the feeling "to have" something, but you don't feel good about having it and don't feel you deserve to have it. Many people destroy goals out of guilt as well.

If we finally allow ourselves to feel the deserving feeling,
we will be able to dare to create all positive vibrations.
Positive vibrations, which show up in positive behaviors,
serving us to create our compelling future.

The new positive vibrations are key, to opening the door leading to your future!

Your genuine positive vibrations and behaviors allow you to feel, express and give gratitude.

Without forgiveness and letting go, we can only express gratitude in certain situations. One situation is your birthday, when you receive gifts and well wishes. You know you are expected to say thank you. In spontaneous cases, when someone opens the door or lets you go ahead in a long line, you won't even recognize what happened. Just take it all for granted.

Without forgiving and letting go of the past, we are handicapped to express gratitude in general.

Deserving is born from self-worth

To feel deserving one must have self value. One must have the "I am worth it" belief.

The foundation for self-value is to have self-importance. Self-importance means that we are important enough to stand up for ourselves. Standing up for ourselves with love, peace, and kindness.

Standing up with peace sometimes means walking away from something or someone silently, or saying only "Thank you." We must learn to let go and walk away in peace. You stay peaceful out of self-worth and self-value. You must love yourself enough to keep your peace in all situations. Your peace is the most precious gift you can create for yourself at free will. So please do so! Please be responsible for keeping your inner peace.

You were born to deserve living in peace.

Every negative blocking belief, is born out of a past event. All of these past events need to be transformed. The transformation process lets us discover the learning in that particular situation where the blocking belief was born. To be the owner of perceived wisdom, you need to do the transformation process yourself. Only after will you convince yourself about applying these teachings in similar life situations today. If you have stressful and painful situations repeating in your life, you must start looking at their root cause and transform them.

The consequences of resentment

In case you still don't have a big enough reason to work on your past, I will show you the possible effects of living with resentment. Be aware of the damage you create for yourself by continuing resenting.

Resentment:

1. Creates pain and illness for ourselves and for others around us. Thinking and speaking out of resentment, we accumulate and dump vast amounts of pain on to others. Words full of resentment are like nails that we hammer into others and especially to our loved ones. The vibration of resentment destroys not only the other person who was targeted, but also you.

    Before I arrived at the point of awakening, I personally wasted a lot of time and effort on expressing my resentment and poking others. Going through the transformations and healing, now, I love myself enough to find gratitude in every event and situation. It is a life long work to be aware of resentment and managing ourselves.

It gives constant vibrations to the Universe to create more events so we can continue practicing resentment.

2. Keeps us living in the past. Resentment is the glue, keeping us stuck in our sad stories. This emotional load makes it possible to keep the extra weight on our body. The emotional burden and heavy stress is destructive to the whole body. The emotional load of resentment eats you up alive. It degrades your immune system and weakens your physique. The body expands, weight increases, - resembling the emotional weight being stuck on the body. The fat acts as an insulation, where the toxic emotional waste is being stored. We lock up the toxins, so we think we don't feel them. We create the illusion that any toxin, which is locked up, doesn't exist. This process is called self-poisoning. As a result, no matter how little you eat and how much you exercise, you can't lose weight permanently. The weight comes right back. Even if we don't eat anything, we feed ourselves with the emotional load. The extra body weight is heavy, just like the resentment caused by the emotional burden.

3. If you can't lose weight or you gain it back very fast, it is because you have a subconscious resentment process, sabotaging you deep within.

I personally know healers, who carry lots of extra weight. They hardly eat, but still putting on weight. They feed themselves with pain. They feed on the client's pain. These healers take up the role of taking the emotional weight off the client and keep it. They are likely to be afraid to let it go. They possibly believe in having self-value equal to the pain they take from others. They live as victims. Being a victim is a good explanation of why they can't or should not let the pain go. A life full of pain is the only precious life for them as healers. The more pain they take off from people, the better the job they believe in doing.

I personally had experience being addicted to pain. I exercised regularly and very intensely to keep the extra weight off. However, If I took time off from exercise due to injury, the weight came on fast. It took many years of healing to put all these down and exchange pain for unconditional love and the ability to let go. I allow others to carry their stuff now and if they are ready to put it down, I am here to help. As a miracle of the emotional healing my body weight stabilized on a healthy level.

No one has to keep pain! Every pain can be transformed and should be transformed to love!

4. It establishes the foundation of life-long bitterness, misery, and depression. The practice of resentment ensures misery to be paid

forward to our family and loved ones. We "poison" ourselves and our family.

5. It ensures a life full of craving and never reaching any goal in life. Resentment sabotages and poisons our own goals.

6. It ensures failure. Resentment makes you suffer from failure feeling, as you regularly turn back and give up your goal before it can come true.

7. It ensures living life as a victim.

Do you still enjoy living in resentment? If yes, you may subconsciously continue living in resentment until you accumulate so much pain that you reach your limit. For some people, the **threshold of pain** comes when reaching the death-door.

Our pain tolerance limit is set to a level, where we finally allow the feeling of pain. We finally stop running away from pain. Now we admit "I had enough pain and anything is better than this!" This is the being fed-up point, where we seek a way out, which I call the door of change. This is the long-awaited time, where you can to step on the road and walk forward with confidence by practicing the changed behavior.

Seeking the way out is your starting point
in your process of awakening.

We have already discussed the power of awareness intellectually. Now it is time to experience it. If you bring yourself to the position, to seek the way out, with every single cell of your body, then you are standing in the door of awakening.

Where are you now in your seeking?

Did you reach the fed-up point that anything is better than living with bitter resentment?

Are you ready to do anything and everything to get out of resentment? If you are, this is fantastic! If you are not prepared, this is also very normal, so go on and read this further, please.

Being ready to put your resentment down is the first liberation from your chains. This liberating feeling signifies the time you admit and accept your resentment practices. You also come to admit that what happened to you so far was all your own doing. The second tier of liberation begins with taking this responsibility. Admit, with the type of conditioned mind you had, resentment was the only possible way to live. Accept it and breathe free!

Acceptance ignites our super-power to go forward. Acceptance makes the road of change visible. How surprising!

> *For real change to take place, you don't have to*
> *want to change, but accept what it is.*

Accepting all the damage we have created with resentment, awakens us and opens the new road to forgive and let go.

Attention!

For those wanting to continue to live in resentment and keep grudges, please know that when we fail to forgive, our life becomes bitter, and we slowly die in misery.

After admitting and accepting, the next step, comes the forgiveness process. Forgiveness is another critical factor in the process of change. Forgiving others and ourselves, cuts us off from our past pain. Forgiveness as one form of love, liberates you from your past. Forgiveness is the foundation of our new road where we can practice our positive behaviors.

Concentration for succes

We have been talking about awareness being a key factor in making a lasting change. Awareness, mindfulness or concentration are all the same and all need to be trained and sharpened.

Change depends on the level of your concentration!

Therefore, the diligent training of your concentration
is the next step to making a lasting change.

You need your concentration to catch yourself on your old behaviors, thoughts, words, and actions. You need your attention to stay aware and mindful about those thoughts words or actions, which are against our goals.

Training your concentration, trains your awareness!

You need your concentration to see yourself being destructive to yourself and others, in thoughts, words, and actions.

You need your concentration to recognize the time to change destructive thoughts, words, and actions to proactive ones.

The higher your concentration level, the sooner you catch yourself on your thoughts igniting destruction and can make the change in your thoughts, words, and actions ("The Future" part of this book will be talking about this in detail.

Why do you need to change your thoughts and behaviors immediately when you see yourself in destructive ones?

You will reach sustained change when you catch the first spark of a negative non-serving thought, word or behavior. Catching yourself and becoming aware, gives you space and time to change your behavior. Change comes with the discipline of being committed to do this work.

Seeing yourself angry and yelling, you become aware. This means you can recognize your bahavior. It is already a significant change. If you catch yourself feeling angry and don't do anything about it and just keep yelling, then where is the change? Once your awareness increases, you can stop your resentment process much sooner. When awareness takes over, it makes you see what you just did. You admit and accept "I expressed my anger."

Awareness makes you see that anger has no use and is harmful to everybody, especially you and you feel awful when you feel angry. Awareness brings the subsequent realization "If I get angry, I will continue to vibrate in anger for hours and days. Do I want this?"

Once your awareness increases, you can ask the question during your anger episode "Is it worth it for me to vibrate with anger for another day?"

The faster you see yourself being bitter, angry and resent something, the quicker you can stop the process and make a change. The sooner you notice yourself being resentful or angry, the sooner the vibration will wear off. The sooner anger wears off, the less harm we cause ourselves and others. The sooner you notice that you are angry and resentful, the faster you realize you need to substitute this feeling with contentment.

The more you practice the vibration of contentment, the faster your life will change to positive. The more contentment that vibrates in you, the more things you attract in, to continue to feel content.

Accept:
As per the law of cause and effect:
Whatever vibrates in you, will continue to
reverberate and have an after effect.

What happens when we are on the road of training your awareness and still create an unconscious negative behavior? It happens, and it is the normal process of the road. Accept it. Re-learning takes time. Be patient!

What happens when we still create negative behavior and become conscious about it?

What do we do now?

We do absolutely nothing!

We need to let the negative behavior run out without a reaction. We need to allow the negative vibration of the behavior wear off.

How do we support this wear-off-process?

Observing breath is our tool to make time and space for supporting the wear-off-process. So the only thing you do is **observe your breath patiently.** This helps you to **stay non-reactive and get back to balance** as fast as possible. There is nothing else you can do to make your unwanted, self-created feeling go away. **Wait it out and breathe.** If you wish your negative vibration to go away, because you don't like it, you practice craving and hatred. The new craving and hatred you create, continues to trickle down and bring you more of that effect. Remember, you are also practicing patience here! Practicing patience is also a vital task when we are seemingly doing nothing.

Whatever happened was also a test for your patience, to practice vibrating with patience and being diligent while concentrating on your breathing. Whatever happened, it was **a test for reminding you of impermanence, that all shall pass.**

The new, positive and proactive behavior is the way out.

Practicing your new behaviors take you forward on your journey towards your goals. This practice is the way out of being stuck.

You must accept and enjoy continuous practice.

We need to learn new positive behaviors so we can go forward in life. It is like driving a car. First, you have to learn the technique of driving, before you can drive yourself and others safely to a destination.

Similarly, practicing contentment and patience makes us become content and patient. Patience isn't available in a pill yet. You need to practice patience and contentment if you want to become a patient and content person.

Let go of your old non-serving behaviors! Thank them for being in your life and serving you in the past. These old behaviors served you, to survive. Today, you have new behavior tools, which are taking you forward on the road.

How long do we have to practice?

You need to practice until the new behavior becomes part of you. The practice is a vital part of your journey.

Without your new behavior becoming automatic, you won't be able to use it in spontaneous and difficult circumstances.

By applying the new behavior, you make difficulty disappear.

Your new behavior is not only needed to reach your goals, but also for sustaining that goal and making it grow. To maintain your goal and make a profit, you need your new behaviors to be on the cellular level.

If you succeed in applying your new behaviors, your goal will come true all by itself. This is an interesting fact about your new behavior leading you to success. We will discuss planning your future in the next part ("The Future") of this book.

Congratulations! You have come so far working towards your full liberation. Now you reached a critical point and hopefully ready to face your fears. If you are still not sure, please read on and learn about fears in general!

IV

The power of your fears

In this Chapter, you find the answer to:

- How to recognize my fears and understand their power over me?

- How to dissect my fears and understand their anatomy and complexity?

- How do fears position themselves in different layers?

- How to open the locks on my fears one-by-one?

We have been discussing the very specific blocks locking up your potential. Now, we finally reached a peak point in our work, which takes place at the deepest level of our mind.

Now is the time to face the most fearful subject, your fears! Don't worry, you are safe, and you are not asked to do anything. We are only talking and learning about fears.

How do we learn about our fears? First, we need to recognize and understand them. Secondly, we need to take out the controlling power of them. The third step is to open the locks on our fears and get wisdom out of them.

How do we recognize our deepest fears?

Fears hide under other fears and keep themselves in great secret. If we want to work efficiently with our fears, we need to work our way down fear by fear until we reach the most profound fear. This deepest fear is the largest block keeping your flourishing talent locked up.

How do you know, that you still have a deep block inside you? It is a very valid question. This is a question asked by many people who have been practicing many different techniques to get over their fears.

You still have blocking fears in you, when you practice your new behaviors, but all of a sudden an intense feeling arises and sweeps through you like a tornado. This tornado sweeps away all your efforts of trying your new behavior. We feel that our trials don't work. Let me explain this through a real-life example.

Do you know how people create drama out of nothing? They create a scene that has absolutely no meaning. The purpose of a meaningless drama is to make one feel important and valuable. One creates a meaningless drama to be the center of attention. We also create drama to prove ourselves.

Whatever the reason to create a meaningless drama, we always feel bad, regret it and resent it in the end.

Take a look at your drama scenario and find the locks you need to open. If you regret and feel resentment afterward, you need to work with these emotions. When you open the locks on your regret and resentment you will reach your deepest fears, creating anxiety. Anxiety makes you horrified. Anxiety disables anyone and begins it's destructive work on your environment too.

How much anxiety do you have?
What are you are afraid of, specifically?

I hope this short introduction to the topic picks your interest up, opens your eyes, ears, and mind. I hope it has been smooth sailing so far and you are curious to see the rest.

If you didn't open your mind yet for the upcoming new information, lets us open it now. Here is the exercise:

Stand up and keep your arms straight in front of your chest. Bring your arms back to shoulder level while keeping your eyes on your hands. Right eye on the right hand and left eye on the left hand. Now keep opening your arms wider, until you can only see your hands from the corner of your eyes.

Now take your arms further back. You can't see your hands, but you know where they are. You can see them with your mind's eye. Now turn your head first to see the right then the left hand. Turn as much as possible without moving your feet.

Congratulations!

You just realized that even if your hands are not visible to your physical eyes, they are there. You can see them with your mind's eye. See, things can exist even if you don't see them physically! Things also can exist when you feel them without seeing them!

> *Opening your mind means, realizing that things*
> *can exist even if you don't see them.*

Now, with your mind wide open, you can begin the work.

The foundation of all fear is "nothing." To begin the anatomical examination of fears and "nothing," we need to answer the following questions:

- *"What am I afraid of?"*
- *"What will happen if my fear comes true?"*
- *"What is the worst thing what happens then?"*

Keep asking these questions until you find the object of your fear. Keep asking the questions above until you get the answer "I don't know." We are simply afraid of not knowing. We are afraid of the "nothing" and becoming nothing. We are scared of "not existing."

Fear is an elaborate illusion. Why? Because only the conditioned mind can make the "nothing" become a reality. How can you be afraid of "nothing," which doesn't exist? Isn't that silly?

However, the conditioned mind can make us believe, that "nothing" has a destructive power over us. "Nothing makes us weak, makes us disappear and become nothing."

Let us continue now with the anatomical examination of fears and to look into the following points:

1. The "nothing."

What is the meaning of "nothing"? Let us examine it by answering the following questions:

- *What is "nothing"?*
- *What does "nothing" mean to you?*
- *How does "nothing" appear to you?*
- *What are the specific causes of "nothing"?*
- *How does "nothing" feel? Do you have any feeling in any body part?*
- What happens as the result of feeling the "nothing"?

Think it over! Who can be afraid of becoming "nothing"?

The only person that can have fear and anxiety about becoming "nothing," is someone who thinks that they are somebody.

What a realization! What did our conditioned mind make us believe? Just what did our mind make us believe about ourselves? We believed all the labels the mind made about who we are. Based on these beliefs, we formed a false sense of self. This false sense of self is called our ego. The ego is our false sense of perception about ourselves and who we are. This ego has been guiding our lives. We have been listening to our ego about who we are and what we should do. So far your ego has created all that you have in your life, but not you. This is a good time to cry your eyes out. Allow yourself a few minutes of crying then come back to reading.

Ask yourself now:

- *"Who am I?"*

"I am a mother, father, brother, sister, athlete, boss, carpenter, Jim, Anna, a teacher, a banker, a businessman, tall woman, short guy, and serious person, etc."

Keep asking this question and write down the answers. Keep writing until you get some kind of response.

Then ask the second question:

- *"Who am I not?"*

Keep asking yourself and keep writing down the answers until you have some.

"I am not a joker, liar, cheater, loud person, aggressive person, gentle person, etc."

All the answers are mind-made labels! The conditioned mind, the ego made these labels! The ego made us believe what and who we are and also what and who we are not.

When we could unfold the trick of the conditioned mind and use objective observation, it becomes visible that we are, as a matter of fact, "nobody" or "nothing" but life, love, and energy. We are "nobody" and "nothing" other than energy.

This realization gives deep inner peace and we finally feel very much at ease and can relax.

The truth liberates and gives peace.

Conditioned-Mind-Made labels, create stress, uneasiness, confusion, doubt, and fear.

2. Fear and anxiety are a subconsciously chosen behavior

As strange as it sounds, fear is a chosen behavior. Of course, you don't recognize that you choose fear, because fear is running automatically and subconsciously in you. You choose fear and anxiety as you concentrate on those life events, where you can practice fear and anxiety. Your concentration is a subconsciously guided process to feed you with fear. As long as the fear program is running in you, it makes you choose fearful reactions.

Can you see your fears in your life now?

How come you have these fearful reactions and behaviors? Why don't you know how to be brave?

The answer is simple. You only know fear and anxiety, because you have fear vibrations running in you. Fear is your only resource. Just like previously, regret and resentment were your resources, now it is fear. Fearful reactions are your single known responses and your comfort zone. When fear is our comfort zone, we feel agitated even if in a safe place. We begin to feel disturbed when we have peace around us. So, when the fear feeling decreases, we quickly create some.

3. Fear is an addiction

How is it possible to become addicted to fear? Fear can be an object of addiction, just like smoking, sex, alcohol, drugs or anything else. Once you create an addiction, you become controlled by it.

The conditioned mind creates fear and anxiety to control us further. When we live in fear and anxiety, we depend on fear and anxiety. Fear is our lifeline. If we are dependent on something, we are addicted to it. So fear and anxiety are also addictions.

Fear addiction means we are craving for the feeling of fear and anxiety. (We will talk about craving in detail in the next point.)

A smoker, who is addicted to smoking would say: *"I will smoke in my pants if I don't have a cigarette fast!"* - or *"I will break something if I can't smoke!"* In the case of fear, *"I will break something if you don't give me something to be afraid about!"*

A smoker lives life between two cigarettes. Smoking defines how much the person is allowed to work or do something out of what he or she wants. Wanting to smoke sensation, will continuously interrupt the life of the smoker.

Alcohol, sex, aggression, and fear control our lives similarly to smoking.

The parts of fear:

4. Fear and anxiety are cravings, and they build inner conflict.

All addictive behaviors are based on craving, like fear and anxiety. Craving builds the foundation of inner conflicts. Inner conflicts result in confusion.

What does craving mean? What are the consequences of craving?

The definition of craving: An obsessive level of wanting, wishing and dreaming for something. We always want something and become sad and depressed by not having it. Craving is also when we still don't want something that we have.

Not wanting something is the way to oppose and express our dislikes. Dislikes progress to hatred. We don't like what happens, so we begin to hate it. For example, a girl really wants to be loved and commented on her good look. She is craving for compliments. When she receives less favorable feedback, she says: "This guy made such bad comments on my hair, it makes me feel so bad! I hate this guy!"

Another example is when we crave to get out of the grocery store fast. However, we run into a long line and say: "I hate long lines, it takes forever to get out of here! Why do I have to wait always for others!"

Being addicted to craving, we are likely to be addicted to opposing and rejecting as well. We run the craving, opposing and rejecting programs automatically. Even if we like a certain thing, we will find something to oppose or reject.

Real life example for rejection addiction: "The food was so nice last night in the restaurant, and we had such a good time, but waiting for the table was so long. I hate that they don't take a reservation! And did you see the waiter making faces when I asked for the wait time?"

Craving and rejection programs run subconsciously. So we look to oppose, reject or criticize, even if we like something. Something only seems valuable if we reject it! One rejection follows the next as we continue criticizing for hours. Imagine a group of craving people together who keep opposing each other for hours, and call it a debate.

When you are rolling in rejection, you will reject, fight, and oppose everything and everyone. Everybody is an enemy, and you are in fight-mode. When rejection program runs in you, you reject your favorite food your wife made you. You deny that she cooked and choose to be hungry. "I don't want it! I am not hungry! Don't cook anything for me ever again!" says the mad, conditioned mind.

Can you see how childish the ego is and makes you humiliate yourself? We really punished the other person by not accepting the offered food! And who stays hungry?

The ego manages to misinterpret something to make sure we can reject it. Rejection is a double-edged sword. The punishment intended for the other person really affects us.

A few hours later when you calmed down and feel really hungry, you realize your childish behavior and feel perhaps some sort of shame. Then you eat the food anyway. More madness of the conditioned mind!

Now let's see the vocabulary of those who express their dislikes, opposition, and rejections. Have you noticed the way people criticize or hate something? Have you noticed their words and tone of voice?

For example:

"I didn't think it was like this!"

"I didn't think you would do that!"

"For sure I would have done this differently!"

"I knew this would happen! I just knew you would do this to me!"

"I dont understand why can't you do it yourself!"

The above expressions are examples or opposing, rejecting, criticizing, regreting resenting and blaming. These negative comments are all full of dislikes, bitterness, and hatred. The bitterness and the low energy of dislikes, will pull anyone down. If you feel depressed after hearing something, it was a hateful criticism.

Craving is an energy vampire. When you do things out of craving you lower your energy level and others as well.

From fear and craving to inner conflict

Desire has many different objects. Being afraid and have anxiety are also objects of craving, just like resentment, anger or smoking, sex, drinking, and spending money.

What does fear-craving look like?

When we don't have the fear feeling, we would do anything to feel it. We crave the feeling of fear. Fear is our comfort zone also. When we reach the goal and feel afraid, craving begins again. The craving this time is to make the fear go away.

Craving now turns into inner conflict. Inner conflict occurs when the object of our fear comes true. When we feel afraid, we start working against it and would do anything to make it go away.

Can you see now, it is not about the fear feeling but the craving feeling? Craving for fear. When the fear comes true, the craving feeling disappears. The conditioned mind can't handle the lack of craving feeling and starts craving something else. In the case of fear, wanting something else is the craving for the cessation of the fear. The same craving and inner conflict processes are valid for the anxiety feeling.

When craving persists long-term, we develop multiple inner conflicts. When craving is constant, we jump between two poles. The first pole is "wanting to be afraid" and the second is "not wanting to be afraid and wanting fear to go away." We keep jumping between these two poles until we wear off. We usually get sick at this point. When we get second tired of the limbo, we will do something about it. However, what do we do then, when we only know to crave?

Craving develops into disliking our own emotions. When we crave, nothing is good enough that we have. What is not good enough, we simply don't like. We dislike what we have, we can't stand the events and people in our lives.

I like to stop here for a moment.

> *It is not the event or the people we don't like. We don't like how these events and people make us feel. So we really dislike our own feelings.*

> **We don't like the fears that we create in certain circumstances or being with specific people.**

Craving makes us dislike our feelings and emotions. Disliking on a long-term intensifies into hatred. We hate our feelings, so we hate ourselves. Isn't this so?

What is next when we hate ourselves? The answer is obvious. We hate others too.

Long-term craving develops into hatred, addiction and numbness.

Hating our own feelings is another layer of the onion. Hatred is another addictive behavior, which takes our attention away from the incredible confusion our inner conflict has created. The inner conflict, which makes you jumping between wanting and not wanting, gets you totally lost in life.

Craving is a feeling, which drives you to do many different "musts." "Must" can be many different things. They can be, a "must smoke", "must drink," "must take drugs," "must have sex," "must express aggression," "must spend money," "must engage in extreme sports" or "must cry." These "musts" are different ways to divert the conditioned mind to get busy with something else rather than looking into yourself.

Finding another addiction is the way out for the fearful conditioned mind to continue hiding. The mind is afraid of being under the limelight. Practicing certain "musts," for a long time, makes us too tired and numb. Being too tired and feeling too numb are new self-created feelings, new excuses why we don't have the energy to look into the root of our issues. Therefore, we continue living in fears.

A real-life example. When a smoker's anger level or fear level increases, he has to smoke immediately to get the calming effect of nicotine. You have seen a smoker shaking just to get a cigarette? Can you also note the relief feeling on them when they take the first few inhalations of the nicotine? Getting the nicotine seemingly moved the smoker to another planet.

So why don't smokers keep smoking one after another? Ask any smoker for the answer: "Oh that would be disgusting". So, just how many cigarettes can you smoke in a row before getting so high or disgusted and vomit? Getting high and feeling nauseous are other layers of excuses, why they don't look into the root of their fears, and anxieties. When the effect of nicotine wears off, the fear, or anxiety comes back, and the cycle starts again.

Craving progresses into multiples of addiction.

When we dislike a specific feeling, we will do anything not to feel it. We would do anything to divert our attention from it. This is the point where we start stacking one addiction on the top of the other. We multiply addictions by adding one addictive behavior to another.

For example: after smoking and drinking we perhaps start yelling, criticizing, resenting, blaming, chatting on social media, or advising people how to run their lives.

Hatred is self-protection

The fear that we diverted into craving, will come to the surface again and again. Fear is so intense that the addictive smoking, drinking, and sex can't suppress it anymore. We don't just hate our emotions but hate one specific feeling, that is our fear.

We learn to hate our fear to protect ourselves from feeling
our fear. Hating our fear is much better for the conditioned
mind, rather than to look into the root cause of fear.

Hating our fear soon surfaces as general hatred. We hate everything. We hate everyone and moreover our own life. Besides generating fears, we also create hatred. We do all our daily activities with hatred. We practice hatred from morning till night and night to morning. We can't sleep out of fear, but not sleeping gives another possibility to express hatred. "I hate that I can't sleep!"

A fearful person uses hatred to defend him or herself.
Hatred is a defensive mechanism, which justifies the
owner to use it for self-protection and survival.

A person who is full of hatred will attack out of fear.

Fear hides under fears

Can you see now, how one protective layer of fear builds on the top of the other?

Can you also see that none of these layers of fears depend on a specific subject?

The more you practice a behavior out of craving, the deeper in your cells craving will ingrain. Living in constant fear and hatred makes you addicted to these behaviors and you become controlled by them. Fear and hatred, like any other addictive behavior, gets into every single cell of your body and shows up in every single part of your life. Fear affects your personal, professional and social life too. When expressing hatred becomes a way of life, we destroy our relationships at work and at home as well. Ultimately we destroy ourselves.

Accumulated hatred is automatically expressed on someone who is not involved. We may not yell out of hatred at home, to our kids, parents or spouse, but we will let off steam, to the lady at the checkout counter. And she had nothing to do with our issues.

Controlling is another form of fear

Isn't it amazing what fear creates in our lives?

Despite the mess fear creates, we still choose
to live in fear and anxiety!

What are we afraid of specifically?

Are we afraid of not having enough money?

Are we afraid of dying from hunger?

Aren't we actually afraid of becoming "nothing?"

There is a chance that we are afraid of all of the above. The more things we are fearful of, the more hatred the conditioned mind justifies you to use. Furthermore, one fear creates a protective shield made out of a particular layer of hatred. And we, of course, have multiples layers and multiple things to hate.

How does hatred infuse our lives?

We hate not having money, because not having money means no power. Having no power means losing control. Losing control means losing identity and becoming dependent on others. Being dependent on others means to become small and nobody. Therefore, we hate to have no money, we hate to feel powerless, we hate to be just like anyone else, and we hate to feel small and inferior. Can you see here the many different fears and multiple protective layers made of hatred?

Furthermore, fear and hatred define our thinking. Fear will make sure to use every single opportunity to show off your power and control by yelling, criticizing, blaming and degrading others into "nothing." We practice all these destructive behavior on others, so they can't do the same to us.

We make money and overeat out of fear too. However, regardless of the amount of money and food we have, we remain hungry for more.

There is not enough money in the entire
world to satisfy a person who craves!
There is not enough money, to make a
craving person feel "good enough."
Therefore, the accumulated wealth is quickly
spent, to keep the craving rolling.

Fear uses hatred to rule

When hate comes from deep-seated fear, it shows up in physical power. This fearful person looks for fights. It is not enough to win over the other person emotionally and degrade him in words. Deep fear has to destroy others physically. No one shall find out this deep-seated fear. All must be kept in fear or destroyed who know our deep fear. The feeling of physical power makes this person acts as God and spread justice.

Our deep-seated fear convinces others about our opinion to be right. Only our point of view is correct! So our point of view has to be endorsed. This deep-rooted fear demands and forces others to do things our way. Demanding forces others to serve us, so we feel superior. Our fear has to suppress everyone into servant status around us. Feeling superior is the only way the conditioned mind feels valuable.

Fear demands respect as we believe to be here to play God. Because we think we are a chosen influential person, we are also convinced that we are entitled. All these negative behaviors are protective shields for the conditioned mind.

What happens inside a deeply fearful person? A fearful person is in constant anxiety to control and rule others. This ruling feeling is the greatest deception making the person believe about their freedom. Ruling others gives illusionary freedom, which shows up in spending or overspending money.

Do you really think playing God, spending, demanding and overspending make you feel free?

Playing God, spending, demanding and overspending are the highest form of self-enprisonment. Using financial, physical and emotional power on others, puts the ultimate chain on your ankles.

> **The magnitude of our demanding, control, destructive
> criticism, hatred, and anger for others is the measure
> of the size of our fears. These negative behaviors show,
> just how much we are afraid of our own emotions.**

All negative criticism and destructive behavior that we express on others, are a reflection of our own fears.

We hate to be afraid. This hate serves to hide our own weakness. Ultimately we are scared of feeling weak.

When you criticize others, you really criticize
yourself for being weak and living out of fear.

5. Lack of acceptance

The lack of acceptance is another element of fear.

When we lack acceptance, we can only reject and oppose things. Let's see how the lack of acceptance develops into fear.

Lack of acceptance, along with all negative behavior, begins with craving. Craving means wanting something else, than what we have at the present moment. We crave as we simply don't know how to use the "now" for our own good.

How can we value the present moment when our only agenda is to practice opposing or rejecting?

If we are addicted to rejecting, we will oppose
and reject everything and everybody.

This rejection process is automatic, so we don't even recognize it. We don't know that the behavior we express is a rejection and hurts others. We only know that by rejecting something we feel valuable.

Do you recognize yourself opposing and rejecting things and people?

If not, then do you notice when others oppose or reject you?

How does it feel to be rejected?

Does it bother you and make you upset? If yes, the truth is that rejection is in you.

Remember, the hurtful behavior of others is a mirror of your own practice. If you are not rejecting others, you are rejecting yourself one way or another.

> *When you grow up in rejection, the only*
> *behavior tool you have is rejection.*
> *We can only behave using the resources we have.*
> ***If we knew how to accept, we didn't have to***
> ***oppose, reject and crave for something else.***

Rejection and opposition are other examples of being addicted to craving.

It is not the rejection and opposing that you really want, but to feel the craving feeling. In this case, the craving is for running the programs of rejection and opposing. Running the rejection program will suppress your craving for a short time. However, when the conditioned mind senses that you haven't rejected for a while, it quickly creates a circumstance so you can reject something or someone. You will also pick on others, so they reject you.

How does rejection relate to fear?

Are you afraid of rejection?

Are you afraid that someone will oppose you?

Do you stay quiet and talk yourself out of your own idea?

Are you afraid to feel rejected or opposed for how you dress, but you wear that way anyway?

Do you find yourself erupting out of anger when someone expresses their rejective opinion of you?

Rejection is the most profound form of fear. Rejection is a protective mechanism. Out of the fear of being rejected we reject others and ourselves. This way, they can't reject us back. Rejecting yourself gives no space for others to reject you more than you already rejected yourself. Rejection becomes a habit or a standard way of conducting yourself to survive.

How could rejection and opposition develop in anyone? Rejection and opposition evolve the same way resentment, guilt and anxiety grew in us. Rejection originates in your childhood when you never felt accepted. You reject because acceptance is unknown to you. You have never seen and never experienced acceptance in your life. No one accepted you at home or in school. So you got used to being rejected. Rejection is the only known behavior for you. Therefore, you reject and oppose everything, which comes to you. You will also reject opportunities as well.

Rejection fills your life with negative thoughts, feelings, and communication. The rejection vibration makes you say the words no, not, don't and never, in almost all sentences. You can't ask for things and say "please." You can only state what is wrong with them.

Highly rejective people make excellent advisors, as they will find something wrong in tiniest detail. They will point out what is wrong or can be wrong. Pleasing them is tough, as they demand excellence. Therefore, negatively criticizing people can be precious assets. We only need to manage their negativity by learning to rise above.

Being a rejecting adult, we reject our spouse, our kids, and parents and anyone at our work. We continuously reject, oppose and hate others, so they can't find out our weakness and our fear. Consequently we have no friends either.

Fear makes us threaten others, so we can feel safe being in power. Ruling situations are valuable. The fearful, rejecting mind, believes it is the ultimate quality controller in life. This illusionary power protects us from feeling afraid of "being nobody."

Acceptance is linked to deserving.

Acceptance, for the conditioned mind means, to take what life forces on you. The critical point here is that the conditioned mind feels that life forces and pressures you to choose something. You are conditioned to "stomach" all that life brings you, as this is what you deserve. The conditioned acceptance means to take everything, even if it's harmful to you.

Moreover, the rejecting mind, that can't accept everything, is harmful. If it wasn't harmful, the mind could not reject it!

When you know only rejection:

- How can you believe that things and people coming on your way can build you and not harm you?
- How can you accept anything to be valuable to build you?

Do you see now the reason why you oppose and reject things out of self-protection?

You reject to make sure you don't get hurt!

As a result of the lack of acceptance, the lack of seeing things happening for your own good, you have never accepted yourself to be a positive entity. Since you are full of pain, you are surrounded by only harmful things. And you must take this pain as the way of life. This is all madness of the conditioned mind!

Acceptance for the detoxified, clear and healed mind, means that all life events are for you. It all happens so you can learn. Everything is for your own good.

Sometimes an event provides an opportunity to accept it, to practice patience. Sometimes a challenging communication happens so you can accept the fact that you have differences in opinion.

Acceptance does not mean you have to agree with the person's opinion!

Acceptance has an old and a new meaning. The old definition is to accept others the way they are. Even if they bring you harm, you must take that pain. This is what acceptance used to mean.

However, the second, the new or higher level of acceptance is, to accept situations and people to bring you something good.

This high level of acceptance also means to accept love from others too. Because you deserve to receive love! When you look at things objectively, everything brings you a form of loving kindness and goodwill. You just have to be able to see it.

> *Acceptance is receiving all that is coming to us, as it will build us.*
> *Whatever happens, it will make you grow.*
> *Acceptance always brings you something*
> *positive to make you more valuable!*

The high-level acceptance opens up new, creative and more compassionate ways in resolving issues. High-level acceptance makes one see and accept the truth about others.

> *What would happen in your life if you*
> *knew a high-level of acceptance?*

If you knew how to accept from a high level, you didn't have to be afraid of rejection and opposition.

If you can accept yourself, knowing that your imperfections

are only in the areas of your life where you need to grow,

then you will also take others for their flaws.

Accepting yourself is the foundation to accept others.

If you accept your journey, you will accept others for their journey of learning. Accepting yourself is the base to accept everyone and everything the way they are and learn from them.

You must learn to work with people on their level.

Working with people on their level means, accepting their differences, rising above them and handle them with loving kindness.

Can you see now, how high-level acceptance replaces rejection and opposition? If you learn to deserve high-level acceptance, you don't need to oppose or reject anyone, or anything. High level acceptance knows that if you reject and oppose, you will only fuel an adverse reaction in others.

Unconditional acceptance means being happy with what we have. Not wanting more, less or something else. When others give us something, we accept that it was their best. We need to be ok with what we get. If we need more, we express gratitude for what we received and ask someone else to do the rest or do it ourselves. We must accept this too.

We must accept that unconditional acceptance doesn't expect. You must use your objective observation of others to see their ability. If you know a person is lacking knowledge, and you expect more from him or her, you just create frustration for yourself. You must rise above, thank the person and move on. Find a different solution. This is your responsibility to keep your own peace.

Unconditional acceptance is the only way to stop
the cycle of rejection and opposition.

Fear of being accepted

The fear of being accepted is a very valid fear among adults. When you have never experienced acceptance in childhood, you possibly grow into an adult who can't accept. You can't accept others so as yourself. This has been previously clear and what we are discussing here is being afraid of something that we have been fighting for. We have been fighting for being accepted, but we have never gotten it. When you become an adult, you form a belief, that you don't deserve to be accepted.

Since you don't know acceptance, you don't know how it feels. So whatever you don't know the conditioned mind makes you afraid of.

Imagine, what would happen if you were accepted but you are afraid of it?

Would you know what to do in an acceptable situation? Or, would you push away the person who accepts you?

What runs through your mind as justification for pushing this person away?

"How can anyone accept me when I believe I am not good enough?" If I were accepted, I would have to stop proving myself. How would I live if I don't have to prove myself? If I would be „good enough" I would have to stop fighting, and I don't know anything else but fighting. If I am accepted, that would be the end of my life."

The fear of being accepted has been serving you to make sure you believe you are worthless. This fear is a perfect buffer to keep you from working on your self-value and self-worth. This fear keeps you away from living your life believing "I deserve to be valued." This fear keeps you away from having an abundance mentality that everything is here for your own good, to live a happy and healthy life.

Accepting yourself to be valuable is your birthright!

You have been given the highest and most precious gift in life. Your breath! Your breath is the most valuable gift ever, therefore your valuable and worth it! Simple.

Our deepest fear keeps the value of our breath hidden and creates the hardest mind-made illusion or belief, that you are worthless.

Have you thought about?

- How would your life change, if you accepted yourself?
- How would your life change if you had the energy of acceptance in your body?

If you had acceptance, you finally stop doing a lot of harmful things to yourself. Having the vibration of acceptance:

- Takes away your ability to reject yourself and others.
- Takes away the craving for rejection.
- Stops you producing events and circumstances to reject others and yourself.
- Stops you from creating behavior or communication, where others will reject you. (I personally used to do this.)

When the conditioned mind is blind from craving rejection, it makes you insert such nasty criticism or opposition that others will reject you right away.

Getting out of rejection begins with:

- Forgiving all who rejected and opposed you.
- Forgiving yourself for rejecting your own inner voice for so long.
- Establishing the bottom line to love yourself on the cellular level.

6. Fear is an illusion

Fear makes you believe all sorts of lies about yourself.

Have you thought about, how much of what you are afraid of is actually true?

Have you noticed that you are afraid of something, which is a projection of your mind?

Fear is a prediction based on an illusion.

Have you noted that fear makes you concentrate away from the present moment and creates a future projection?

A projection is not reality, it hasn't happened yet!

A projection anticipates something to happen, based on past experience. You learned to react with fear, so fear became your only tool. Therefore, the fearful mind projects out events to the future so you can practice your fear.

Have you thought about how different your life would be if you concentrated on other things in life, other than feeling fear?

Have you thought about how different your life would be if you were not thinking about thoughts, which creates fear and anxiety? What if you thought of something else? What else would you think of?

Where would your fear be now?

Exactly. Nowhere!

If we concentrate on fear and looking for the opportunity to be scared, we can ensure ourselves to practice anxiety.

Fear creates an incapacitating illusion

Fear takes the essence of our life away. Fear makes you believe that life is about being afraid. Through our fear experience, we learned that life is about "never to be good enough," craving to be "good enough," and being afraid to "not being good enough." As a result, we learned to deserve living in fear. We learned to use fear as self-protection. We continuously created fear to feel safe in the comfort zone.

How can we come back to reality in an instant?

Getting out of fear for good makes you go through the transformation process. However, there is a useful tool here to help you get out of fear in an instant.

Look back into your childhood where your fear was created. Look at the event objectively. What happened there? See all the participants in that event and note their resources. Now come back to the now! And remind yourself: "That was then and now is now." You are not there where your fear was learned!

How does chronic fear and anxiety affect our body?

We must understand the destructive process that fear creates in our body so we can develop a big enough why, to let the fear go.

Fear is the number one destructive emotion. Fear destroys our health and life. Fear used to serve us in the past, but not now! Now fear is dangerous to our lives.

Fear literally grinds us down and eats us up inside out.

Fear runs the stress process and **makes you gain weight**. While stress runs the body, the body works for survival. The stress process pauses all our healthy functions. Life-threating fear **takes away the appetite**, so you stop eating. A lower level of anxiety **may make you eat all day**. The stress process, however, starts storing energy. Storing energy means storing fat, so you start holding onto a lot of weight.

The stress process is driven by a hormone, called cortisol. A high level of cortisol during the stress process ensures our survival.

Excess cortisol from stress keeps your fat storages locked up, so fat can't be used for energy. Those with constant low-level stress, eat mostly sweets. And a lot of sweets! Anything consumed in excess is converted to fat and stored on your hip and tummy.

Cortisol, anxiety, and **fear break down muscle** for energy. Stress, therefore, eats you up alive. You are in so-called autocannibalism.

The healthy level of cortisol keeps us active during the day.

If you want to lose your excess weight and protect your muscles, you must look into your stress level and resolve it. This book gives you the guidelines for resolving your stress and lose weight without really trying.

Stress **affects your immune system.** As long as you are stressed from your fears, you wear your immune system down and start getting colds and flus. Stress washes magnesium (a mineral used in 325 places in the body) out of your body, so you start **getting muscle cramps**. You are lucky if the muscle spasm is just tension in your neck or cramp in your leg. If the muscle spasm is in your blood vessel, which constricts it's muscles, the result is high blood pressure. If the spasm occurs in your heart muscle, you have a heart attack.

Deficient magnesium level affects your **blood sugar regulation** and develops insulin resistance and diabetes. Stress **causes insomnia**. The lack of rest **makes you eat more sweets** and carbs, so you put on more weight. These are just a few symptoms of anxiety.

Please remember, as long as you are running the stress process, you can't relax even if you wanted to. Only exhaustion or getting ill can knock you off your feet, so you finally rest.

7.   How did we learn to be afraid?

The next characteristic of fear that it is learned. Fear, along with our behavior, is a result of conditioning. Conditioning is a learning process. We have learned to be scared, practiced being scared, so we developed anxiety in childhood. The childhood tension carries forward to adulthood and can accompany us for the rest of our lives.

I like to show you some examples of the objects of fear in childhood and their appearance in adulthood.

Please feel free and add your own experience to this list.

Examples of fears in childhood:

- *Being scared to go home because of the tension of my parent's fights.*
- *Being scared to go home because dad will beat me up out of his frustration and anger.*

— *Being scared that my father will beat my sibling and our mother in front of me.*

— *Being scared that mom or dad leaves us again.*

— *Being scared that mom will take dad back and they will fight again.*

— *Being scared to move out of the house as mom leaves dad again. Being scared of the instability.*

— *Being scared that my parents belittle me for my ideas. They say I am stupid and they laugh at me.*

— *Being scared that there is no food at home and I stay hungry. I am scared of going to bed hungry at night.*

— *Being scared of going to school, as I am small and I get beaten and bullied. Being scared that mom or dad will drink too much alcohol again and they will beat us up.*

— *Being scared that I am not allowed to study what I want. Being scared of being forced to study what I don't want. I am afraid of my parents choosing my carrier.*

— *Being scared to show my school report because my parents will degrade and devalue me.*

The object of fear in adults:

— *Being scared that I won't be able to make enough money for the family.*

— *Being scared to go home as my spouse is angry again, will blame me even if I didn't do anything wrong.*

— *Being scared to get sick and die.*

- *Being scared to get old.*

- *Being scared to lose money.*

- *Being afraid of people as they are all against me.*

- *Being scared to be cheated.*

- *Being scared to be alone.*

- *Being scared to eat and become fat like my parents.*

I am sure you also have a story about your fears.

The process of learning fear

Once you learn to be afraid, fear soaks through your entire life. Fear grows into anxiety, and it becomes a normal daily condition.

Since fear is the only known condition and emotion for us, we believe that this is what we deserve.

The first imprints of fear

When we first experienced fear, we had no idea what it was. We didn't know what we should do.

Watching people around us living in fear, we learned to copy them. We copied their shocking fearful face and tense body. Copied those who stopped breathing, or those who screamed loud and lost control crying, We copied others who ran away or those who froze in silence. We copied those who beat up others. We copied those who allowed others to beat them. We copied those who got sick. We even copied those who fainted.

When we personally experienced fear and realized it's unpleasantness we chose to fight back with a reaction. We chose from the reactions we saw from others. We also learned to dislike unpleasant feelings like fear. We also understood from others that hatred is the general remedy for anxiety. Therefore, we also began using hatred toward our fear feeling.

From a fearful person a painful society

Once the fear and hatred reached a certain level, we must download it to others. We must download fear and hate to feel better. We learned that fear and hatred has to be downloaded to someone else. Therefore, expressing hatred became a pleasure. Our accumulated hatred can makek anyone the recipient. We especially look for those, who seem happy. A happy person doesn't have any hatred, so let's give them some. "If I feel miserable then everyone else should."

The fearful mind will do everything and anything,
so we don't feel our fear or anxiety.

Alcohol, drugs, cigarettes and sex become other layers of dependencies, remedies or aids for our fears.

Fear makes you get attention

Do you know why children do all sorts of stuff to get attention?

Do you know adults that always want to be in the center of attention?

Wanting excess attention roots in a specific fear.

When a child is ignored and grows up without acknowledgment, he or she will learn to do naughty things to get attention. They must prove themselves by getting attention to feel valuable and worth it. They will continue to do the same in their adulthood. Negative attention is better than being ignored and not getting any attention.

Feeling ignored makes one feel worthless.

The feeling of worthlessness is a powerful motivating factor do to something by which we feel valued. The fear of being worthless pushes you to prove yourself.

Some people will get engaged in naughty things, others seek excitement to feel valuable. Seeking excitement makes one enjoy fear. They enjoy the limbo of being found. Being addicted to the excitement of being found out, drives many people into affairs. For them, the affair is a game and provides great fun.

Fear and emotional dependency

When we grow up in emotional scarcity, not seeing and experiencing love, we become dependent on others for love.

In a relationship, we depend on our spouse to give us love. The fear of not being loved creates jealous anxiety when our spouse is out of the house, and we can't control who they give attention and kindness to. Jealous anxiety makes you believe that you are the sole owner of your spouse's loving kindness. As an extension to this jealousy, we get terrified, if our spouse falls ill, and can't serve us. "If my spouse can't serve me means I am not loved. I married my spouse to serve me, so he/she makes up for the lack of love I have for myself."

When the anxiety grows to our golden age, we create fears hour by hour. If not in our personal life then we create fear in our professional and financial lives. Some people manage to have these severe anxieties until they die.

The advantage of fear being learned. The good news about fear being a learned process, is that we can unlearn it. If we discover the antidotes of fear, we get out of our fear!

Getting out of fear is possible

The first level to get out of fear is **the intellectual level**. This is the level of the mind. The second is on a **sensation or cellular level**. The complete eradication of all irrational fears happens on the cellular level.

The intellectual work makes a vital first step for most people. We have to make sense on the intellectual level, which is why we need to work on the emotional or cellular level.

We will discuss both of these levels next.

V

The way out of fear and anxiety

In this Chapter, you find the answer to:

- How do we resolve fear and anxiety on the intellectual level?
- How do we resolve fear and anxiety on the cellular level?

---

1. Resolving fears on the intellectual level

The conditioned mind allows you to work on your fears intellectually. This work is inclined to convince the conditioned mind to make sense about a specific action to take.

Intellectual work starts by reading lots of self-help books, watching videos, and listening to lectures on this topic. You may have chosen this book too for the same reason.

The intellectual work on the mind is based on asking questions. When we ask questions, the brain starts to look for answers. By looking for answers, the mind works itself out. The questions need to be specific, so the mind recognizes the self-made illusion in the form of fear.

Here are a series of these specific questions. Answering the questions helps to examine the reality and the belief behind a particular fear. (Robert Dilts one of the top NLP master in his book "Sleight of Mouth" talks about in detail, how these beliefs formulate specific behaviors and how communication can help to resolve these issues.)

What are you afraid of? – take one of your particular fears and ask yourself the following questions:

1. How do you know your fear exist? Do you have any specific feelings in your body?

2. What causes the fear or this specific sensation to appear? What has to happen specifically for this fear to surface up?

3. What are the consequences of using this fear? What do you get out of having that fear? What are the positive and negative effects?

4. Define what you are afraid of in this situation? What are you afraid of specifically? What is the precaution or action you have to take to avoid that fear?

An example:

"I am afraid to be alone."

1. Q: How do you know that you are alone? What kind of body sensation do you have, which tells you that you are alone?

   A: *I have a tightness in my stomach when I feel I will be alone. I also need to eat chocolate or something sweet.*

2. Q: What are the reasons you are alone? What are the reasons people don't want to be with you? Is there any specific behavior or way you conduct yourself why people avoid you?

   A: *I don't really know why people avoid me. I think I am valuable for others as I tell them the truth. I am always helpful and advise them on how to do things. I may have a critical tone of voice, but I mean well. Maybe people don't like that I suggest them all the time, and I seem to be the "know it all expert."*

3. Q: What are the consequences of being alone? How is your life living alone? How do you feel living your life this way?

   A: *When I am alone, I feel very lonely. I have no one to talk to. Even if I had a problem, I don't know who to call. All people after the first few interactions with me back off and don't answer my call. I really don't like living this way and with this feeling.*

4. Q: What does it mean being alone, specifically? What do you have to do to avoid it?

   A: *Being alone means I am an outcast of society. I feel hated, and I don't belong anywhere. I think I have to learn to be friendly and listen to people. I need to listen to others more than talking to them. I overwhelm them with my advice. I act like, "I know it all." I need to learn to feel important and valuable without providing advise. If I allow people to talk, and I listen to them patiently, they can just work their problems out. I need to learn to listen with understanding instead of just proving my opinions. I think I would want someone to listen to me when I have a problem. I think people need emotional support, so they don't feel alone in a dilemma. Supportive, encouraging words can ensure them and increase their self-esteem. Encouraging words can strengthen their self-trust to do a particular task. I would want to have the same support as well.*

I went through these questions and answers many years ago. You can ask how it was? Reading my answers was shocking and life-changing. You can read my answers to these questions above. These questions made me face a huge mirror. I got the picture of myself right in my face. I am alone because I push everyone away by telling them how wrong they are and what they should do. I had to express criticism and put others down to feel secure, valuable, and important.

By answering these specific questions, you can find your blocks. The questions bring the blocks to the surface. The answer to these questions enforces you to resolve these blocks. Giving honest answers to these questions makes you find the solution too. When the big "Aha" happens, about your blocks on the intellectual level, you realize that you need to conduct yourselves differently. The question is: What can we do when we only know fear?

Fear comes from not knowing a specific "how." With these questions and answers, we get the "how." The answers are the new tools that we have to learn and put into practice. Applying the new life instructions we put our lives into our own hands. And the fear disappears.

> *Fear comes from some sort of knowledge deficiency.*
> *Missing knowledge can cause fear.*

> *When we don't know what to do, we chose fear.*
> *Fear comes from not knowing a specific "how."*

If you find the "how," you don't have to use fear ever again.

The antidote for being alone, for example:

Loving and accepting yourself, being friendly and accepting to others. Listen to others by seeking understanding, and you will always have people around you.

1. Resolving fears on the sensational level

Resolving fears on the intellectual level is an efficient preparation for the deep-seated work. Addressing fears on the sensational level detoxifies our cells from fear and completes the eradication.

For the efficient resolution of fear, we must understand:

Not the object of the fear is essential, but the fact
that our body cells know the vibration of fear.

Fear and anxiety are automatic, subconscious vibrations,
which control our thoughts, communication, and behavior.

The first step in resolving fear on the cellular or sensational level is the practice of awareness. Your sharpened awareness will be essential to catching your feelings and a specific fear program. You can only change something that you are mindful of. Even if you know the antidote programs, without awareness you would not know when to apply it. Let's take the inferiority complex as an example. The inferiority complex comes from the fear to stand up for yourself and being afraid to be valuable. You may possibly know you need to apply self-confidence and self-worth. Without awareness, however, you don't know when to use self-confidence and self-worth.

Fear keeps its antidotes hidden from you. It is not a surprise, because one role of your fear is to keep your inner knowledge in secret. As a matter of fact, fears keep all your inner wisdom locked up.

Does it make sense now why we need to go deeper than the intellectual level if we want to eradicate fears?

If not, then please go through the questions above one more time and answer them honestly. Going through this intellectual exercise will make it obvious to look into the body sensations.

Fear and anxiety come in specific body feelings.

Even if you have not noticed it until now, fear and anxiety have body signs. For some people, fear shows up as a tightness in the chest or neck. For some people, fear comes as back pain. Some people carry fear in visceral organs, like lungs, so they cough or can't breathe. For some people, fear appears as pain in the stomach, gall bladder, or the intestines. Some people have inflammation in the knee or hip so they can't walk. Some people have shoulder, elbow, or wrist pain so they can't even lift their arms up. Some people get colds and flu in a fearful period.

Whatever is our body sensation of fear, the first step, is to accept these feelings. Take a look at the following exercise.

Look at your fear as a feeling objectively now. Pull yourself out from the fear sensation. Step back from the fear sensation in your stomach, neck, back, or knee. Step out from the knot, the tension, the pain. Look at the feeling and observe it. Observe the area of the sensation and see what happens over time.

- *Where is the sensation exactly?*
- *How is the shape of the sensation?*
- *How big is the sensation?*
- *How is the intensity of the sensation?*
- *What is the color of the sensation?*

Don't judge your sensation, just observe it objectively. Observe what you actually experience. Don't look for causes and don't ask why that sensation is there. Accept it. This is the only thing you need to do. This is your first opportunity to practice acceptance. So do it now! Accept the fear sensation for what it is. Don't want to make it go away! Don't want it to have any other sensation instead! Observing your fear sensation objectively and without any expectation. Slowly you will notice that fear sensation begins to change.

This practice of observation and acceptance will affect your entire life and health. If you can practice acceptance as a body sensation, then soon it will grow into accepting yourself. Accepting yourself is the foundation to accept others and get out of fear. What a simple solution acceptance is!

2. The application of gratitude, love and the permission to move on

After accepting your fears unconditionally, you need to apply gratitude and love on them. I know this sounds strange. You would never expect that you need to be grateful for your fears! I still ask you to keep practicing love on your fears. Perhaps you want to hug and even caress your fears too.

Now tell your fear:

"Thank you fear for being here and serving me for this long! Now I let you go. I let you decide if you want to stay or go. If you decide to stay, I still move on."

This exercise gives permission to your fear to go. With this permission, you break the obsessive clinging to the fear sensation and prepare the process of letting go. Now, allow your fear to go. Allow it to go with love. Give your fear to the Universe. Trust the Universe that it will do the best to manage your fear and help you to have wisdom. You hand over your fear to the Universe as it no longer serves you.

When you let your fear sensation go, finally you
will have room for your new sensations!

When we begin working with our fears on the cellular level, the entire fear-complex becomes visible. All the sudden, you can see what fear has created out of your life. You will see the decisions you made out of fear. You will see all the decisions you made to block yourself moving forward.

The next challenge is to admit:

"I created and limited myself by listening to my fears. Now it is my responsibility to make better decisions and create something else." You must experience the self-liberating effect of this sentence.

- *How painful is it to live in your fear?*
- *How incapacitating is your fear for your life?*
- *Would you like to get out of the cycle of subconscious fear-creations?*
- *Would you like to get out of out the control what fears have over you?*
- *What are you ready to do, to experience something else than living in fear?*

Are you still hesitating? Do you still have doubts that it is possible to get out of fear?

Did you know?

Our deepest fear is:
being afraid to live without fear!

I know a lady, who said: *"I am afraid to be happy and live without worry. If I let go of my worry, something bad happens".* She continued: *"If I worry about bad things, then I am not disappointed at least when they happen. So you see it is easy to live with my anxiety as it gives me a comfortable feeling. The last time I let my fear and worry go, my husband got a heart attack."* The above sentences show that fears serve her. She used to get physically ill and asked for my help. Unfortunately, my advice was not enough. The meditation exercise made her feel relaxed, but she said: *"I am afraid to stay calm like this."* She always felt back to her comfort zone of living in fear. The deepest possible fear is: to be afraid to live without fear.

Did you realize your fears and their power over you? Are you ready to change?

Here is a way out:

- *Pick up your fear and hold it in your hand. Look at your fear objectively. Put a smile on your face and welcome your fear. Embrace it like your loved-one, who you haven't seen for a long time. Accept your fear, show your gratitude, love, respect, and appreciation. Now say out loud: "Thank you, dear fear! I appreciate you, I love you, I respect you!" Cut your ownership of your fear and pain and let it float up. Watch it floating up to the Universe.*

Being grateful and respectful for something,

which is causing you pain is the most

important step for letting go for good.

This is also possibly the first time in your life, you changed your reaction towards your fear or pain caused by fear. Instead of hating your fear shift your response to unconditional acceptance and love. You must change your feeling toward the powerful feeling inside you what you have been hating!

If you hate any feeling inside you, it makes you hate yourself.

I know exactly how you feel now! I know, how your ego fights and sais: *"What a stupid exercise this is? Why am I doing this? What? I should actually love something that I hate in myself? I should love my fear, which made my life a misery?"*

Allow these doubtful questions arising, observe them objectively, and accept them. Now continue focusing on your goal to resolve your fear.

Accomplish the above gratitude and letting go exercise on all of your fears.

Being grateful and letting go is the first step getting out of your self-limiting fears forever.

As you practice loving kindness on our fears, you realize that there is an opportunity to live differently than in fear.

Do you have anything to lose by practicing this exercise?

Absolutely nothing! You can only gain learning to love our own feelings, hence ourselves. This exercise is called: **Fear resolution by loving kindness.** Here is the entire exercise, step by step:

- *Take a big breath and - just for this one time and for this exercise sake-, accept your fear and say. "Hello fear, I accept you here in me. I know you are here, and it is ok with me."*

- *Next, thank your fear for the service. Your fear has been protecting you. Tell your fear: "Thank you fear for your protection and saving my life! Dear fear you did a great service to protect me! I appreciate you very much!"*

- *Now let your fear go and tell: "I let you go now dear fear as your service ended here. I have love and kindness to protect me."*

- *Wrap your fear up in a beautiful box, put a colorful bow over it. Make a wonderful gift.*

- *Lift your hands to the sky and give your beautiful box to the Universe with love and appreciation. Show your appreciation as the package helped you to learn loving kindness. Keep looking at the package as the Universe takes it from you. When your hands are empty, put them down.*

- *Now watch as the Universe transforms the content of your package into love and all kinds of love energies. Write down all the antidotes of your fear what the Universe sends you back.*

- *Follow this process with your mind's eye. Now take a paper and colored pencil and draw this process. Use colors to demonstrate the letting go process. Use different colors from a specific fear to go into the Universe and draw arrows out of the Universe with the particular love energies that you received.*

For example: Let go of the "fear of standing up for myself." The Universe sends you back the antidote of this fear: "self-confidence, self-esteem, self-value, courage, and deserving." Celebrate what you received from the Universe! Show this celebration with bright colors. Coloring and drawing make the process of letting go and solving problems much more comfortable.

- *Acknowledge that the particular love energies are now your tools to protect you. You may draw on a separate sheet of paper the specific love energies to be your protective shields.*

Important:

Once love (acceptance, gratitude, respect, and letting go) vibrates in you, they will actually push out all the leftover negative vibrations (obsessive defense mechanism of fear and hatred). You really don't have to do much, but to love all your vibrations. When you apply acceptance and gratitude on all your negative feelings, they love from you. You are consciously practicing loving kindness on your emotions. You cut the cycle of fear and hate. It is your own freedom of choice to give love or hate vibrations to your feelings.

The above process is how you generate your own positive vibrations. According to the Law of Attraction: you attract in more, what you already have. So practice acceptance and gratitude, so you have more things in your life to practice acceptance and gratitude. You will see that the number of fearful events beginning to drop. The events are all prompting you to find something to accept and be grateful for. The number of occasions where you practice loving-kindness will grow. Life will change as you apply loving kindness. You enter into a temporary learning phase now as you are consciously building love into your life.

I am very grateful to my mentor Tedi Ware for realizing this above described healing process. I asked her to help me get rid of my anger and hatred. We had a magical session. The next day I woke up realizing that I don't have to wish my anger and hatred to go away. I need to only apply love on them hence on myself. Anger can point me to the directions in life where I can bring change! So I began to use love and kindness on my own feelings and sensations. I applied loving kindness on myself the way I am. I realized, if I apply loving kindness, I don't have a chance to express anger or hatred!

I genuinely wish all of you to have the life-altering experience when you apply love on all your sensations and feelings!

3. **How does fear fall apart? What does the realization of "I am nobody" brings you?**

The last part of the fear-process is the complete disintegration. The complete disintegration takes place when you realize that you are "nobody."

You are made out of sensations. You are made
of all different kinds of feelings.
Will you give a name to each sensation and call yourself that?

Realize that your fear made you believe that you are
"somebody," who is entitled to things in life. Entitled to
accumulate money, fame, cars and being served by all.

When you realize, you are made of sensations that you have been identified yourself with, the "I," "me", "mine" all disintegrates. You finally experience what you were so afraid of: becoming "nobody" and "nothing!"

The titles fall off. Money, car, clothes are all gone, and you stand there "naked" and vulnerable. The only thing you have is your breath.

Now you tell me how valuable your breath is?

Dear Reader,

Everyone has the free choice to be grateful for every single breath or not. Some people will reach this point when they lose health and become deadly ill. Some people have to enter the "death door" to realize the value of every single breath. Do you have to wait for this point?

I know, you agree that waiting for the "death door" to occur, is a waste of time! Isn't it?

Please take the time to reread the above and sink into yourself. Please also cry as much as you like!

Then accept, the fact, "I am nobody!" Don't worry, because we are all "nobodies!" So welcome! The conditioned mind made you believe you are "somebody."

Accepting that you are "nothing," therefore you don't own "anything" is a massive step in getting out of your fear.

> **Accept that you simply exist! Moreover, accept**
> **that you are "good enough," because you are alive!**
> **Accept that it is your free choice to be happy to make**
> **your existence the most valuable thing ever.**

With the realization of the "nothing," our true self-value begins to develop. Your self-value no longer depends on money, car, clothes, titles and the people you know. You accept yourselves precisely the way you are because your existence is the first and foremost treasure. You exist because you breathe. Your breath is the most valuable treasure!

Your conditioned mind has been putting on labels on you and trying to make you more valuable.

You can't possibly buy anything more expensive than your breath.

Shift the value of your breath to the top of your priority list and see how your shopping habits change. You will focus on quality and have the patience to search for the best price. If something comes on a higher rate, and it provides the necessary quality for you to reach your goals, then buy it with a clear decision. I personally pay good attention to the quality of the shoes I ran in. Running serves my health on multiples of levels; therefore, the purpose, -injury prevention-, justifies the product. I look for sales and discounts and buy running shoes in advance before the previous wares off.

There is a difference to own things to define who you are or to own the same expensive items, to serve you reaching your goals.

Attention!

Not all expensive things mean quality. Seek quality. You will be surprised to find good quality without a very high price tag. Once you have modesty and moderation as a value, you seek quality in your life.

Congratulations, you reached the point to become a human being now!

You became a self-assured and self-valued person. Now you realize that all things are here for you to use! Buying something doesn't mean you own it! Therefore, you need to treat everything and everyone for the service you receive from them and practice genuine gratitude.

When you truly value yourself, you will begin to value others. You will value others, as you will see the service in all they do. It is eye-opening to see, just how much others do for you!

What happened with your strong self in this process of ego-disintegration?

All the sudden, you realize:

You didn't "die" becoming "nothing." You experienced your true self.

You just found in yourself who you are! You are the energy of love, acceptance, and gratitude!"

Since you don't own anything, the whole the whole world is yours!"

Since you were brave enough to become "nothing" and now can accept, love, appreciate and respect these feelings, you experience your re-birth.

We are re-born with the practice of acceptance, appreciation, gratitude, and respect.

You can find your true self under the complex and multilayers of fears. Your true value becomes visible when you become "nobody" and "nothing."

Be brave to become "nothing," and you find your true self and your true value!

This is the point where the deepest root of fear and anxiety disintegrates.

How did fear paralyze you up to now?

If you have not realized until now what fear has done in your life, then let's talk about it.

Fears paralyze the expression of genuine love. Living in doubt, we can not express our love. Showing love for the conditioned mind used to be toughness, giving criticism, and pushing our agenda. Expressing love used to be proving our uniqueness, smartness, and superiority.

What happens with the complete disintegration of fears? When limiting fears disintegrate, we can speak softly and listen patiently. We feel comfortable in silence. We can handle things outside of us, without taking things personally. We can see the truth in others and see them through compassion. We can honestly,- from the depth of our heart-, hold someone's hand, caress their back and give them a hug. We become helpful and can offer help. Helping others and be at their service no longer makes us feel inferior.

Service, serving others becomes the way to elevate ourselves.

Service means, helping and lifting others
without wanting anything in return.
We also experience that the higher we lift others, the higher we rise.

Lifting others is the most unique growing experience
to become humble! The level of humbleness while
lifting others is the only measure of our growth.

Gentleness and humbleness are the highest forms of strength!

You can indeed be proud of yourself if you developed the strength to become gentle.

Congratulations on learning what love is and reaching your healing power.

Were you able to cut the cycle of pain from fear? Did you find yourself under the disintegrated ego?

Did you realize that you are an equally important part of the world by being "nothing?"

You are like everyone else; hence, you are the world!

The summary of the way out of fears:

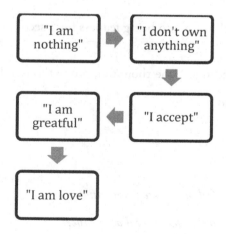

Zsuzsanna Fajcsak-Simon

Are you still in doubt?

If you still haven't done the exercise, loving your fears, - it is ok. Stay with us and read on.

I still encourage you to look into the next exercise: the **what ifs**.

- *What if you could put your fear down?*
- *What if you could give a chance to yourself to experience life without fear and anxiety?*
- *What if, you could put down all your dependencies?*
- *What if you could give a chance for yourself just this one time and put your fear down for 5 seconds?*
- *What if, you could give yourself permission to feel loved for 5 seconds?*
- *What if you could give yourself a chance to express your love for 5 seconds?*

Be brave right now! Jump into being fearless for 5 seconds!

Count: 1 one thousand, 2 one thousand, 3 one thousand, 4 one thousand, and 5 one thousand.

What happened?

- *How did it feel being free from craving?*
- *How did it feel to be in total acceptance?*
- *How did it feel to be in the now, for 5 seconds?*

Are you ready now to step on your journey? If yes, then here is the next exercise for you.

- *"What do you have to lose by putting your fear and anxiety down?"*
- *"What do you have to gain by letting your fear and anxiety go?"*
- *"What do you gain by not letting your fear and anxiety go?"*
- *"What do you lose by not letting your fear and anxiety go?"*
- *"If you live in the control of your fear and anxiety, then who is the boss? Who controls you and your life? Do you allow your fear to control you?"*
- *"What if you can control your own life?"*
- *"What if you can count only on yourself to control your life?"*

Yes, you can only count on yourself! Get used to it!
It is normal to count on yourself!

Cry your eyes out but accept it! You are the world
with all the knowledge inside you! So be quiet
and start to listen to your inner voice!

This is the foundation to live without expectation.

When you give up your wantings and expectations, the right help arrives. You have no idea how many different kinds of support can come when you don't expect anything!

When you don't have anything, what can you lose?
When you are "nobody," who can lose?

Here we go again, our fear of "nothing" and "nobody" creeping back. Remind yourself: only fear can lose!

Do you see now, as the ego falls apart, as you don't have and own anything? As a result, you can't lose anything!

What is really "yours?"

The Whole World! When your fear falls apart, you only gain! You gain the realization of love!

Accepting to be "nothing" doesn't mean to live in the forest as a monk. Some people, however, chose to be a monk. Most of us, ordinary people becoming "nothing" can own a car or decide not to own a car. Have a house or don't have a house. Your self-value remains the same, regardless of the things you own.

Everything is here for our service and for our own good. Everything is here to help us reach our goal. Even a life-lesson, which is not so favorable, serves us. A life-lesson is a lesson you can't buy in school!

If you still haven't done the exercise treating your fear with loving kindness? Then there is the time to turn the page back. Let's do it!

4. So what is next when every breath is a success?

How does life look like with the daily practice of acceptance and gratitude for each breath?

Acceptance and gratitude make life a smooth sailing while crossing the Ocean! Congratulate yourself every day!

You are truly successful when success feeling runs in you unconditionally. The next 1000 steps come after this. The good thing that you don't care about the length of the journey! You are successful, regardless of how many steps you took already. Success is independent of the number of steps you take. You only care for the very step, that you are taking right now.

Put down all your dependencies one by one or all at once. The application of loving kindness on your fears makes you drop your dependencies one by one. Let go of being dependent on fear first!

What else should you let go next? Your intuition will give you signs, what is the particular fear or dependency you should let go. It doesn't matter the order. Just listen to your inner voice, your inner feeling. Your intuition is your internal GPS and tells you what to do.

> *Put your addictive behaviors down, so the ego*
> *has no way out to bring your fears back.*

What else shall you let go? Besides fear, let go of your anger, hatred, yelling, criticizing, resentment, guilt, and blaming. Let go wanting to talk about your feelings! Let go your cravings! Let all go with love!

Then let go that somebody owes you something and you are entitled!

All knowledge is inside you! Look inside yourself for what you need and fulfill it yourself. Your inner voice, your intuition will help and guide you to filter out who will be a help. Your intuition will tell you where you need to look for help. Your intuition is your knowledge to choose who or what will be helpful for you. In the age of the internet, filtering out the available information is real knowledge!

Let go playing God. Accept that your role here
is to love and allow God to this his job!

God lives in you; therefore, you have all the divine knowledge you need for reaching your goals. All this knowledge is accessible through your intuition channel. Your intuition guides you the right way, the divine-way.

Your intuition is open when you are aware.

Remind yourself again, when your conditioned mind brings you stuff:

"I am not God, God lives in me! I let God
do his job, and I do my job."

"I am love! I am made of love! I was made to love!"

Here the conditioned mind disintegrates!

You are only an existing human! You are Alive, so it is just enough to be very grateful for.

Learn to practice acceptance, observe, and shift focus. Now you put your life in your hands.

Choosing suffering or gratitude is your real freedom.

Happiness has been all inside you! You have been successful! The grip of fear and anxiety is gone!

No more fear only objective observation, acceptance, and gratitude. Now begin to work with what you have!

The more gratitude you feel, the more things will happen for you to be grateful! The more gratitude you express, the happier you will be!

5. How do we spend the rest of our lives?

How do you think it makes sense to spend the rest of your life? In gratitude, of course! And yes, Of course, it makes sense too! Nothing else makes sense but living in gratitude! Why? Because expressing gratitude makes you happier!

Living in gratitude doesn't mean you sit home, keep saying, "Thank you." You are leading your life and working for your goals, while continuously expressing gratitude for the smallest goodness coming to you.

Gratitude changes our vocabulary. We will get used to saying, "Thank you," -happily. "Thank you very much," and "I am grateful."

I like to note here that expressing gratitude never can be abbreviated. So "Thanks," "Tks" "tq" don't do it.

Besides gratitude, we spend time to listen compassionately. We realize that sometimes the most prominent expression of our love is to stay silent and listen compassionately.

Another progression on the journey of loving kindness to become humble and speak less. We no longer feel good to talk about ourselves and to make ourselves shine. We no longer need to push and force others to get something out of them. We can accept what is freely given. We only say things that build others.

Living in gratitude has an effect not only on our personal life but also on our professional life. Imagine the abundance what follows if you live with the abundance feeling.

The abundance feeling has no expectation. We only have humbleness and gratitude for using what we have. We also take care of the things and people in our lives. One part of our abundance goes towards building society. It is not financial giving, but we donate our time and our knowledge. We give because it lifts others, and lifting others lifts us further.

I wish you to reach these realizations and to step on the journey to heal yourself and practice loving kindness. I wish that you cut your chains off and experience your truly successful existence, where you connect to your potential; the potential you never imagined you have!

VI

The transformation

In this Chapter, you find the answer to:

- How do we prepare for the transformation process?
- How does the transformation process look like step by step?

Finally, we have arrived at the long-awaited chapter about the transformation process. We will discuss the process in such simplicity so everyone can do it at home. Going through the transformation is a huge step on your journey and prepares you for the work on your cellular level.

The fastest and the deepest transformation requires one-on-one work with an NLP coach (certified in TimeLine® Therapy). An NLP coach is specialized in asking personalized questions, which we are unable to ask, due to our conditioned mind. These questions are necessary to find the deep-seated answers in ourselves.

This book helps to look at the past and your difficult life situations yourself. I intend to help you to see your history from another point of view, which allows you to take out positive life instructions. You learn to look at a past painful event with your adult self and with your knowledge today.

The first step in the transformation process is to establish the TimeLine®. The following two questions will help you.

1. Where are the past events in reference to your body?

Your past events can be possibly behind your back, at your side, above or under you. Your past events can be diagonal in any direction to you, or they can be inside you in some body part. So if you were to know where your past events are, what direction or place would you point at?

If your past events are any other place than behind your back, you have to move them there. Place your past events with your mind's eye, behind your back, in chronological order on a straight line.

Creating a straight line of your past events is a vital step for the effective transformation. I had clients whose past events were in the heart, in the chest, or around them in a circle. I had someone who had her past in front of her. Imagine those whose past is in them or in front of them! Just how stuck are they pushing their past in front of them? One of the main reasons people can't get out of the past is because of their TimeLine® is curved or takes any other shape than a straight line.

Now make your timeline straight behind you and place your past events on this straight line in chronological order.

Attention! You are not shoving your past behind you! You arrange your past events in order, so they become manageable. This exercise on your TimeLine® is done in your head, with your mind's eye.

2. **Where are the events happening in your future?**

If your future is at anywhere else than on a straight in front of you, then make your TimeLine® continue ahead. Make it a straight line and render your future events again in chronological order. This work is done again with your mind's eye. Create a straight TimeLine®.

Your TimeLine® originates from the back and shall go through you. If you don't feel yourself on this line, then put yourself on it. The line should not go above or under you or next to you. Your TimeLine® must go through you. This way, you put yourself in-line with time. Otherwise, your life will pass by you. If you are done with your TimeLine® work, we may proceed further.

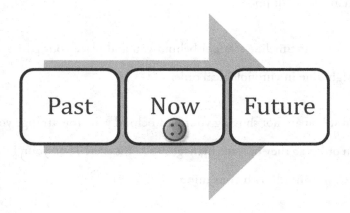

The preparation for transformation: calming yourself down

Getting unstuck calls for re-visiting the past, which used to be difficult. We must calm down for this exercise. We can only use our objectivity and take out positive life instructions from the past, if we are calm. Practicing breath observation twice a day helps to establish the first level of your calmness.

Attention!

Breath observation is not a breathing exercise! It is an exercise to work on your focus and teaches youu how to re-focus continuously. This exercise is an essential, introverted, meditation exercise. Practice 5 minutes in the morning after waking up and before going to bed.

The breath observation exercise, or meditation

Please read the following exercise thouroughly until you gain a good understanding. While reading it, try out each step on its own, then add it all together. If the written form of the exercise seems difficult, click on the voice link of the meditation later, at the end of this segment.

Sit in a comfortable chair or on the floor. Choose sitting on the floor either cross-legged or sitting your heels. Set your watch or timer for 5 minutes.

It doesn't matter what position you choose, the most important thing, is to stay in that position for 5 minutes, if possible.

Promise yourself to stay in your chosen position and with your eyes closed, for the entire 5 minutes. Now, close your eyes.

Let's begin by observing our thoughts now.

Observe your thoughts like you are watching the clouds in the sky or watching a movie. Sit back and watch the show. Allow your thoughts to be there. Let your thoughts come and let them go. Accept each thought. This is another opportunity to practice acceptance.

Thoughts come and go. They come and go continuously all the time. It's ok. Make peace with yourself about your thoughts. Accept each thought the way it is. Don't ask questions about or criticize them. Don't answer the questions either that the mind brings you. Don't make any reactions to your thoughts. Don't wish your thoughts to be something else and don't fight against them. Allow the flow of your thoughts. Accept each thought the way it is. Allow your thoughts to be there. Allow your thoughts to come and go.

Now bring your focus of attention to your physical feelings, your body sensations. As you sit, you feel your seat touching your legs. Or you possibly have a physical feeling from the position you are sitting. Allow these physical feelings to be. Allow them just as you did with your thoughts. Accept each feeling the way it is. Don't ask questions about it, don't criticize it. Don't make any reactions to your body sensations. Don't fight against your feelings and don't wish to change them. Allow the free flow of your physical sensations. Accept all your physical feelings.

Now bring the focus of your attention to your heart and soul. Accept each emotion there. Allow each emotion to be there. Make peace with your emotions. You have been fighting against your emotions by wanting them to go away or wanting other emotions instead. It is time to stop hurting yourself and stop generating reactive emotions to the ones you are feeling right now. Allow the emotions to come and go. Accept them. Don't question them, don't criticize them. Don't make any kind of reaction to them. Stop fighting against your emotions. Simply allow your emotions to be there and accept them the way they are. Allow the free flow of your emotions as you stay non-reactive.

Now bring the focus of your attention to your nose. Start observing your breath as you inhale and exhale through your nose. Observe the occurrences of inhalation and exhalation. You don't need to label "It is inhalation" and "It is exhalation." Quiet down your talking mind and observe the occurrence of your breath. This is how you practice your awareness. In this exercise, you are observing the presence of your breath.

Observing the occurrence of your breath is your first step in learning objective observation. You don't change your breathing. Allow each breath to happen naturally.

However, your mind quickly jumps and starts thinking about something. When you realize that you are thinking about something, bring your attention back smoothly to your breathing. The conditioned mind jumps in every few seconds. Your job is to bring back your attention to your breath, continuously. Bring back your attention without any kind of reaction. Your mind wants you to be angry and frustrated and unable to focus.

Your task here is practicing refocusing. Keep bringing your attention back to your breath.

If you get angry because your mind took you away from observing your breath, you practice anger. You must stay aware not to express any emotions or reactions if the mind pulled you away. This exercise gives you the first opportunity to practice staying non-reactive when something unexpected happens. Continue refocusing. Continue your work and observe your breath. Your task is to keep bringing your attention back as smoothly as possible.

The conditioned mind wants to control you by pulling your attention left and right. Bring your focus back without any reaction. You will be rolling in thoughts if you allow your mind to control you. You want to observe your breath and not think about this or that. Discipline your focus and practice refocusing.

After a few minutes of observing the occurrence of your inhalation and exhalation, bring the focus of your attention to the edge of your nostril. Begin to feel how the air is touching the entrance of your nostrils. You may follow the air traveling inside of your nose. As you inhale, the air is traveling up, and as you exhale the air is traveling down. If you don't feel the air touching the inside entrance of your nostril, then please take a few harder breaths. Once you feel the air touching the entrance of your nostrils, return back to natural breathing.

The mind continuously jumps. It pulls you left and right, up and down. Practice diligently and keep bringing your breath back to your nostrils without any kind of reaction. Practice refocusing. Your mind jumps all day. The mind keeps pulling your focus away from your task and keeps you wondering. So train your mind with this exercise to do what you want to do. As a result, you will become more and more aware when your mind jumps and pulls you away, in your life too. Observing your breath allows developing your awareness over your mind.

Through the observation and non-reaction, you can come out from the slavery of the mind. Observation helps you to take control. It is your responsibility to decide to wonder and think or come back to observing your breath. This is the only control in life one should apply.

> *The control of your own reactions is the only real*
> *control, which serves you to build your life.*

Here is the voice link of the breath observation meditation by Mr. S. N. Goenka, who reawakened the vipassana meditation:

https://youtu.be/Oh5ii6R6LTM

Make an effort to learn this voice-guided meditation then practice it yourself.

Dear Reader!

No one can do this exercise perfectly. So don't put unrealistic and perfectionist expectations on yourself. Those meditating for many, many years also just sit and practice. We all continue bringing our focus back from wondering and thinking to our breath.

If you feel sleepy and drowsy during the meditation take a few deeper breaths to wake yourself up. Consider this exercise as a time invested in practicing training the mind, training your diligence and persistence. This is why it is recommend to sit with a straight back and practice morning and evening.

Practicing breath observation in bed while laying down is an excellent way to fall asleep. Practicing breath observation before falling asleep at night, ensures your quality sleep. Allow yourself to become drowsy and fall asleep. You will have a sound sleep and wake up refreshed.

When you wake up at night and can't sleep, practice breath observation. Your body will sleep and regenerate, even if you are not sleeping. This also helps you to get up in the morning refreshed. Your body sleeps 6 times as much with this meditation as actual time spent sleeping. So practice breath observation during the day, and your body rests in the meantime. Breath observation helps you any time you feel uneasy, stressed, or tired. You feel the refreshing and calming effects of this exercise immediately.

Five minutes of breath observation equals 30 minutes of sleep.

You can only discover the effects of this exercise by tryinging and experiencing it. Explaining is impossible. So best wishes and do it now!

The transformation

Welcome to the actual transformation exercise. This exercise helps you to visit your past safely. I recommend practicing the breath observation exercise for a few days before beginning the transformation work. Breath observation meditation makes the transformation smoother, because it reveals both, your fears and your hidden wisdom, faster. Remember that the mind wants to keep a very tight lock on your fears. The breath observation practice, will help loosen up your fears so their intensity decreases. It is much easier to manage a fear, which has lost some of it's power.

The first step

Give yourself permission to transform your old non-serving, unwanted emotions. Fear, anger, hatred, guilt, resentment, humiliation, rejection, betrayal, sadness, abandonment, sorrow, blaming and injustice, will transform into positive life instructions.

Ask yourself: *Do I allow myself to transform this unwanted emotion into positive life instructions? Now answer: "Yes."*

You need to be ready from the bottom of your heart to say yes for this question.

The second step

Familiarize yourself with the next exercise, by reading it first. Only then begin the work.

This exercise is done in your head.

Remember the first time you felt and experienced this unwanted feeling/emotion?

When was this first event?

You don't need to recall the event in detail. It is not important what happened there. The only important thing is how you felt in that event. Was this the first time you felt fear, anger, shame or sadness, etc? If yes, then use this event for the transformation work. Find the first event you felt a particular emotion. If you can't recall the first, use the first one you remember.

Now fly up from your TimeLine®, slide back or float back like a cloud on the sky and stop above the event. Slide back on your imaginary straight TimeLine®. Looking through your own eyes look down at the event. You, as an adult today, look at this event. Look at this event like you are looking at a movie that contains the child you use to be. Look at this event as an adult that understands now.

It is very possible that the first event happened between 0-7 years of your life. If you can't remember anything between this time interval, then any event that you remember will do. Work with the earliest event as possible. When you work with this event, your mind will likely open and you will see an earlier or the first event.

It is prohibited to speak out what happened in the event.

You must NOT say anything that was too painful!

INSTEAD:

Look down at this event as an advisor. *Tell those who are involved, what they should have done differently in order for you to have left this event fully loved. Advise them how they should have behaved, instead of their hurtful behavior.*

List all the people in the event, that should have avoided this difficult situation with the child.

What kind of personal growth, do adults need to reach, before they can handle situations with a child, so that the child can walk away lovingly and with a positive experience?

What kind of person listens to a child to make sure they build the child up?

Look down at the event as your adult self now and look at what happened objectively. Describe all that you feel or what you think should have happened there, so this difficult event never existed.

The transformation: Visiting the past event

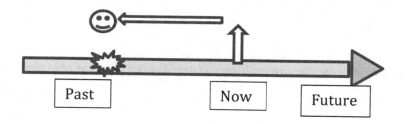

Fly up from your timeline from the Now. Fly, float above your TimeLine® and slide back to the chosen event. Stop above the event floating and look down with your adult eyes. Write down all that should happen there. How differently should the involved characters behave there?

Write down everything that should have happened there. Write positive statements or life instructions, which point to the future.

Example of wisdom from transformation:

Love the child and listen to him or her with understanding. If the child makes a mistake, explain to him or her what is happening, patiently. Show calmly, the acceptable way to behave there. Make sure to hug the child. Explain to the child that it is ok to make a mistake. Explain that all life is about learning. Make sure the child feels safe and not blamed.

Keep writing until you feel that if all of that, came to pass, you would have walked away feeling loved. If all that you wrote down would have happened, you would never have felt an unwanted feeling.

While you are writing, observe the old unwanted feeling or emotion as it is getting lighter and lighter. Now you remember this event for the teaching that it contained.

Can you see how the original story changed when you use objectivity and compassion?

Make sure your notes are positive statements. All statements shall point to the future and regard you. If you have a statement such as "Don't yell at the child," then rephrase it immediately to: "Be patient and talk kindly in a loving tone of voice to the child."

These statements become Universal wisdom when you generalize them as follows:

"Love everyone. Be understanding with everyone. Listen patiently, always. Forgive everyone, as people can only do their best. If anyone makes a mistake, explain it to them patiently."

Reread your generalized sentences. What do you notice by reading them again and again?

The statements you gained from the transformation are your life instructions! Can you see it? Do you realize that you have never been patient, understanding, or compassionate?

The past events contained all of life's instructions about how you have to live your life, from now on. If you live your life while being understanding, patient, and compassionate, your life will change.

Up to now, you have only known demanding and harshness which has produced the type of angry life you have right now. Do you want to continue creating a bitter life?

Change becomes long-term when you use the changed behavior with everyone. Imagine yourself behaving with the change now! See yourself behaving kindly with everyone, including those you used to consider an enemy. I know this excercise may sound strange, but give it a reasonable chance!

—⟋⟋⟋—

Complete the transformation exercise for all of your past, painful events. Continue the transformation until only understanding, compassion, and love remain in you.

It is beautiful to discover the object of our fears. You have been afraid of the knowledge locked inside you. The conditioned mind kept you in fear to keep you away from this gift, your wisdom. Once you have this wisdom, the conditioned mind-made fear dies.

Your conditioned mind-made self, the "I" dies.

So tell me, did your life end? Did you become nothing?

Do you see how disillusioned your conditioned mind has kept you?

The secret of successful transformation

Successful transformation requires a clear, first event. Can you remember when you were exposed to the specific negative emotion the first time?

Do you recall how old you were at the time of the first event? Who was there in this particular event?

Was this event the first time you felt fear or anxiety?

Where and when did you experience first anger, hatred, rejection, pain, abandonment, betrayal, injustice, humiliation, guilt, blaming, and resentment?

When did you first believe that you were not good enough?

To find out about the specific emotional pains from your childhood, I recommend Lise Bourbeau's book: "Heal your wounds and find your true self."

The five most painful emotional wounds that a child can experience from the parents or the guardians are:

1. Rejection
2. Abandonment
3. Humiliation
4. Betrayal
5. Injustice

The deepest wound for the child the absence of one or both parents. It doesn't matter how loving the guardians of the child are, the lack of birth parents causes the most profound emotional wound.

I got acquainted with Lise's work in Malaysia in 2009. Finally, I received an understanding of my emotional issues. I could finally realize what hurt and could find the root cause. I also realized why I chose certain negative behaviors as self-protection. This understanding helped me greatly in the healing process.

The five emotional wounds

It is not important what happened, but
rather how we felt in that event.

Some can feel totally different in a similar situation. A
completely different situation can cause others to feel the same.

Let us see the emotional wounds in the chronological order of their awakening.

The first wound is **rejection**. This emotional wound awakens from conception to one year of age by the parent of the same gender. Rejection can begin with an unwanted pregnancy. If the mother didn't want the pregnancy the little girl is already rejected. If the father didn't want the pregnancy the little boy is already rejected.

Anything can happen, between conception, to one year of age, which triggers the emotional wound of rejection. The rejection feels like: *"They stay in one place and push me out of there."* Rejection is not always a physical rejection but a feeling, an emotion.

Emotional wounds are protected by behaviors, which serve as shields. The function of these shields is to protect us from feeling a particular painful wound.

The behavioral protection for rejection is withdrawal. If a child removes him or herself, "shuts the door" and locks people out, he or she is practicing withdrawal. The child protects him or herself from rejection by applying withdrawal.

The most common form of rejection is criticism. If the child grows up in criticism, he or she will learn to criticize. The child can only relate to the world through criticism. By applying criticism, the child provokes rejection. No one likes to be with the child as he or she is so bitter from rejections.

Negative criticism devalues the child, who begins to lose self-value or self-worth. As a result, the child learns to reject him or herself. Self-rejection is the process, which helps children to convince themselves that they are worthless. If the child believes he is worthless, no one can reject him anymore.

The body sign for rejection is a slim, skinny body. Rejected children and adults have a very fast metabolism and are unable to gain weight. Building muscle is a challenge even when doing weight training. They can eat anything and not gain any weight. A fast metabolism is a sign that they reject everything from themselves, even their physical bodies.

Abandonment is the second emotional wound. This emotional pain awakens by the parent of the opposite gender, between 1-3 years of age. This emotional wound feels like they left, and you stayed in one place, stuck. Absence of the parent of the opposite gender caused this wound. If this parent lives in another country for work, or due to divorce, the child will experience abandonment. Emotional abandonment is when the parent of the opposite gender doesn't support the child's ideas and actions- causes the same pain as physical abandonment would.

The behavioral protection for abandonment is a general dependency. If we depend on others, no one can leave us. We make others depend on us, so they won't leave us. We are the first, however, to leave others. Practicing abandonment, before the other person can leave us, is also a protective shield. Some women think, that by becoming pregnant, they "hook" their guy, by becoming dependent. Some men keep young wives pregnant, - one baby right after another-, so they won't leave.

We practice abandonment on ourselves when we abandon our dreams, intuitions, and ideas.

The body signs of abandonment are sagging body parts like breast, tummy, or buttocks. An abandoned child grows into a very painful adult, going through many painful relationships. An abandoned adult is always on the run but doesn't know where is he or she is running to. It is very difficult for an abandoned person to let go, because letting go means death. The result is *"I can't live with you or without you."*

The third emotional wound is **humiliation**. Humiliation means belittling and making fun of the child at about 3 years of age. The emotional pain is generally awakened by the mom. When moms say out of frustration: *"You dropped food on your clothes again! You eat like a pig! You see the floor is so dirty under you."* Or making fun when the child has an accident. *"You peed your pants! Babies do that, you are a big girl now."* These expressions destroy the child's developing self-worth at the root. This way, the child will unquestionably believe that he or she is worthless. Belittling or humiliation is a painful wound and it begins to store pain.

The behavior protection for humiliation is masochism. Humiliation stores pain. The child begins to inflict the accumulated pain to him or herself. If they hurt themselves, no one can hurt them more. A humiliated adult dropping food or drink on their shirt or having their pants ripped, exposing themselves when they bend over.

A humiliated person humiliates others out of self-protection. Giving pain is another way to protect themselves from getting hurt. When pain infuses the life of a humiliated person, he or she begins to punish others. When the level of the accumulated pain reaches a certain level, it must be downloaded. We must give pain to others as we are unable to hold it in any longer. Holding pain, in the form of anger, would cause our death.

Punishing others and giving them pain is the worst self-punishment. Punishing others ensures resentment, and the body weight begins to grow. We hold on to every single bit of pain. Our body weight increases grossly, so we humiliate ourselves even further. A humiliated person takes up space from life in proportion to the love they want to get from others. The only source of love for a painful person is food. Lots of food and especially sweets. A humiliated person can't lose weight. If they lost weight, their conditioned mind would sense that they are at "loss." This is the reason the lost weight is quickly gained back. They put on even more weight than they had before. Experiencing loss in any form for a humiliated person means "I don't have anything." A humiliated person looks for pain and suffering in everything and anything. They are victims of living with self-sorrow. The humiliation wound makes the body soft from the accumulated fat and inverts the knees, showing sexual closure. The humiliated person, however, is addicted to sex. They will belittle themselves by making sexual jokes. They go after the opposite gender and ask them for unsolicited sex. When their sex request is declined, they burn in humiliation and shame.

A humiliated person believes: *"I only deserve pain, I am a victim, and everyone takes advantage of me."*

The fourth emotional wound is **betrayal**. Betrayal awakens at 4-5 years of age from the parent of the opposite gender. Similarly to the other emotional wounds, we use betrayal on others so they can't betray us. We also begin to lie to ourselves, to practice self-deception.

The behavioral protection to betrayal is control. If we control everything, then no one can betray us. If we control what we eat, then we won't gain weight.

However, we gain weight immediately when skipping exercise and overeat from losing control.

Strenuous exercise is one way to put control over ourselves. We betray ourselves that pain is good for us. So we ensure physical pain through exercise.

A betrayed person controls the other person in a relationship too. The signs of control are excess jealousy and envy. If a woman can't have control over her husband, she will inflict control over the children. If there are no children, she wants to control anyone who is perceived to have less power. It may be the girl at the check out counter or the customer service desk.

Dear moms and dads,

Who can recognize themselves here?

A betrayed person will often have an excessive sex life. A sexual relationship allows them exceptional control. Control the other person to have sex and control even further through the type of sex one chooses, to feel empowered.

A betrayed person can typically cheat on everyone to feel in control. This behavior is totally natural to them. God saves those who try to cheat them in personal life, financially or in business.

Betrayal is built on the abandonment emotional-wound. If you feel emotional betrayal, look for the abandonment, emotional wound too. The body signs of a controller are large muscles and big shoulders, and intense sexual organs.

"I know how to do everything. I am always right! Everyone shall do as I say" –
becomes the life motto of a betrayed person.

Injustice is the fifth emotional wound, completes the installation of a child.
Injustice awakened by the parent of the same gender by 6-7 years of age.
Injustice makes this person rigid. Injustice means something is unfair.

Rigidity is the behavior protection of a child who experienced injustice. The
person loses flexibility and can apply ruthless injustice on others as self-
protection. They feel like God and make justice everywhere.

Injustice is built on the top of rejection. If you feel injustice is an upsetting
pain in your life, then you have to look earlier and examine your rejection
wound. The body signs of injustice is a very thin and very unflexible person.

Do you understand yourself and the other people around you now? Can you
see them better? Can you hear and feel their pain?

Does it make sense why you did certain painful things in your life?

It is an eye-opener seeing others differently now, whom made you feel upset.

Can you see people with their brutal childhoods, and it makes sense for them
to commit unforgiving crimes? The most dreadful thing to realize: If you
went through the same brutal childhood conditioning, then you would be
the same person committing ruthless crimes.

Be very grateful it is not you!

We have an incredible responsibility towards ourselves and our children! We must filter through the information that we allow ourselves and our children to receive. We also have to take responsibility for sifting through our own words and actions, which others observe. We must consider others who listen to our words. The vibrations of our words not only affect others, but you too.

Your expressed anger will affect the other person and consequently you and is the biggest self-punishment! Anger continues to vibrate for hours and days in you. What do you do during this time, so you don't harm others?

Anger must be contained and managed. The management is done by objective observation. Objective observation allows one to transform anger and learn from it. This is why we meditate and do the transformation technique.

Look at your behavior, then note the emotional wounds. Which ones are the most relevant? Which ones are the most painful? Which ones make you upset if someone else does it to you?

It is very possible that a combination or all of the emotional wounds are running in you. Complete the transformation exercise for every emotional wound present in you.

The transformation exercise is a huge head start to your healing journey.

If you reach more difficult parts of your transformation, seek professional help. Look for an NLP coach who is certified in TimeLine Therapy®. The mind can lock up your emotional pain so deep, that you may need a professional to bring you out of depression. .

The conditioned mind is responsive to questions. So if your conditioned mind receives a very unique question, then your block dissolves as you realize the answer. To have these exceptional questions, you need an NLP coach.

Emotional wounds cause craving. Transforming your emotional wounds that cause resentment, anger, hatred, aggression, fear, sadness, guilt, or depression will be significant for ending your craving. Transform everything and anything rising to the surface. Take your time and work patiently!

I feel that rejection and abandonment are two emotional wounds that almost all of us have to deal with.

It doesn't matter if we only remember adulthood or teenager events, transform those too. The conditioned mind allows the transformation outside, in. Only by transforming these outside layers, will the conditioned mind bring the deeper painful events to the surface. Our body cells remember everything! The body stores the painful memory deep down. Our protective compensation numbness pushed these memories deep down.

I had a client who used to feel nothing. He said *"I don't even feel hurt anymore when something happens, I go numb. However, I always see the bad in everything. I did an excellent job shoving my stuff under the carpet."* After many months of attending my yoga classes, he started to feel the air passing through his nostrils. After participating in the "Recharge your life" camp, he bagan to feel emotions on day 2. He finally remembered and felt the painful emotions from his past. While feeling the air passing through his nostrils, his painful memory slowly began to open up.

Not remembering your painful past is entirely normal. You possibly shoved all those memories under the rug and rendered them non-existent.

Suppressing memories deep down is a protective
mechanism of the conditioned mind.

Good thing your mind allows you to remember such depth, in a way that you can handle. So no need to worry. A worry here is merely another layer of fear coming up.

Disconnecting the first event by the transformation process, makes your painful past fall apart. The emotional wound falls apart.

If you still feel a particular emotional wound present, you have an earlier event to transform. Meditate with the breath observation, and in due time, you will be able to remember the earlier event.

The transformation process becomes a daily practice. Transform your past events as they come up one by one. Then begin transforming upsetting events what you experience now. Perhaps you see something on the street or in a movie, which feels upsetting. Use these as reminders, why you have to behave with loving kindness in similar situations. Expressing only love and kindness can ensure that you create a supportive, harmonious environment around you. This is how you can create a peaceful life.

Understanding all the above, I wish a very successful transformation!

Loosening up your fears prepares you to take the ultimate journey to discover yourself fully. This journey begins with attending a 10 day- vipassana course. This course is free and offered in 165 places in the world. See www.dhamma.org for more information.

Making long lasting change

The energy invested in the transformation process also makes the foundation of your empowering future.

Making change is one thing. Making long lasting change is another. To sustain the change you made, we have to discuss an essential part of your journey here. This important part of your journey is the **transitional phase**.

Most people fall back to old habits because they don't understand the importance of the transitional period. This is the phase when you learn to handle your own emotional ups and downs.

It takes time and practice until change builds into your character. The new life instructions and behavioral skills, will become part of your life step-by-step.

What does this step by step process look like? Let's see for example, in the case of anger. If you can stay in the center and can stay non-reactive one out of ten times, you are progressing. If you can stay awake and focus on your breathing instead of getting angry, one out of ten times then your anger is fading. Keep practicing awareness and you will be able to increase the use of your new behavioral skills.

> *It takes 1.5 - 2 years, until a new behavior becomes automatic and becomes a part of your character. It takes dedication, diligence, and perseverance to reach complete personal development.*

Practicing awareness and objectivity brings a gradual result, and you feel better and better. The number of your emotional ups and downs decreases, and their intensity becomes milder. This is the result of increased awareness brought to you by the daily breath observation meditation.

Who am I?

During this learning process a fundamental question arises, *"Who am I?"* We begin to ask this question because the habitual "I" is missing. The disappearance of the habitual "I" is another step forward.

The purpose of the transformation process is to change your habitual "I." This is what you wanted to happen, isn't it! You have been fed up with your old self, your past behavior patterns, which have been creating so many miseries. Now, this old "I" is not there. In other words, your behavioral change was possible as the underlying "I," "my," "mine" fell apart, faded away, and disappeared.

Our biggest fear was actually to experience the "I," falling apart. Fear wanted to believe that you are "nobody" without your fear.

Now ask yourself: *"Who am I not?"* Any further answer is another intellectualization from your mind.

When you get used to being a "nobody" your "I" falls apart. So who is there instead? Your new "I-less, I."

Becoming a "nobody" empties out your stored emotional load from your heart. The love begins to flow into your heart and shows up in a sincere smile.

The realization comes *"I am not who I thought I was."* The conditioned mind uses labels that lose validity and importance, because we realize deep down who we are.

We are the observer.

We are love, and we are the source of love.

Love is not outside of us!
Don't look for love in others, because love is inside of you.

Now let's go to the level of sensations and examine the effect of "I"-less. If there is no "I", how is it possible to have my sensation, my feeling and my emotion?

Emotions and feelings are the imprints of your past pains on the cellular level. These imprints coming to the surface, bring us knowledge.

Conditioned sensations or emotions, just like your thoughts, are reactive and controlling you subconsciously. Sensations however, just like thoughts, come and go. If thoughts and sensations come and go, how can they be you?

It is revolutionary to realize that we are not our thoughts.
We are also not what we believed about ourselves.
We are also not our emotions. We are also not what we feel.

What you believed up until now, is the result of your conditioned mind. You are not your subconscious feelings and emotions!

You can't own your conditioned emotions! Emotions come and go. Therefore, wanting to hold on to feelings makes no sense.

All our feelings and emotions are
temporary. Please get used to this.

We are the mass of vibrating atoms, which are continuously changing.

If we could be our emotions and feelings, we would continuously disappear when sensations or emotions go.

We are not our body either. If we were our bodies, our bodies would defy who we are. If we are not our body, then the sensations, which are felt on the body, are not ours either! Your body sensations, like pain and illness, are there to bring you knowledge and not to be an object of ownership.

Let go, depending on your subconscious feelings! Let go, allowing your emotions to define your mood.

Let go, allowing your sensations to direct your thoughts, words, and actions.

Let go, allowing your subconscious emotions to determine your future and destiny!

Let go of possessing your body! We have received this body to practice, learn, and take care of it. Now we learn to observe the sensations coming up from our own body and learn temporariness. Everything passes away. Our sensations and thoughts and all that happens in life, passes away. If we can observe our inner feelings and emotions objectively, we will be able to observe ouselves through difficult life events. If you are able to observe your inner feelings, then you are able to recognize their changes, due to outside circumstances. With this objectivity, allow things to happen, stay in the center and remain non-reactive.

Let go of wanting to feel! Let go of wanting to feel this or that! Millions of feelings are running in us due to the conditioned mind.

You must understand that you can't choose your subconscious sensations, which come to the surface.

What you can do is choose your reactions to the sensations coming up from your subconscious. Observing objectively is your free choice, allowing you to stay non-reactive. This remedy allows the subconscious sensations to come to the surface and fade away. The objective observation is the way to change and free up the power of the mind.

It is an enormous experience, while the "I" falls apart. And we no longer ask *"Who am I?"* The question itself becomes irrelevant. The answer is automatic. We are the observer. We feel gratitude for every feeling and sensation in us, because they allow us to practice objective observation.

If you are aware, every sensation serves you!

Let go of giving importance to your subconscious thoughts and sensations. Your only task is to observe them objectively. This is the way you are progressing as you are sharpening your awareness. The more aware you are, the more you can handle the subconscious sensation, rising up to the surface.

We can sense, and we can learn. Therefore, we can also learn to manage our sensations. You have received this body to clear out your past emotional imprints. While taking care of your body, you can complete this clearing work as much as possible. Once you have succeeded with the clearing, then use this body to create a meaningful life, which contributes value to society.

Let go of the feeling of pain!
There are other sensations besides pain,
that you can sense and experience!

YOU are NOT YOUR SENSATION,

therefore, you are NOT YOUR PAIN either!

Give up feeling pain and thinking pain is the only sensation, that exists!

Let go of believing you deserve only pain!

Let go of your fear of living without pain!

Let go of being identified with your pain!

Give up suffering! Give up being identified with your suffering!

Give up all your expectations and wants!

Now just observe objectively your pain, suffering, expectations, oppositions, and wants, coming to the surface.

You have been hard as a rock. You have been hard on others and also on yourself. As an adult, you have transformed into a rock. A rock who doesn't feel anything anymore. You became a rock, however, don't have to continue living your life as a rock!

Give up the hardness and being a rock! Give up building stone walls as protection to feeling any pain!

It is time to learn to be gentle. It is time to open the locks on your fears and let love, kindness, goodwill, and gentleness come to the surface. Remove mind made fears, and you find true love there. Be brave to live out of love! Express the love that you are made of!

You are made of love!

We are all made of love!

The greatest love of the Universe, created your life. Your life is the greatest gift anyone can give you.

> *We don't feel love, because we search for love outside*
> *of ourselves. We don't feel love because we have not*
> *opened the locks on our fears deep within us.*

Imagine a world, where everyone started to be gentle to each other, or animals or plants?

> *How would your life be, if you expressed your*
> *kindness daily to at least one other person?*

Can you see the change in your life if you expressed your kindness to your family? Imagine the difference in the world if everyone practiced kindness at home!

Most of us had rock hard, parental conditioning. We had to be strong, so no one could hurt us. Being gentle was a sign of weakness. Therefore, we developed a thick layer of hard shields so no one could see our weakness.

True strength and power are formed from awareness, objectivity, and compassion.

Living with awareness dissolves all layers of fear and
we can see the consequences of our actions.
Awareness allows our natural responsibility to
develop for our words and actions.

We begin to choose our words and actions consciously
while considering others. We will be able to
consider our loved ones and our relationships.

We can reach our goals without hurting others. We must choose the higher road and generate value for all involved in the process. Developing this mindset helps you to drop unfair business peacefully and with gratitude. There is no use for negative criticism, yelling and sarcastic tones of voice. Anyone who does incorrect business won't hear and understand our critical words anyway. These people have no concept for differentiating between right and wrong and driven by their conditioned mind and in a hallucinogen illusion. Talking to a person in this illusionary state, is like talking to a wall. You waste a lot of time and energy. Recognize people who live in delusion and choose your actions accordingly! Let this person realize his or her loss. However, it is none of your business if the person realizes it or not. Only those will hear us, who are ready to listen. And this is not everybody. Remember, it took you also a long time before you were ready to listen.

Let go of wanting to teach everyone! Remember, that everyone behaves right based on the resources they have in their head. People also close their minds due to fears. They are afraid of you and everything you say. Remember, fearful people hear everything you say as a threat and feel inferior. They simply don't feel good enough the way they are because you keep telling them to change. You need to accept a fearful person the way he or she is, so they won't feel threatened by you. This is the time when they possibly open up and may listen to you. It will take a lot of love and communication skills to get through to them. Patience and acceptance goes a long way and empowers them to ask for your help. Practice change in your life and let your work talk for you. The biggest motivation for a fearful person to ask for your advice is seeing you looking good, healthy, and happy. Your increased awareness made the changes in you and slowly begins its work in others around you.

Awareness brings many amazing and incredible changes in our relationships. If we are asking for advice, we will be able to wait patiently while the other person finishes what he or she had to say. Even if you don't like the answer, you can look at it objectively. You can use this event to practice patience and gratitude. The person took the time to explain whatever he had on his mind, regardless of your disagreement, Accept what others say. Thank the person for his or her time and effort and move on. This event was not about the advice itself, but your chance of practicing patience. The answer from the other person was irrelevant. This event was about allowing the other person to speak. Remind yourself that you are practicing acceptance and patience. You give time for another person to talk because you have time. So you practice abundance as well. If you live in abundance, you have an abundant amount of time to be patient.

Awareness does great clearing in the people who are around you. Only those stay in your life who positively serve you living a conscious life. People who are not meant to remain part of your life, will disappear. The wrong business will fade out too. It is possible that your income will somewhat decrease from the trillions to millions, however, all who are involved in your business, will win. Everyone must be in abundance. Agree only to abundance in business for all, as this feels right.

The more of us that can live our lives with kindness, the faster a new society will grow. Living consciously your mind concentrates on solving issues more efficiently. The solutions will serve all and promote the growth of society. These solutions are the innovations to use renewable energy, alternative green methods to build and protect and rehabilitate the environment.

Get started living your life in kindness

Here is the exercise:

Wake up in the morning, look in the mirror, and caress your face. If it is a strange feeling, it is entirely normal. It means you need to go back and work on your deserving. We need to build the deserving feeling, into all your cells from the top of the head to the tip of your toes. If you haven't felt the deserving feeling, please ask the Universe to show you.

You deserve to be "good enough," is your birth-right!
You have received your life as you deserve it!

Experience deserving through caressing your own face. Increase the number of caresses from 3-5-10, then be brave to caress your face for 1 minute. Caress your face gently. Add the genuine feeling of gentleness, acceptance of yourself, and taking care to caress youself. Be grateful for receiving this caressing.

Take a look at your face. Can you see a genuine smile? Can you see your skin and the possible wrinkles smoothed out? You deserve to be handled gently and with care. Use this reference experience to conduct your life as you talk about yourself to others. Experience what the power of gentle, loving care can do for you.

If you are not brave enough for this exercise, it is ok, continue reading.

Opening the secrets

Going through the transformation exercise, allowed you to open some of the locks. In this chapter, we reveal all the secrets, which are locked up inside.

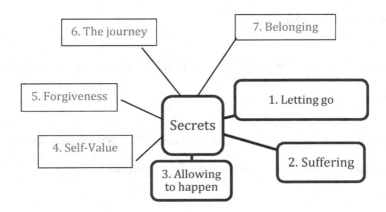

The revelation of these secrets came to me in a series of downloads as well. The first significant download about fears, came to me in the middle of the night at 3 am, then continued through all different hours of the day. Life was becoming crystal clear like the sound of a bell. The specific objects of emotional craving became apparent. I could also see and feel what steps we have to take to come out from the grip of these cravings.

My Vipassana meditations opened the channel to this wisdom. Through this wisdom, I also received the instruction to share this knowledge with the world.

The first secret: Letting go

Let me begin with an annoucement!

Today is the International Day of "Let go and Be Kind." Yes, it is today! Whenever you read this chapter, it is this day. So start letting go now!

Why today?

If not today, then when?

Why you? If not you, then who? Who will start putting your emotional loads down?

Haven't you carried this heavy load long enough? How long do you want to reject opportunities, things, and people from your life?

Just how many of us have tried to keep and hold onto beautiful people, beautiful memories, and beautiful illusions? Why are we so frightened to let them go?

Why do we reject letting go?

Why have you been rejecting to let go? Why have you been doing everything else than letting go?

We are afraid to let go because we believe that by letting go, we lose. Holding onto things and emotions, we have an illusion that we have something. Without holding on, we have nothing, and we are no one.

Can you see here another fear created illusion? A fear of letting go. So it is time to transform it!

Look back in your life and see how many beautiful things, people, and events were present. Since you could not be grateful for these beautiful things and people at that time they vanished. We only realized what we received from them, after they were gone.

The fearful mind can only have it, if it is a possession. Therefore, we are holding on to every crumb of those memories. Imagine that these events happened to give you a chance to let go.

The fearful mind is the one holding one. The fearful mind can only possess, rule and control to make the illusion of having.

Realize, if you expressed gratitude instead of control during those painful times, you would still have those things and people in your life. If you could live in the state of letting go, those people would still choose to be in your life. Please cry for 2 minutes now that you understand how your possessiveness pushed people out of your life! You possessed because you had no other tool!

The dependent possessing made you forget to appreciate what you received from those who were in your life. You didn't know the value of what you received at that time. Nothing was ever good enough! You only knew to demand more. You were unable to let go of wanting and be content. The only thing you knew is craving and wanting more.

When I look back at my life, I can see the events where I was holding on. These events screamed loud from my craving. I wasn't able to express appreciation and gratitude. Moreover, I was afraid to show appreciation and gratitude. I was scared to let go of my dependency on craving. I was afraid to understand the truth within me.

I was holding on to beautiful memories. I was holding onto illusions, which I made my memories. I lived in a complete fantasy. I had a specific illusion about people (especially relationships) and illusions of my expectations towards them. I lived with the illusion of hope. I subconsciously created more pain with my illusions. I was not able to let the pain go.

I had a conviction. *"If it comes through pain, it is worth it. All valuable things must come through pain."* This painful conviction was the result of my childhood conditioning. And just how many of you have it?

It is possible that sports only deepened this conviction. Every single training must have been painful and had to end with exhaustion. I remembered feeling valuable and deserving when I felt dead tired from physical fatigue. I was convinced that I did an excellent job, and this is how life was supposes to be. Painful.

I was holding on to my inflated hopes about people because within these illusions I felt like a somebody. I was dependent on my illusions about my emotions, things, and people. I was afraid to let illusions go. I believed that if I let pain and illusion go, I would become nothing.

The illusions and pain made the foundation of my massive anxiety, which I cured with a long run in the morning. I worked the whole day and fell to bed, dead tired at night. I continued the same routine the next day and every day for years. I felt good only at work where my mind was fully focused. I repeated this routine and called it a life. A live lived in self-inflicted pain and suffering. Pain and illusion were my protective shields and justified why I shouldn't look into my fears. Fears? What fears! I didn't have any! Only weak people have fears, and I was strong! My mind convinced me that I was fearless. I was untouchable and so strong that no one could beat me at anything. Lol.

The biggest self-created misery is to reject letting go. We reject letting go by looking for all sorts of illusionary solutions instead. We practice chanting, stare at candles, take all kinds of nutritional supplements. We take pills as a remedy for our anxiety. Some people reach out at this point for substances. A substance, which numbs the pain and gives temporary happiness. The second step is then becoming dependent on the substance for a happy feeling.

I ask everyone: Please let pain go! Let go today, let go right now! Give up rejecting yourself, and others! Give up rejecting this opportunity to let go!

> *Be brave and take the very first step your mind is*
> *afraid of, but your heart says is the right thing!*

Give up being hard as a rock! Let go of your thick protective shields around your fears and your inner self.

If you have not able to succeed with the previous exercise using a mirror, then here is the time!

Take a small mirror or use the selfie camera of your cell phone. Look in the mirror. Lift your hand, and like a loving mother, touch your face. Now move your hand softly and caress your face. Look in the mirror and see how you are caressing your face lovingly. Express all your gentleness to yourself. Be brave and caress your face! Yes, you deserve it! Let go of holding onto the initial strange feeling and continue. You will get used to it. Continue this exercise even when your mind tells you: "This is so stupid and so meaningless." Accept these mind-made thoughts and let go of holding on to them. Continue the exercise. If you don't do this exercise, you won't have the experience of breaking through your ego.

Smile! Allow a genuine smile on your face. Accept everything! Let go of all your negative convictions and beliefs about yourself. Be kind to yourself and be gentle. Today is the International Day of Let go and Be Kind. Right here, and right now! And guess what? Tomorrow is another day to let go more! Tomorrow will bring another today. So continue and practice this exercise. Practice every day until the process becomes smooth and natural. Continue the practice, so you ensure some time for yourself every day. Practice and remind yourself how important, how worth it, and how valuable you are!

Now caress the head or the face of someone else in the family. Then caress the face of your friend and then someone you don't know. If this step is too much for now, then express your appreciation by a smile. Be brave to show your acceptance and appreciation, regardless of how this person looks. Don't worry, it is natural that your mind is making comments, like "What if this person thinks I want something from him or her? What if this person gets angry?"

Remind yourself that you don't want anything from this person. You want to give something. A smile and acceptance.

Caress the person who you have been holding onto, with love. Thank them for the wisdom and wish them the best. Let go of holding their hand. Now caress all the emotions in yourself, which don't serve you. Thank them for being there and let them go. Let them transform into love and kindness.

Make this above exercise a challenge for the next 6 weeks or 42 days. Use this opportunity to let go of being a rock. Let go of your fear of expressing love. Begin with showing kindness to yourself first, then to others!

Letting go of rejection, criticizing, blaming, will show up in your tone of voice and words as you speak. Pay attention to how your words will change towards yourself and towards your environment.

Letting people go from your life is not the end of the world!

Letting people go is the beginning of your new life! Once you let go of dependent relationships, you make space for healed people to come into your life. Now the difference, is that you don't want to own them. You don't want to control them and rule them to keep them in your life. You can allow them to stay in your life at their free will. Your rigid possessiveness, criticizing and blaming pushed them out of your life. You realized that keeping people in your life is only possible if you stay in the state of letting go. Welcome them to be in your life and treat them with gratitude. Wish them well if they want to leave.

When you handle others through the feeling of letting go, you give them permission to be themselves and decide to stay or leave. The state of letting go creates space for expressing gratitude every single day for those who freely choose to be in your life.

How would you want to be in somebody's life? Do you want to stay when you feel expected? You want to stay longer when it is not expected. You want to visit someone when they treat you with gratitude for your presence. Don't you?

Be brave, let go and be kind!

How many of you have the instant reaction to the above title: "It would be great if it were easy." This statement is completely natural from the conditioned mind. The conditioned mind only knows the difficulty. The conditioned mind is convinced that all has to be difficult and hard. Since the conditioned mind made you into a rock, then everything has to be hard as a rock. Remember the conditioned mind is fighting for it's right to convince you, that change is hard, you die in the process. Let go of your fear of letting go!

Complete the let go exercise with all your fears now.

Wrap up your fear of letting go, caress it with your hands, add gratitude, then lift your hands up and give it to the Universe. Thank your fear for serving you this long. Give your fear to the Universe! Let the Universe transform it into loving kindness.

Complete the letting go exercise for all your specific fears. You may have a fear of poverty, illness, poor health, being alone, living without fear, responsibility, deserving, love, acceptance, criticism, abandonment, the future, etc.

The Universe transforms these fears into loving kindness and empowerment. So now write down the opposite of those you let go. If you completed the transformation exercise in the previous chapter, you would know exactly what the opposites of your fears are. The opposites or the antidotes of your fears, are some sorts of positive life instructions coming from love and kindness. These will be your new tools. Imagine, all this knowledge has been inside you!

Let go of rejection. Wrap up rejection, criticism, and the fear of rejection in a beautiful box. Caress this lovely package and thank the content for serving you up until now. Now let it all go. Watch it with your mind's eye as it flies up to the sky. Let it transform into acceptance, appreciation, freedom of choice, kindness, and responsibility. The new life instructions or your new tools are acceptance, freedom to choose, kindness, and responsibility.

Write these antidotes down and color them with bright colors. Your life will change for the better in an instant if you use your new tools.

Let go of abandonment. Take the wanting to run away and the fear of being alone and wrap them up nicely in a pretty package. Lift the package up, thank it's content for serving you and then let the Universe take it from you. Let God take the package, so He can transform it into love and kindness. The specific tools or the antidotes of abandonment are: awareness, objective observation, acceptance, seeing clearly, and patience. Please add anything to this list that you feel will be an antidote. These antidotes are your tools, which will help you to wait out the passing of any "storm."

Moreover, you are part of the Universe, so no one can leave you! You are always in unity with the Universe.

Take a few minutes to let your pain go. Take another few minutes to let go of punishment, harshness, rushing, forcing, criticizing, yelling and speaking in an elevated tone of voice, resentment, sorrow, inferiority, humiliation, blame, control, pride, boasting, superiority, and sarcasm.

Let go of each of the above. Now continue letting go of the list below. Add any specific thing you need to let go personally.

- *Let go of betrayal, cheating, and injustice!*
- *Let go of your ignorance!*
- *Let go of not caring!*
- *Let go of your fear of responsibility.*
- *Let go of all of your fears!*
- *Let go of abandoning others and yourself!*
- *Let go of your doubt!*
- *Let go of your inner weakness.*
- *Let go of your resentment!*
- *Let go of living your life in difficulty!*
- *Let go of expressing your dislike and hatred!*
- *Let go of opposing and fighting back!*
- *Let go of being defensive!*
- *Let go of being always right!*
- *Let go of wanting to be the center of attention!*
- *Let go of being a victim!*
- *Let go of obsessive wanting and craving!*
- *Let go of being obsessive aboout becoming something or someone!*
- *Let go of making people your slaves!*

- *Let go of making others serve you to feel loved!*
- *Let go every kind of obsessive craving!*
- *Let go of allowing your cravings to control you!*

What does it mean to let go?

Letting go doesn't mean to give up planning and working. It doesn't mean to give up your dreams. Letting go is a feeling just like the other feelings or vibrations, which are required to behave kindly. The feeling of letting go shows up in your thoughts and communication. You let go of people who drain you and don't serve you.

Letting go means making space for the new. After the clearing part of the letting go, you will enjoy a temporary emptiness. By creating this space, you allow things, circumstances, and people to come to you.

Letting go means knowing how to accept. Letting go means having the mindset that all that comes to you, serves you. All that comes to you makes you more. So letting go means opening for abundance.

Letting go sets your entire journey. It brings a sequence of events, which is your life journey. How do your goals come true on this journey? Your old self used to work until you reached your goal. You worked possessively to reach your goal. You worked and worked and worked and forgot to live.

Now, when you make a goal, let that go too. Work on the steps reaching a goal and let those go too. Your focus comes in applying your new life instructions daily and achieving a balance between life and work. The Future segment of this book will discuss this balance in detail.

Work on your relationships and practice all your wisdom from your past.

Practicing your wisdom from your past will make your goal come true by itself. It is unbelievable to hear this at first. Allowing things to come to you is your new journey.

In the new journey, we let go of working on our goals obsessively. Letting go of pushing through people to reach our goal. Letting go of being inconsiderate and learning to care for all involved! Let the Universe bring you what is yours. Whatever the Universe brings is yours! Another surprise is that the Universe brings us an even better version of what we make into a goal.

What do you have to do, to calibrate the law of attraction for your goal? The great thing is that you don't have to do much, just be aware.

Applying awareness tells you precisely what you have to do at any moment. If you look at things patiently, objectively, and out of compassion, you will have an answer.

Focus on becoming a good human being. A good human being, who can handle everything kindly. Work on your relationships first. Become a good human being to your plants, pets, and family members.

Allow the free flow of love between you and your plants or pets. Accept their unconditional love. This is a good start, working on relationships. Personally, I have a fantastic experience about the free flow of love between me and our dogs, Rocco and Albert the past two years, since they are in my life.

So, take a leap and let go! Let go and allow yourself to be kind! Let go of buying more clothes! You probably have enough! Be kind to the clothes that you do have! If you don't use them, then let them go and donate them. Give your unused garments to those who have a use for them. Let go of your clothes with love and kindness, let them make someone else happy.

Letting go step-by-step

- Sit down for 1 minute. Close your eyes and choose one thing or one feeling or emotion to let go. sadness, fear, resentment, hatred, or obsessive wanting.
- Let go of your chosen feeling and give it the Universe for 1 minute only.
- If you were able to let this feeling go for 1 minute, then increase the time for 3, 5 then 10 minutes.
- Now practice letting go for as long as you can. Test yourself and challenge how long you can stay without your chosen emotion. The duration of your state of letting go increases with your awareness.

    When the particular non-serving emotion creeps back, then observe it, say thank you and then let it go again with love.

When you let go of any of your negative emotions, you free up space and create time to use one form of loving kindness. It is huge progress, to reach 1-3 - 5 or 10 minutes of letting go feeling every day!

Let go of obsessive exercising. Exercise is a compulsion for many people. Exercise becomes compulsive when you use it as a compensation for your overeating, keeping a specific skinny look or training to punish yourself.

How many personal trainers give punishing exercises to their clients, and the clients love it?

Exercise becomes compulsive when you use it to make yourself stronger to withstand more pain. You are possibly familiar with the old saying: "No pain, no gain." If you exercise out of self-inflicted pain, you use physical pain to suppress your emotional pain. Let go of all painful training! Be kind to yourself and your body! Choose the kind of exercise or physical activity, what you enjoy doing. Be brave and give yoga a try! Dance at home, go for a walk, or take a hike while enjoying nature.

Personally, I used to exercise and especially run, to beat myself up. I made these exercise sessions so hard that nothing in life could be harder than what I inflicted on myself. When my body couldn't take the wear and tear, I had to stop the crazy routines. I reached this point in early 2001. My Naturopathic doctor advised me to stop running and strength training. He recommended to walk and do yoga. The recommendation came as a big shock! What? Stop running? But I did! And I also gave yoga a try. My friend gave me a sheet with drawings of yoga poses and said, *"Do this while you do deep breathing through your nose."* I followed her instructions because I wanted to go back to running later. This was the beginning of my yoga career. Surprisingly it all worked out. I became a big fan of yoga, later became a teacher and then a teacher trainer. I am convinced now that yoga is a masterwork for the body. Deep nasal breathing, coupled with yoga poses, provides such a workout for the body, that no other form of exercise can!

Stop wanting and start doing!

Craving comes to you to teach you to let go. You only crave for things that you have to let go. A wanting feeling awakens when you have to practice to let go of your old behavior of wanting.

You are craving for things that you have to let go of!

Letting go of wanting, craving, dislike, or hate is necessary to allow the flow of kindness and love in your heart.

Anger and hatred don't fit together with kindness.

Until you clean out your fears and cravings, your kindness remains on the surface, and it is conditional. Conditional kindness will quickly turn into hatred when something doesn't go according to your expected conditions.

The second secret: Suffering

Suffering is a strange secret. Gautama, the Buddha recognized suffering to be a key part of the change process, 2500 years ago. One must learn to recognize suffering and observe it objectively to receive the necessary learning outcome. This is one essential teaching of Vipassana meditation.

You can only let go of your suffering if you recognized your own pain.

We have to recognize our thoughts and emotions, feeding our suffering. We have to make this recognition ourselves.

The second step in the recognition is to admit:

- We create our misery and suffering.
- Suffering is the only way we can operate in our lives.
- We create suffering day by day, hour by hour, and minute by minute.

We create suffering by:

- The way we answer specific questions.
- The way we address a particular issue.
- Being ignorant and inconsiderate of others.
- Not thinking before talking or doing.
- Being careless.
- Being self-centered.
- Getting engaged in something we don't want, because we can't say no.

- — Looking for problems, faults, and mistakes.
- — Looking for expressing our blaming and resenting.
- — etc.

We keep up suffering all day long by keeping ourselves rolling in the same suffering causing thoughts. We allow our rolling thoughts to come out in our words, in our tone of voice and in our facial expressions. These negative expressions will certainly get the same kind of reaction from others. Our unconscious words, tone of voice, and facial expressions make others reflect back what we have just expressed. Our unconscious words and behavior will ensure others will suffer. This is what addiction to misery looks like. Our unconscious suffering expressed by our unconscious behavior, causes misery for others if they don't know how to handle it.

Being dependent on misery drives the unconscious creation of pain. When the level of misery gets low, one unconsciously decides that it is time to practice a little suffering. We must practice suffering from time to time because this is what we deserve. This is what your unconscious mind wants you to believe.

Awaken to your suffering!

Take your two minutes and cry if you needed!

Then breathe and continue reading.

Let me show you now a few life examples of misery-dependency in the case of rejection. Rejection can be expressed in many ways. Words, tone of voice, and body language. Your expressed rejection affects others who can't handle it. The consequences of our criticizing communication and disgust showing facial expressions provoke others to reject us. This is the mirror effect.

Are you aware of your own facial expressions?

Would you like to look at someone with the same
facial expression, who looks like you now?

Would you want to spend time with someone
who behaves the same way as you do?

Our subconscious mind-driven behavior provokes others to behave the same way we do. We receive precisely the same behavior that we display. You can see your own behavior reflected back on others.

My husband has an excellent metaphor for misery creation. He says, a person behaving poorly to another, might as well put his head on a cutting board and say to them "cut here."

Realizing the mirror effect is a tremendous experience, which drives change. I remember very clearly the day I recognized the mirror effect in myself. It dawned on me, how my rejective behaviors and expressions provoked rejection in others. Astonishment, being shocked then numb. A chill ran through my spine. Everything was so clear! Life events ran through my mind's eye. I had been provoking others to reject me! My provoking behavior was crystal clear, which caused my broken relationships. Because at that time, the only response to everything in my life was rejection.

Note: our mind blindly rules our behavior when we allow others close to us. When we open up, we become vulnerable.

Let us have a deeper understanding of suffering. Suffering is hidden behind an even bigger secret lock, than our fears. At least this is what your fear wants you to believe! This is another big tabu!

In this book, we open up every tabu and myth that the mind makes. So let's see further.

We suffer, and we are also afraid to suffer. However, we continuously suffer. A crazy cycle. We begin to be afraid when the level of suffering is a little more significant than what we believe we deserve. If the suffering is smaller than what our belief dictates we deserve, then we create some more. Now we can suffer from our fears and anxiety too!

Our most immense anxiety is about letting go of our suffering and pain.

The question is:

When did you decide to deserve pain and suffering?

When was pain installed in you?

When did you believe that whatever happens, you have to turn it into suffering?

When did you believe that whatever good things and opportunities are coming to you, you must reject them and turn the situation into the suffering of resentment?

Open up the door on your suffering! Open the lock you placed on this door first. Open the door by writing down all that brings you suffering. Be honest! Write down events when you caused your own suffering. Write as many of these events as you can.

When you are done, you more than likely realized just how big suffering is a part of your life!

We are suffering from being alive!

When did you believe you deserve suffering?

Find the answer!

Another example of misery creation when we talk about the weather. When the sky is blue, and the sun is shining, we are already talking about the upcoming storms or possible droughts.

Why can't we stay happy while the sun is out? And why can't we stay delighted when it is raining? When did we decide that our happiness depends on a condition?

When did you decide that something has to happen to permit yourself to feel happy?

Find the answer!

The third secret: Permission for deserving

After realizing our suffering the next secret is permission.

Answer the next question, honestly, please.

- Are you worth it to permit yourself to tell the truth to yourself?
- Are you afraid of what others might say when you finally speak the truth about yourself?

You are not alone. The "I don't deserve it" program, in my opinion, causes the most emotional issues in children who grow into painful adults.

The deserving is also a conditioned program. As children, we copied the "being worth it" program from those who we grow up with.

You copied your environment, to define how much
you allow or permit yourself to deserve.

Please stop here for a minute and reflect on your life. Just how many times did you stop short because of your level of permission to deserve something?

The permission program sorts out in life: *"This is mine, this is not." "I can take this much."* or *"This is something I can't even touch."* The mind also reasons *"This is what I can say, this I cannot say."*

Let's see the permission program through an example of buying shoes. We buy a $10 pair of plastic shoes, without a thought, because that is "ours." The $80 leather shoes we can't afford.

I bring this example up to demonstrate how the permission program works, irrelevant of the object. I also bring this example as I am a woman who likes shoes and used to buy lots of them. Most of you reading this book can be like me.

Let's look at this story objectively. The plastic shoes wear out in 2-3 months, the leather shoes 3 or more years, if we take care of it. We buy 4 plastic shoes in one year, which is 12 pairs of shoes in 3 years. Do the math. The cost of plastic shoes for the 3 years is $120. It is $40 more than the price of the leather shoes.

Apologies to those vegetarians who only wear synthetic or cotton. I could make this example of comparing a synthetic shirt with an organic cotton one.

The point here is the craving. We crave again and again to feel deserving and turn to our permission program. Our buying strategy is based on the low price and not sustainability. This has been proven by research looking at buying behavior. Buying behavior, is markedly different from what people say or do. Even though there is a tendency to buy second hand, the bottom line is that fewer people care about sustainability and the shoes in 3 months end up in landfills.

What is the importance of the 3 month time? It allows us a brief enough time to rebuild our craving for new shoes. It becomes totally rational in 3 months to buy a new pair. Something else to consider is before buying the new shoes, it is entirely neccessary to visit every shoe store possible. The searching time of 2 weeks is also crucial before we actually make the purchase. We don't care about wasting 2 weeks either. The 2 weeks of searching allowed us to stay craving.

What else do we deserve? We deserve to be ruined, worn out, falling apart. We need to have the worn out feeling to justify our craving and buy new. The worn out feeling is the driver to permit craving.

The shoe industry recognizes this buying pattern in women. This is why the industry makes more synthetic. A shoe manufacturer friend of mine told me. *"We are happy to fulfill the desires of women, wanting to have new shoes every 3 months."*

The permission program has more secrets. Permission to have something is only one type of permission. When we practice opposing and fighting, we permit ourselves to be in situations where we can oppose, resist, and fight.

Permission to accept, appreciate, and express gratitude is also specific permission programs. Permission is also when we permit an event to happen without opposing it. We permit things to happen, and we accept it.

Permitting an event to happen is based on our abundance belief. Even if the event is seemingly fearful, and we used to express opposing, defending and blaming-, now we simply allow it to happen with the mindset of gratitude and abundance.

"I permit all coming to me. Everything is for me! I
have everything in me to handle any situation."

The fourth secret: Self-value

Permission reflective of your self-value. If you don't value yourself, you can't permit things to happen. If you can't allow things to happen, you must look one layer deeper and examine your self-value. This fear makes you afraid to be valuable.

Unconsciously we simply become afraid to be valuable enough to live!

Do you have doubts about you being valuable enough to live?

Are you afraid to be valuable enough to permit and
deserve to live your life in happiness and love?

The origin of your doubt to deserve and permit a happy life comes from the first emotional wound, rejection. A child is already rejected if coming from unwanted pregnancy. Rejection is the emotional wound we experience from conception to one year of age. Rejection creates the most destructive beliefs and convictions. If these beliefs remain untreated-, we can destroy our lives.

Are we worth it to live?

Do you feel worth it to live?

You are again not alone with your negative feeling as an answer.

> **You are worth living because you received life. If you were not worth it, you would not receive life!**

> *You received your life because you are valuable enough to allow love to fill you up and live out of this love. This is the secret belief, which opens up the next lock and creates your healing on the cellular level.*

Yes, you are worth it to live!

We are all worth it to live!

The fact that conception took place means we are worth it for the most valuable gift ever! This is your life! Being Alive justifies your success!

Selfishness or self-value?

These two words are often interchanged by the conditioned mind. I like to clear out the difference between these words.

Self-value does NOT mean *"I am the only one who is important, and all is mine."* Unfortunately, we have been conditioned to believe that those who are worth it must be loud, ruling and controlling. These are the signs of selfishness. Selfishness comes from the complete deficiency of self-value. This person has conditioned worth, based on the ratio of their money, knowledge, jewelry, car, or other possessions. Or perhaps their connection and power socially or in business. How do we recognize selfishness further?

A selfish person:

- Lives by the "Everything is for me and nothing is for others" – belief. This illusion makes the person feel that they have the right to take everything from others.

- Believes they are entitled. Everyone owes them a favor, and everyone serves them.

- Delegates without doing work. Will not lift their little finger. If this person needs to get his or her hands dirty from work, he or she feels that life is over. They must get everything done by others. They will manipulate or use force to get things done.

- Steps on anyone in their way.

- Is unable to give. If they gave anything, they would lose themselves. They have nothing. Everything they have, even the love they feel for themselves, is based on what they receive from others.

- Always makes themselves shine and expresses their own pride to feel valuable.

- Is unable to ask. They can only demand and take. They expect everything to be done. If it is not done, they punish.

- Has self-worth and self-value, defined by their behavior and their possessions. Without their rejecting and demanding behavior, knowledge, and properties, they are "nobody" and worth "nothing."

- Lives in chaos. They live with multiple cravings and materialistic dependencies.
- Lives in constant stress, pain, and anxiety.

I used to depend on my knowledge to feel valuable. I used my studies, career, and exercise to generate pain. Through these painful times, I felt important. I felt worthy. It took lots of transformations to be able to come out of this painful life.

If I did it, it is possible for you too to come out! The work was worth it!

After dissecting selfishness, let us see true self-value.

The person with healthy self-value:

- Stays quiet, works diligently, and lives in high awareness. This person simply does what he or she has to do. They know when, and what and how much they have to say and do.
- Lives by impermanence and abundance. Everything happens for their own good. They are happy for everything and are able to transform all to abundance. They are truly happy for the happiness of others. They live in the present moment.
- Is able to express his or her appreciation in words and giving. If they work in an executive or directorial level, they will help on any level needed.
- Gives because he or she has and can. They give because they live in abundance. Their self-value and self-worth are independent of their

clothes, cars, possessions, and connections. They give freely without expectation. They give as much as they freely can.

- Excess is waste. Whatever they have comes to them on its own. They don't need to fight for anything.

- Humbleness, humility, and modesty with good quality is a life motto.

- Able to ask kindly. They accept with gratitude and respect. If they receive a "no" answer, they don't take it personally. They accept it and move on. They keep going until they find a solution.

- Will value human relations over everything. Therefore they take good care of their relationships. They build others and their employees. Building employees means building a business. An employee who is taken care of, takes good care of the company.

- Stands for his or her rights and knows his or her self-value and respect. Their time is more valuable than to waste it on demanding and criticizing. If needed, they walk away quietly or don't call back. They let the silence speak louder.

- A self-valued person takes excellent care of his or her health. They live an active life and take time out for exercise.

- It is a pleasure working with a self-valued person. They are grateful for everything and express their gratitude on a daily basis. People feel more while being with them.

- Everything they do, they choose it, therefore, like it.

- Life is based on truth and honesty. They keep high etiquette at work and at home too.

How much do you recognize in yourself from the above list?

Is a self-valued person weak or the one who is really strong inside?

Developing self-worth and self-value, the exercise

The value of your breath gives the value of life and yourself. For developing self-value, so you need to work with your breath.

Can you be grateful for every single breath?
Can you feel genuine gratitude in your heart?

This exercise helps to develop a solid self-value based on generating a genuine gratitude feeling in your heart. Once you developed genuine love in your heart you can express it for every single breath.

After the 5 minutes of breath observation exercise add another 5 minutes of sending gratitude for every single breath. One inhalation followed by one exhalation and say "Thank you." Now quiet the mind down and send gratitude as feeling for this one breath.

Do this exercise twice a day, morning and evening. Practice anytime of the day for as long as it feels right. You will feel the effect of this instantly.

Taking one or two deep breaths during the day and saying thank you, is another excellent way to interrupt your racing mind. Focusing on your breath makes you come back to the now and in touch with yourself and your worth. Practice focusing on your breath anytime you forget just how valuable you are.

A good time to practice gratitude breathing is when you are facing someone in his or her rejection mode. When someone is criticizing and blaming you, just keep breathing and say "Thank you" after each breath, to yourself. If the gratitude part is challenging at this time, keep your focus at least away from the other person, and observe your breathing.

You must realize that your life is the most important. Being grateful for your life ensures your self-value, self-worth, and to feel the "I have." Appreciating your life while being thankful for your breath is the best reminder for your self-value and self-worth.

Allow and permit yourself to be valuable and worth it!
Permit yourself to deserve to be valuable and worth it!

How do we deserve suffering and misery when we have received the most extraordinary and most valuable gift ever - our life!

As long as YOU feel GRATEFUL FOR your
BREATH, you are WORTH IT and VALUABLE!

The fifth secret: Forgiveness

Forgiveness gets you out of your past pain.

You can only get out of your past and stay healthy if you leave things behind with love. If we don't let go of our past with love, we leave the roots of the pain intact. The good thing is that we have the transformation exercise. So go back to those past events and keep transforming them. Keep letting go of all un-serving feelings and beliefs.

Letting go of un-serving beliefs, seems to be the hardest for most people. It is impossible to let go of your past if you don't apply forgiveness.

The secret of letting go of your pain forever lies in forgiveness.

What do we have to forgive?

We have to forgive others and ourselves. We have to also ask for forgiveness from others, who we hurt.

We have to forgive every single hurtful thing in our lives.

Now it is your turn to go through the forgiveness exercise.

The forgiveness exercise

The first task: Make a list of those people who hurt you.

Now forgive each and every one of them. You have already transformed the actions of these people. If you have left anyone out, then please transform their action now. Write your learning from the transformation beside their name. Now write below the sentence substituting XYZ for their name:

"Dear XYZ, I know you did the best you could with the resources you had at that time. I forgive you. Thank you for letting me have wisdom from this experience.

I am grateful to have learned from this and I let you go and set you free from me. I let the Universe take you! I wish you all the best!"

See this person go to the Universe and be transformed into loving kindness.

Now internalize your new tools and new emotions that you learned from them. Practice the new emotions vibrating in you. Complete your forgiveness by going through everyone on your list the same way described above.

The next part of your forgiveness exercise is about asking for forgiveness. Make a list of those people that you have hurt. Count yourself in the list too. Surprise surprise! This list may be as long as the previous one. Realize, you not only feel hurt by others but hurt others too.

Write beside the person's name that you learned from in the situation. Transform your own behavior and action. Now write beside the person's name:

"Dear XYZ, I know I have hurt you. I did the best I could at that time with the resources I had. Please forgive me! I learned from this and have new tools.

I also forgive myself because at that time, I had limited resources. Now I have the tools and I'm devoted to living by these teachings.

Thank you for teaching me (make a list). Now I let go of self-blame and hurting myself. Let it be transformed into loving kindness."

> *If you can't let go of something from the past, it's*
> *because you still have something to forgive.*
> *Meditate, and you will know what it is!*

Life is about learning to manage our emotions.

Learning to manage our emotions is a great task in life. We don't need to manage anything else but our emotions. If you manage your emotions, all will be well.

Isn't it the lack of emotional management, that all conditioned minded people have? Weren't Adam and Eve locked out from Eden for the lack of emotional management too? They were punished and exiled to live on Earth, in a place of suffering? Let me continue with my other, middle of the night revelations.

Adam and Eve tasted the forbidden fruit. They tasted life based on the senses. They "tasted" life but had no tools to manage the sensations. They had no idea what to do with these senses, so they reacted. They had no idea what a reaction was and what to do with it. I think these reactions turned their lives into suffering. So craving was born. Craving back then was for apples. Today craving has many more objects beside food. Craving for smoking, drinking, drugs, sex, gambling, owning cars, and spending money, for example.

To explain craving further, I like to share with you my learning from the advanced course of vipassana meditation, called Sattipathana sutta.

Craving gives birth to four other dependency creating emotions. These emotions are the foundation for all shades of behaviors that make our lives a misery.

After **craving** the next dependency creating emotion is aversion. **Aversion** means opposing something and disliking it. Anything we dislike we hate. So the behavior levels are dislike, hatred, resentment, sorrow, envy, jealousy, guilt, punishment, blaming, and irresponsibility.

The second dependency creating emotion or feeling is **drowsiness.** The variation of drowsiness: numbness, sleepiness, low mood, and laziness.

The third dependency creating emotion is uneasiness. **Uneasiness** comes in the form of excessive moving, hyperactivity, worry, tension, fear, anxiety, stress, and being obsessive about being on the road. A person with uneasiness can't stay put.

The fifth dependency creating emotion is **doubt**. We doubt because we have no trust in others or ourselves.

If you sink into yourself now and see how the above list creates the root to your behaviors and emotions. These basic five emotions are reactions to something experienced in childhood. This is why it is possible to feel and react very differently in the same situation. One person may be afraid, someone else gets angry and criticizes. A third person may stay quiet as he sees the truth in the situation. This third person stays calm and practices patience.

> *We don't react to the event or the situation itself. We react*
> *to the feeling and how the situation makes us feel.*

We react to life events the same way we learned it the first time we experienced it.

If the first experience was pleasant, we would want to have more. If the situation was painful, we learn to oppose it and dislike it. The reaction to this situation is one form of hatred.

These are all the wisdom Gautama, the Buddha realized 2500 years ago. Gautama the Buddha also received wisdom, how to come out of this self-created misery.

The Buddha name means "The Enlightened." Anyone can be a Buddha who reaches a state of enlightenment. Gautama was the first one. He received divine knowledge: Applying objective observation on physical or emotional feelings one can experience impermanence. If we stay non-reactive to our inner feelings or sensations,- the imprints of our past emotional wounds-, come to the surface and get eradicated. If we don't make new reactions and continue to observe the old emotions objectively, they get eliminated. If we continue to react to our body or emotional feelings, these imprints get deeper, and pain storage becomes exponentially larger. If we learn to manage our emotions and feelings objectively during our meditation, then we will learn to manage our feelings and emotions created in life events. Managing your inner feelings is the way to manage your feelings while interacting with others.

Objective observation is the path to freedom. This is the way out from the life based on the senses. This is the path of happiness. Objective observation is the tool to keep you centered while the old storage of your painful imprints fades out. Under these painful imprints, you find love, kindness and goodwill, compassion, peace, and harmony.

These are the teachings of Vipassana meditation. This meditation technique of objective observation can be learned in a 10-day residential program. I have been talking about this course all throughout the book. This meditation has been helping me to work on myself continuously, since January of 2011.

The word Vipassana comes from two words: Passana means "seeing," Vi means" as it is." So the Vipassana word means, *"Seeing as it is. Seeing something as it is and not as it seems or appears. Not what you like to see. But seeing the truth within. Seeing what lies behind everything."*

This course is free. The course is covered by the donations of the students who participated in the course earlier. They paid for your course. They paid their blessing forward. Someone paid for their course as well.

The course gives you a wonderful clean residence to stay and vegetarian meals. The course is served by those who have done the course previously. They cook and clean in the course. The servers donate their time, 10 days of their life for your benefit. This course can be done more than 165 places in the world. See www.dhamma.org for locations internationally.

The breath observation meditation described earlier as a preparation before the Transformation is the first step of Vipassana meditation. It is called Ana Pana meditation. The breath observation is the first step to teach someone to concentrate, to develop awareness, start seeing things, people, and life from another point of view. The other point of view is seeing things objectively.

Breath observation gives time for you to see the tools when it comes to managing others. Without observing your breath, and using objectivity you would yell back. The management tools of patience, peace, honesty, genuine kindness, love, compassion, and good-will brings a positive resolution. We begin to experience our lives in inner peace and harmony.

Managing life peacefully, allows you to feel your inner calling to do something with your life and something for society.

There is a way to eliminate fear. Applying objectivity is the first tool. This is what we used in the transformation process too. Simply apply objectivity in your life, and you create your happiness, in a life based on the senses.

From this, the question arises. Does happiness come from not feeling? Does a life without senses equate to joy?

These questions can come from a conditioned mind, that can't see clearly, the concept of objective observation.

Happiness and joy coming from senselessness is the creation of fear deep within. Without feelings and emotions, we would be robots. Let us clarify feeling and sensing, as it relates to happiness.

What happens when emotions take over and drive our lives? This is a life lived in emotional dependency. Emotional dependency is a clearly visible phenomenon. Look around and see it yourself. Emotions define people when they say things like *"I feel good now, I am in a good mood so I am happy and worthy."* They may also say *"I feel awful, I am not in the mood for anything, so I am unhappy and worthless."*

Linking the state of happiness to a certain feeling, is the foundation of self-created misery. The misery begins with certain cravings. By wanting a certain feeling to last forever, we spend most of the time craving a certain feeling. *"If only I was feeling happy," "If only I felt free," "If only I felt loved," "If only I felt rich."*

Unable to feel the craved emotion and the object of the craving, we begin to dislike or hate our feelings. We try to sweep unwanted disliked feelings under the rug and pretend they don't exist. Pretending the feeling doesn't exist is how numbness develops. The best strategy for a fearful mind, is not to feel anything we dislike. Feeling the unwanted disliked feelings would be painful.

Ask yourself: *"What would happen if I just observe my feelings and don't react?"*

What if it was possible to not react?

> *Objective observation makes non-reaction possible. It makes*
> *you see all that you need to see and feel, to live your life alive!*

Imagine that you don't react but instead observe objectively. What happens when you look at something objectively? You see the truth.

Seeing the truth helps you make the right answer in that situation. The truth behind certain difficult situations, is immediately visible if you look at it objectively.

Objective observation makes it possible to solve difficulties proactively because you have space and time to apply compassion, kindness, and good-will. Your life will become really full of sensations. You finally permit yourself to feel! You permit yourself first to feel the piles of suppressed stuff that you have been accumulating for many years.

Objective observation brings wisdom. After looking at those piled up feelings objectively, you will see the wisdom in them.

Imagine underneath your painful stuff, you have been carrying all that wisdom too! The reason why events happened in the past, was to show you this wisdom. Objective observation takes away the fear from your own feelings and creates feelings between you and your friends.

Objectively observed feeling, brings wisdom, so you can celebrate your feelings!

> *Objective observation lets you become your own advisor. When you need advice, simply sit down, remain quiet, and look inside yourself.*

Looking at your feelings objectively helps to see others objectively. Objectivity and compassion make you feel and see the truth behind other people's behavior. You will be able to feel their fears and handle them with loving kindness.

How do we sort out our feelings?

Which inner feelings can we listen to?

How do we manage feelings arising from our painful emotional storage?

Very relevant questions. The mind still wants to keep you in doubt about your feelings. Your mind still questions that you can safely resolve your own feelings.

Every one of our managing tools begins with training our awareness. Becoming aware of your sensations, emotions and reactions are the first steps before you can observe them objectively. When you are aware of your sensations, the sensations no longer drive you to do something emotionally or physically harmful to yourself and others. Being aware of your sensations, means that you understand the current thoughts and emotions. You know by reacting to those sensations you will create an unwanted consequence.

Once you are aware of your sensations, you need to accept them. Acceptance means allowing them be there. Don't label your feelings, don't crave for more or different feelings, don't hate your feelings and don't wish they would away. Accept them. Remain conscious about the presence of your feeling, observe it non-reactively.

When you are aware and observe objectively, you can choose your behavior consciously. Now you are able to ask the question *"Do I want to have an unwanted consequence if I choose my old reaction, or can I rise above and come back to the original task I was doing?"*

One example might be, that you are walking on the street, a dog is barking at you behind a fence. Accept that the dog is barking and keep walking peacefully. Similarly, accept the feeling of fear and keep walking. Your fear feeling will be gone in no time.

Handling your fear of addressing a difficulty

How does emotional management look like in a difficult situation?

Example: You need to talk to your boss, teacher, or spouse, but you are very afraid. What do you do?

It's good that you are already aware of your fear being present. Accept it. Don't fight the feeling! Now, observe your fear and rise above it. Once you have, you will see the tools you need to apply here, in this situation. You need courage and communication skills. Start using the courage feeling!

Breathe! Now, walk up to the person and ask for an appointment (this is the communication part of the tools). Show up precisely at the time of the appointment. Breathe, breathe and breathe. Now say respectfully what you have to say and offer a solution. Apply self-confidence! You are no longer practicing fear and swallowing down your words. You breathe and calmly say what you want. You need to know in advance the outcome that you want. Saying what you want, instead of what is wrong and who you blame, is another communication tool that moves you forward to reach a solution. Continue to breathe and wait for the answer patiently and gratefully. Say: *"Thank you for your answer,"* regardless if you liked it or not. If the answer is not suitable, ask for permission to offer another solution. Offering a solution and asking for permission from the other person, such as *"Is this ok with you?"* - is another communication tool. Continue your negotiation until you reach a win-win for both parties.

Accepting the unwanted feeling means accepting its presence. Allow the feeling of being there without reaction. So allow the fear feeling to be present without reaction. Don't give any energy to it. Despite the fear, re-focus on your goal and talk to the person.

Open your fear and allow it to bring you wisdom. Fear was calling your attention to something you didn't know. Fear showed you a *"know how."* You needed to learn acceptance, self-confidence, patience, respect, and gratitude. Fear showed you how to ask a question about a problem and get a solution. Fear taught you how to create a pleasant conversation for both parties.

Managing the feeling of laziness

Laziness is another common feeling you need to manage for Living your Life Alive.

How do we recognize laziness? How does laziness feel?

The lazy feeling is like drowsiness and having no mood for anything. Laziness makes you feel like a big lump that doesn't feel like moving or doing anything. When laziness takes over, exercise or any sport is out of the question.

How do we manage laziness?

Accept this feeling. Don't label it, don't criticize it. Accept it with awareness and with no reaction. Observe the feeling objectively then rise above it. Now step up to your laziness and say *"You are a feeling, and I accept you. You are welcome here to stay, however, I will carry out what I want to do and concentrate on what I want to do, now. I am going for a walk. I breathe. I stand up. I put on my shoes and coat. I open the door. I walk out the door. Open the gate and walk out on the street. I walk for 15 minutes, and I observe every single step. I observe all that I see and feel from the environment. I breathe and I take one step after another."*

Execute these actions with crystal clear concentration. Stay aware of every single movement. Rise above your unwanted feeling continuously and concentrate on taking small steps. Complete your 15 minute walk. Goal accomplished! Now walk for another 5 minutes for a bonus feeling of even greater accomplishment!

Small steps lead to the entire goal. Going for a walk can be broken down into tiny goals.

Fill your day up with tiny goals and keep getting it done!
When you have a goal, you have a reason for your actions.

Feel every single step as the muscles move all the way through your walk. Observe the process objectively. The goal is to transfer objective observation from your walk to your daily tasks. Stay aware of what you want to do and do it. There is no room for laziness, only objective observation and accomplishment.

Another favorite example of laziness is our washing dishes story.

Imagine a pile of dishes after a family function. You have to wash them alone and by hand. You really don't want to wash them. You are aware of your laziness combined with the fatigue, anger, and hatred feelings. Now breathe and accept each and every one of these blocked feelings. Observe the feelings objectively and rise above. Concentrate on what you need to do. Continue breathing, step over the unwanted negative feelings. Start moving your hands, lift up one dish from the pile, wash it, put it down on the drying rack. Feel your muscles working as you take one dish at a time and complete the wash. Breathe, breathe, and breathe! And you are done! How tired did you get? The surprising fact is, that you are not tired. You stayed awake and stayed in the present moment.

What makes washing the dishing so tiring?

It is not washing the dishes, which is tiring, but creating the opposing dislikeable feeling. The small voice in your head continually asking *"When will this be over, I hate it so much!"* This makes washing the dishes tiring. Neutralize your conditioned mind-created dislikes, by accepting each and every movement of the task.

Welcome to the world of sensations! Feeling yourself is the point of your re-birth. You learn to rely on your inner feelings to guide you in life. This is living your life guided by your intuition.

To feel your intuition, you have to practice awareness and objective observation over your subconsciously stored painful sensations. These painful sensations are blocking your intuition channel.

Based on your intuition, you will always know
what, when, and how much to do.

Your freedom is choosing to react or observe
your inner feelings objectively.
If you observe your feelings objectively and wait
patiently, your intuition shows you the right path.

Your intuition always brings an answer with the feeling of peace and calm. If you don't have inner peace, then stress, anxiety, tension will come out of the ego, the conditioned mind. Applying objective observation to the uneasiness, reveals wisdom.

Living in the now re-forms your life and makes it very livable. By staying in the now, you make room for practicing love, acceptance, patience, abundance, good-will and compassion.

Living in the now you find your home.
Your home is your heart, which is the channel to your intuition.

The sixth secret: The journey of sensations

The next secret is the journey of sensation.

Any journey has the same characters. It is a continuum, it has different stations, ensures a series of changes, teaches the importance of time and the effectiveness of patience. Let us see how the journey applies in the case of getting rid of our fears and reaching the happiness within.

The first important revelation here is that fear plugs up love and happiness.

Do you realize how much of your happiness has been blocked by your fears?

Can you now see the specific locks? How many of them did you open so far? How many new life instructions did you find?

Your love and happiness come from applying your new life instructions.

How valuable do you think these life instructions are?

They are so valuable that they are locked up under many locks. Life instructions are your treasures!

Opening the locks and getting to the treasure is a critical process of your journey. This part of the journey is like entering into the vault of a bank. You need to open many locks and doors to reach the gold, the treasure. You need to open the doors one by one. You can't open the second door before you open the first one. Breaking into the vault or opening the locks over your fears involves using the same process.

Opening the locks takes effort. Don't expect the locks to fall off by themselves. They won't! You have to apply patience, diligence, as you open the bolts one by one. Your craving wants to open all locks at once. The process takes time, and it requires you to practice great patience. *The locks open up one by one.* The locks become visible to you in the order of the difficulty of their content.

Trust the process! You will only face fears, that you are ready to meet.

Facing fear takes awareness, objective observation,
patience and rising above. Staying in the higher state of
rising above, allows you to choose your action consciously.
This is how transformation comes into life practice.

Developing patience is a key factor before you can meet your fears. Awareness and patience are your tools to prevent your fears and doubts to take over.

The only fears that come up are the ones you can manage and transform. Fears can come up at any time of the day or night. Anything can awaken them. Take your life in your hands and be aware, accept your fears and apply objective observation to them. Breathe, observe patiently, calmly, and quietly until the storm passes. And go back to what you were doing. This is how simple it is!

Observing a fear objectively in the middle of the night helps to fall back to sleep waking up rested. If the fear was coming up during the day interrupt your task, do your transformation work on the fear and go back to your previous job.

Opening the locks is an irreversible process. When the locks fall off, there is only one way to go, that is forward. This is the process of awakening! Awakening is irreversible!

The more locks you open, the better and lighter you feel and the more freedom you gain. You feel better as long as you are aware. So keep practicing!

The duration of your awareness extends day by day with your practice. This is the journey. Don't crave for the end. Don't let frustration take over. Remind yourself that impatience and frustration are fears and lead to hatred. Observe your impatience and frustration objectively!

Breathe!

Accept that life is a practice! Accept that you will
practice all your life! Make peace with this fact.
If you practice awareness, you progress on your journey.

Living with awareness makes you walk forward and upward. Developing your awareness cuts off the emotional chains of your fears and bring liberation from your self-made-prison.

Taking the path of awareness is the
secret to reaching freedom!

Remember!

Fears have many different shades. Fears come to the surface in various forms and ask for your attention. Always stay aware and observe them objectively. Continue practicing!

Let us summarize the 5 dependency creating emotions or thoughts, that we have to stay very aware of:

1. Craving
2. Hatred, aversion
3. Drowsiness
4. Restlessness (worry, tension fear, and anxiety)
5. Doubt

Another part of the journey is becoming aware of your sensations, feelings, and emotions. With your awareness, you can sort through the five dependencies. I found it helpful to name a particular emotion and know it's root cause. It is helpful to recognize: *"Right now I feel uneasy and it is coming from doubt. I admit this as truth at this moment. I allow this feeling to be here. Let me observe it objectively."*

However, just like any other thought or feeling these dependency-creating feelings shall pass. Observe your feelings objectively as your feelings come and go. The feelings and thoughts arise, stay for a while, and pass. This is the entire change process, which runs continuously.

Everything changes.
This is the Law no1 of the Universe: Everything is temporary.

Your feelings are also temporary.

Your life markedly changes for the better when you apply temporariness to everything that happens. We can have a better understanding on temporariness, if we learn about the nature of sensations.

The nature of sensations

Every sensation has the same nature. Observe them, and you will note them arising, staying for some time, then pass away. Stay focused the entire time. Allow the sensations to come, stay, and observe them going. Observe the entire process objectively.

Take a headache for example: Be aware of your headache coming, staying, and going. The tricky part is staying aware as long at it persists and is gone.

What do we usually do when we get a headache and don't practice awareness? Living unaware, we only note the *"My head hurts"* - sensation. We become upset because we don't like this feeling. This is the hatred reaction to the headache. If it hurts enough, then we take pain medication and sometime later we realize the headache is not there. We actually know the pain is there but the drug blocks the feeling of pain.

Practicing awareness helps you to recognize the entire change process on all your feelings. You will note the arising part and the passing part too. When you are aware of the rising portion of your stress and the headache, you understand it is a signal for hydrating, calming down and taking a rest. If you do what your body signals tell you, you take care of the root cause of your problem and won't have a full fledged headache. If you stay calm, hydrate normally and eat well during the day, you will never have a headache from stress.

I find it very beautiful how Buddha reminds us to stay aware all day. This is how it sounds *in Pali* language, - the language of those days:

"Atape Sanpajano Sattima"

"Always and continuously stay aware"

As long as you are aware, you are on your journey. As long
as you are aware you can feel the truth within yourself and
can act accordingly with kindness and compassion.

We have been talking about fears, their eradication, and transformations. However, it is time now to highlight what fears do to our sensations on the cellular level. I like to discuss this again, from a different aspect to bring you more reasons why you need to work on your fears.

The role of your fears in sensing

A unique role of your fear is to block up your inherent emotions of love. This block prevents you from looking inside and connecting with your feelings, sensation, and emotions.

Fear keeps your head in constant noise. Fear stops you from being alone and quiet. Fears keep you away from the kind of circumstances that disintegrate. The most feared situation for your fear is being alone and being silent.

Fears prohibit you from sensing and feeling yourself in general.

Fears drive numbness and creates an illusionary state in you.
Fear keeps that state alive in you, so it can control you.

How does our sensation return?

Our ability to sense our feelings, returns with the transformation process. Resensitizing our body is also a part of the journey. We feel lighter, we have inner peace and then later we feel physically tired. Feeling tired is an entirely normal process as we allow ourselves to feel. You have been spinning on a high wire, so feeling weary with the feeling of peace and inner lightness, is a strange sensation. We finally allow our sensations to guide us and take a rest and take care of ourselves more.

As our sensations return, we stay aware of our arising negative emotions and observe them, so they no longer drive us blind. We are no longer dependent on creating non-serving feelings either. Behavior dependency ceased.

May I share with you my personal experience managing a non-serving fear. This fear transformation occured on my 8th vipassana course, in March 2018. This particular fear was loosing the positive emotions that I receive from others. I was holding on to devotion and belonging feelings that others created in me, by being in my life. I felt valued when I felt others were devoted. I stayed aware and recognized hitting bottom on losing this condition to feel valued. Then the question all the sudden arose: *"Do I have any feelings that are mine?"* A strange emptiness came when I realized that nothing is "mine," therefore, a feeling is my property. I have realized the loss of ownership regarding my loved ones earlier. The level of this realization was much deeper. It dawned on me that not even the love feeling received from my dog's devotion is mine! If this sensation was mine, then I had to be the owner of it, and it has to be my property. If the feeling was my property, I would get dependent and would crave for this feeling. What an incredibly strange and liberating experience this was! I can't say more about this, since you must experience this void and emptiness coming from losing ownership of your feelings.

This hollow feeling came from my ego falling entirely apart.

I realized the only way to live is with awareness. Give freely out of compassion and without expectation. Stay living in a state of "letting go," which is the foundation of living without attachments.

Every feeling and sensation comes and goes. Precisely the same way thoughts do. If you could observe and get over your lazy feeling and go for a walk or wash dishes, you could observe all un-serving feelings and do something pro-active.

If you are only happy when certain things happen
and make you feel a certain way, then your happiness
is dependent on that particular feeling.

What happens if that certain feeling persisted all the time? Would you be happy all the time?

Let us examine this dependency in a real-life example: Having sex all day and night for days and an entire week. No work, no food, no shower, no toilet break. Would you be happy?

Another example: Smoking cigarettes non-stop, from morning until evening. Lighting up and smoking one cigarette after another. How long would smoking this way make you happy? How would you feel at the end of the day?

How about the example of alcohol, drugs, and behavioral addictions, like expressing anger and hatred all day long. Would it make you happy?

Did you realize that you are not craving for sex, cigarettes, alcohol, etc, but craving the feeling of the "craving" sensation? We crave for the sake of the feeling itself.

If you smoked, had sex, took drugs or drank all day long, then when would you have time to crave or wish or want these things? After practicing one dependency behavior for a while, your craving subsides. The dependent mind can't live without craving. This particular behavior is no longer good enough, we just want something else. This is how multiple dependencies are developed.

What do multiple dependencies look like? Say you had sex, felt satisfied, then felt bored and started craving a cigarette, a drink, or certain food. It is also possible that once the satisfaction took place, you start talking about the new car you will buy or the holiday you want to go on. Crazy, Isn't it!

Happiness continuously flows in the state of awareness.
Happiness flows in the now. Happiness flows right
now because you permit yourself to feel the now.

If you genuinely feel grateful for your life, you begin to feel sensations in your legs, arms, and entire body. Be grateful for these sensations. Be grateful for the fact you can feel! The small vibrations or buzzing sensations come and go through all your body parts. You can't stop them, just observe them and be grateful to sense them objectively. This is your life, the greatest gift! This is where your happiness lays. Observe everything with gratitude and you realize your happiness is in the now.

You have an infinite amount of Now!

Permit and allow yourself to feel. Feel more and more of your sensations. Be grateful for them. Those sensations have been there all your life, you just blocked your sense with fear. So Live your Life Alive and feel Now!

How many breaths can you take in one "now?" Yes, only one. If you pay attention to your breath, it keeps you in the now. Observing a simple tool to stay in the now.

How does commercialism drive your sensations?

Life today is based on creating sensation dependencies, from your sensations experienced through your senses. Let me show you what I mean. Imagine the beautiful, colorful, and mouth-watering displays in a restaurant. Adding low music to the visual experience designed to keep you in the mood to eat more.

Take a look at the youngsters today. What kind of music do they listen to and how loud? What kind of emotions run in them while listening to this "noise?" All ranges of anger, aggression, opposition and fighting.

Look at the visual experience that magazines or billboards display. Pictures, that create sexual illusions and fantasies to raise desire. Everything is sold through sexual desire. Whether perfumes, cars or cosmetics? The ads of these products are there to develop excitement and craving. They are all there to create the "I want feeling."

The role of an advertisement is to take over our rational sense, which tells us, "I have enough." An ad needs to convince you about the "I want it" feeling.

How can music and exercise become an emotional suppressor?

Advertisements, watching TV, videos, listening to music, or being on social media are forms of feeling suppressors. I used music to suppress my feelings. I exercised to loud techno music through an earpiece. Why? To push my limits. The musical beat took over my feelings and finished my exercise regiment for me. The music made me finish my workout even though I had no energy to exercise at all.

The beat made me push through hard training day by day. I suppressed my fatigue feeling with music. I was training to become tougher and stronger. I was training myself to be stronger than anything that could happen to me. Of course, I had many sports injuries from this type of training, from my back and hips to my feet. The overtraining and the physical and mental stress together affected my stomach.

I trained myself for toughness. Why? Because I had the belief that life was hard and difficult. I learned to expect difficulty, so life brought me everything through difficulty and complication. I reached all of my goals though, and proved myself tough.

Hard training was my stress management tool. If I didn't train hard, my stress would have eaten me up alive.

Dear Reader, this type of exercise training is not healthy. It is a punishment, which has nothing to do with health. It has been almost a decade now. I spend most of my time practicing yoga, doing light weight training, jogging and walking. I learned to exercise by enjoying every minute of it. Alternating jogging with walking at different intervals is also fulfilling. Through exercise, I enjoy feeling my muscles working and all other body sensations. When I move, I feel my body sensations talking to me. My body sensations tell me when and how much I should exercise.

I stay very aware and observe my body sensations through the exercises objectively. I have days I start my run with slight discomfort in my knee or hip. I slow down and observe the feeling objectively. If the pain persists, I walk. If the pain goes away I return to running.

Healthy exercise based on body signals

Your body talks to you through sensations. One day your body tells you more and other days less. Using objective observation one day, you exercise more, the next day less. Based on my body signals, I can take a break and have a rest day. A rest day means doing some yoga poses in the morning to warm up my body.

Being calm is critical for the body to use stored fat. Emotional calmness represents itself in physiological calmness. Physiological calmness means a balanced hormonal state, so the stress hormone, cortisol doesn't go over the roof. When your body is calm, it has no reason to store fat for later. Being calm is the easiest way to start losing your excess fat.

Being calm regulates what you eat. You will start eating less all by yourself. Your food cravings stop. Food turns into nourishment. Whatever you eat, you will enjoy eating it. You learn to use food to nourish your body. Your body will sort out the food you will eat. There will be time for ice cream and for a piece of chocolate cake, which will make up for a meal. You no longer need to treat yourself with food and replace self-love with food. Soon you will see that even one bite of the chocolate cake will be enough.

More people choose a less strenuous exercise for activity now. The reform in the choice of physical exercise is noticeable. People don't want to fall apart and "die" in physical exercise. More people choose a fun-filled physical activity, like dancing, pilates and yoga, to build their bodies and stay healthy.

What is your emotional suppressor?

Just how much do you use your feelings experienced by senses, to suppress your emotions and behavioral addictions?

What do I mean? I used loud music, so I could not sense the fear of being weak. Some people eat sweets, so they don't feel alone. Some watch movies, so they don't have to face their fears of standing up for themselves or getting out of a rut. Some people get hurt and become sick, so they get attention and receive sorrow. They use pain, so they don't have to face the fear of deserving to live healthily and work on themselves. Some people create negative behavior, like blaming others and holding them responsible, so they won't have to face their fear of responsibility and build their own lives.

Fear to sense creates an insensitive world

By concentrating on your senses you don't give yourself a chance to observe your inner feelings. The information overload through the senses masks the vibrations of the cells storing emotions from your past. Are you afraid to feel your inner emotions?

I can confidently say from my experience that we are afraid to feel what is stored in our cells from our past memories.

If we are afraid of our own sensations,
aren't we afraid of our own self?

What kind of fearful world do we live in?

Why would we want to build a society of
people who are afraid of themselves?

If people are afraid of themselves, then of
course they will be afraid of others!

The word is becoming an insensitive place. Why? Because fear uses insensitivity, pretending, and ignorance. Fear blocks the heart and takes people's courage away from caring. Only the portals through our senses are open. We learned to crave certain feelings and hate those feelings we sense through these portals. We are restless, live in doubt, and mostly stay in a drowsy state. And let me say, the pharmaceutical industry has a pill for every one of these symptoms above.

The seventh secret: Belonging

The feeling to belong is one of the greatest secrets. Not belonging anywhere or to anyone is one of the deepest, fear driven cravings.

In my opinion, the lack of belonging, is equivalent to the lack of deserving. The desire to belong drives us into a havoc of misery in our lives and forces us to create vast amounts of pain. The desire to belong to someone creates dependency and justifies why someone stays in an abusive relationship.

Look back at your relationships.

- *Do you remember the sacrifices you made because you wanted to belong to someone or to something?*
- *When did you decide that you are only worthy to be loved if you belong to someone?*
- *Are you afraid to be alone because you only feel whole if you belong to someone?*
- *Do you have to belong to someone to feel "good enough?"*
- *Do you have to belong to someone to feel valuable enough to receive their love?*

- *Do you need someone else's love to make you believe that you are lovable?*

- *Do you need to have another person's love to make you believe that you deserve to be loved?*

Answering these questions shows that besides the belonging dependency, we need to address the level of our conditioned deserving. The level of deserving represents the level of self-value and the level of self-love. **The lack of self-value makes you:**

- Dependent on someone else's opinion about your lovability status.
- Believe that the source of love is outside of you and love must be received from someone else.
- Expect love from everyone.
- Develop conditions for love.
- Lose touch with yourself and your love deep within.
- Develop fear to feel your own love.
- Develop fear to feel any emotion except fear and pain.
- Develop fear from love you are made of.
- Develop fear from yourself.
- Develop fear from others.

What do you think of people who live in fear?

What can you learn from people who are afraid of others, fearful of their own inner feelings, including their free flow of love?

Zsuzsanna Fajcsak-Simon

Isn't it fear that you learn from them?

> *Awakening moment:*
> *Realize that you are the only one who can give yourself*
> *self-love. No one else can provide you with self-love! Only*
> *you! You are the only one who knows the exact forms*
> *of love you need to feel. And yes, you may give this love*
> *to yourself, for sure! You are made of love! Feeling this*
> *love energy inside you is your conception/birthright!*

Can you see why people craving love? Can you see your behaviors are craving love?

We have been made to believe that we are not valuable enough to love. Therefore we learned to expect love from others. We learned to believe that others should know how to love us. If they love us, they should know what we need. It is their job to love us. If others don't express their love for us, we learned to demand it and get it at any cost. What mind madness makes us believe that we can practice demanding and craving?

Awakening to accept:

> *Others simply can't know how to love you!*
> *This knowledge is yours exclusively.*
> *You can't give anyone their self-love. You must accept these facts.*

The transformation work makes you get in touch with yourself and the love you are made of. When you transform your fears, you open up the locks and let go of holding onto pain, and reach your self-value and self-importance. And at last, you allow yourself to feel the unconditional love flowing in you. This is the point where your craving for belonging is healed.

When you found your self-value and self-importance, the awakening comes: *"I don't have to belong to anyone! I am complete and whole as I am the part of the Universe."*

The Universe lives in you. You are everything, as you are part of everything.

Allowing yourself to feel complete makes you empowered to feel your own feelings and emotions. You are completed with universal wisdom, which helps you observe everything objectively. This is the point when you can feel your true needs and permit yourself to have them. You simply start taking care of your body and give yourself what you genuinely need.

Now you realize who you can rely on for love.

You can only rely on yourself! You can only give yourself what you want. And this is completely ok! This is good enough and it feels natural. Your expectations are healed right here.

Giving yourself what you truly need to stay healthy and happy, doesn't mean that you will live alone in a cave. This means that you can live with others without expectations. You don't expect anything from anyone. You are independent emotionally and can keep your identity.

The constant flow of your self-love allows you to give freely and receive what openly comes to you. Everything is based on free flow. Free flow of giving and receiving. You accept that everyone gives their bests, so stay grateful. What you received was not sufficient to your measures, complete it quietly yourself or find someone else who will. Interestingly enough, when you live by the free flow, you freely help others, and more people come forward to offer you help.

How do you recognize the difference between craving and intuition?

A fundamental question to be clear about the answer.

You have transformed so much of your past, opened the locks and about to build your future. You are on this beautiful journey where you learn to be universally guided by your intuition. Your compelling future depends on your strong intuition. What happens when past fears and doubts still creep in? Why are these doubts coming in?

Doubts and fears are powerful reminders for you to use your new life instructions. They can also cause temporary confusion and allow craving back. Therefore we need to talk about the difference between craving and intuition. Let me give some examples so you can recognize both in yourself.

The first sign of fear or doubt that they bring confusion a feeling of restlessness. Some of the leftover crumbs of fears can still question your self-worth and self-value. Bits of doubt can even want to make you crave to belong to somewhere else than yourself. Some of these fears wish to talk you out of doing something new. Some of these fears can pull you back from opportunities. The bottom line, fear always brings an uneasy and stressful feeling, along with other negative friends like resentment, blaming, anger, guilt, etc. When these feelings surface up, you must know, it is time to meditate. Spend some time to be alone and stay quiet. Transform and let go of all the things that are still needed.

Intuition brings you thoughts and dreams with ensuring, pleasant, and peaceful feelings. Any idea, that makes you feel at peace comes through your intuition.

Anything, that comes from your intuition, comes with the power to make it come true. This is a real goal. If your goal builds the society, then that is a true goal. If you feel you are worthy, valuable and deserve to have this dream, then you are the one whose role in life makes it come true. This goal is calling you!

How to avoid falling back to an addiction when you found your calling in life?

Finding your calling in life is an empowering moment for anyone. You feel the burst of energy and the impatience to get it done. When impatience surfaces up, it makes you feel uneasy and want to take over. If you practice awareness, you can recognize this moment and know to apply objective observation. Proceed with the practice of patience and calm and to let your goal go to the Universe.

The letting go-process keeps you detached from craving. Entrust the Universe with your dream and come back to the "now." Enjoy your life! The Universe takes over from here and brings people and circumstances to you accidentally and out of the blue, to lead you to your goal. You only need to stay aware and notice the opportunities. This is how the Universe works.

Letting go of the obsessiveness about the goal is possible with our new abundance belief: *"If the goal has to come true, it will. I am good enough, and I have enough either way."* Letting go of possessiveness is the key to allow things to come to you quickly and easily.

Your new intuition based life begins when you stop your dependencies and expectations. You learn to count on yourself. Relying on yourself means taking responsibility for the things you have to do. Putting down your expectations ensures sufficient space around you and in you to allow things and people to come to you.

Welcome to your self-managed life! Yes, it is possible to manage yourself and your life by managing your emotions! Managing your emotions makes it possible that everything comes to you easily. All comes to you based on the Law of Attraction. Whatever is inside you, you will get more of it. The key, not to expect it, and keep letting it all go!

Being in the letting go state creates space to receive. The state of letting go arises from abundance. Stay aware and treat every "Now" as a gift (present), which contains something for you for your goal.

Does it make sense now, and do you understand why is it essential to deal with your future? Can you see how important it is to see your goals crystal clear?

Can you feel how important it is to tap into your intuition to see your future?

Your future and an entire lifespan will become visible when you are re-born "I" less, or conditioned mindless self.

Congratulations to those who reached this point reading this book! I am very proud of you!

Congratulate yourself for completing this massive chapter and reaching your true self! Whatever level you achieved in the realization of becoming a self-managed individual, is fantastic!

Take a short break and digest what happend to you and enjoy your new self. Celebrate your life each and every day!

Living by your intuition will show you the right time to continue your work.

The next chapter deals with building your empowering future and an your entire lifespan! Wishing you a pleasant journey!

THE FUTURE

THE FUTURE

How can the Future follow the Past?

You are perhaps a bit surprised seeing "The Future" chapter, right after "The Past?" Where is the now? Doesn't the present come after the past? I beg your indulgence and kindly ask for your patience, that I may explain.

The cleaning of the past, transforming the toxin, sets forth your healing. You begin to feel lighter, more peaceful and conduct yourself calmer. The healing of your emotional wounds makes visible changes in your body. Muscles relax, eyes brighten, skin glows, wrinkles soften as a genuine smile returns. Once this initial state passes and it is normal to feel physically exhausted but emotionally empty. The fatigue and the emptiness come from putting down the emotional load and being brave enough to feel again! Congratulations!

Healing continues by putting our wisdom into practice. Forgiveness and the "let go" phase, wrap up the healing. Learning to let go of your past and also your future. Letting go of the past ensures you resolve all bitterness. Letting go of the future ensures an addiction free life, living in the now.

Living a crave free life means living in high awareness. Living crave free allows space for you to live by your wisdom, which slowly becomes part of you.

> *The wisdom gained from the past gives you tools for the*
> *Now. Your job in the now is to practice this wisdom.*

> *The application of wisdom, using your new behavioral tools,*
> *defines your Now, and ensures your empowered future.*

No one can tell you what to do in the now. This wisdom is inside you. To be the owner of this wisdom, you have to do the work. Working on your past and making the transformation, will tell you what to do in the Now.

Committing yourself to this diligent practice, means everything in your life will fall into place. This commitment is the only commitment you shall make in your life. Commit yourself to yourself and to live by your wisdom. This commitment means you will automatically work on your relationships and solve your problems.

Commitment means:

> *Being committed to using your new behavior tools every*
> *single day. Use them in every hour and every minute.*

Why do you need to plan your future?

The reason behind people not planning for their future is still an emotional wound. *Some children have never seen parents who planned anything, so they just drift along in life and continue craving.*

Fear of rejection, fear of failure, fear of being valuable and a deep undeserving from lack of self-worth are lying behind a life lived without plans. We will discuss the consequences of living without plans in a bit.

When you come out of your past fears you will have a temporary time of emptiness. It takes time until all wisdom goes into your entire life. Be patient and practice awareness. You will notice the changes in their own due time. You need to build your self-worth, self-value and deserving back, before you can begin planning.

Let's take writing a book as an example of preparing the prerequisites, planning and executing, step by step to reach a goal. If you want to write something, you need, paper pen and the know-how to write. If you don't know how to write, you need to learn. The writing process begins with learning to draw straight lines, curves, and circles. Once you master drawing the shapes, you begin to form the alphabet. Connecting alphabets together, you create a word. Adding words together to form a sentence, needs a little grammar. Putting sentences one after the other creates a story. Arranging the stories in an order, you can write the entire book.

Planning our future is like writing a book. Writing a book is the goal. If you put your learning about writing into action, the book will be well written. The book is a meaningful end result. The book gives a big enough "Why" you need to practice your learning throughout the writing process. One seems to be a lot more keen to learn to write, when there is a goal and a book involved. Learning to write and just writing sample sentences is not as meaningful as having a goal. You might want to write a letter to a person or be able to write legal letters to sort your issues out.

Making and reaching a goal in life gives the same opportunity as learning and practicing to write. A goal gives a meaning or the purpose of practicing new behaviors purposefully.

If you had many failed relationships, a goal could be, attracting a loving partner for life. You need to fulfill the prerequistes, making the changes in yourself to reach this goal. Your goal may be a new career, which also requires some changes in your beliefs, so you can become financially stable.

"There is no life without meaning" - said Dr. Viktor Frankl. (He was an Austrian psychiatrist, a Holocaust survivor. It is worth it to look up his work.)

Living your life Alive means also living your life in a high purpose. Which means doing everything consciously and purposefully. If you stay conscious, you will stop doing trivial things.

If you don't have goals, you will build someone else's goals.

If you don't make goals, you will have to depend on others who make goals. Without a goal, you drift in life and build other people's goals. It is an awakening moment to be clear on this.

You may have a goal to help others to reach their goal. However, you help others with full consciousness, and the action makes you happy. Be clear about your role in helping others and make it your goal. Most people reach the social contribution of assisting others later in life. Reaching our personal goals and maturity, leads to contributing socially. This is when other people's goal becomes our goal.

Charitable contributions and helping others reach their goals happily, creates the most meaning in life. One needs to achieve a particular selfless state for making such a social contribution.

Working for others and resenting the work you do, sooner or later, will cost you your health. Working for others and staying healthy assumes that you find meaning in the work you do. Therefore, finding meaning in your work, even if it is temporary work, is a must for your health. Temporary work can serve you with an opportunity for future reference that you add to your Resume.

Finding goals in every part of your life serves to give you a meaning-filled life. Goals, whatever their size, serve you.

When you invest your time continuously into meaningful things, you produce value consistently.

Every goal carries responsibility. This responsibility also serves us and further increases our self-value.

Reaching any small goal means success. Reaching any small goal gives a reason to practice recognition and acknowledgment. Anything acknowledged in our life calls for celebration and expressing gratitude.

From the point of choosing goals, planning the steps, and reaching those goals, you create a life where all positive life instructions are practiced.

Choosing your goals in different parts of your life, will bring a balance between work and life. The scope of this chapter is to give you all the tools to create a work-life balance.

Balanced life is born out of our goals

In this Chapter, you find the answer to:

- What kind of goals should we choose to create a balanced life?

- How do we have to phrase our goals, so that they come true?

Objective observation for choosing your goals

Objective observation is also a potent tool for choosing your goals. Observing your feelings and sensations objectively, helps you recognize what should be a goal and what is only craving.

Goals coming from your intuition come with inner peace. It is your calling to make this goal come true. You are meant to complete this goal.

Craving comes with uneasiness and stress. If you observe this sensation objectively and without expectation, at some point, you will understand and feel the message it carries. A craving sensation may bring up a leftover fear. This fear may be a reminder to practice a new life instruction, or needs your loving care to transform it. Regardless of the type of sensation, emotion, or feeling you have, it shall pass as well.

Objective observation continues to serve you on your journey while working toward the goal. As you are progressing while making your goal come true, some of your very deep-seated fears may surface up. These deep-seated fears are for feeling undeserving. Undeserving feelings need your immediate loving care, so they won't block the goal from coming true.

Other deep-seated fears may also come up, so continue with your transformation process. Be aware of your old fears, manage them, so the fear has no effect on making your goal come true. The continuous fear treatment is part of the journey.

Awareness and your goals

We have been talking about the importance of your awareness. Sharpening your awareness strengthens your objective observation. Practicing awareness is vital to catch the awakened irrational fears and treat them with objective observation.

The conditioned mind can ask at this point "I have been practicing my awareness for months. How long do I have to practice?"

What do you think?

Is practicing making you impatient, frustrated, and hesitant? If yes, you need to still work on the feelings of impatience, frustration, and hesitation. These feelings are still the residual of your deep-seated fears, and their role is to ensure you further about the message they carry.

Not treating your continuously awakening fears, will make you regress and you end up talking yourself out of your goal. If you back off from your goal and you feel uneasy, know it is the doing of a deep fear inside you. Some people back off from making the goal come true in the very last moment. For them reaching the goal will be no longer important, but rather the practice of the automatically awakened undeserving. Practicing undeserving comes with the practice of resentment and self-pity. Stay aware, when this happens.

Awareness and objective observation will be
your treatment tools on the journey!

Awareness also makes you really determined, dedicated
and focused over your goal. Awareness keeps you completely
mindful over everything happening in your life.

I apologize for repeating myself about awareness and objective observation. Developing awareness and objective observation are vital before you begin choosing your goals.

Your increased awareness can help you to sort out your behaviors. You can recognize which one of your behaviors serve your goals and which ones don't. With this level of awareness, you choose your behavior freely to reach your goals.

TRAINING your AWARENESS is

a LIFE-LONG PRACTICE.

How do we build the future?

I found it very useful, how Brian Tracy divides our lives into 7 major areas. His work helped me 25 years ago on my journey.[2] To plan our future in

---

[2]   Brain Tracy was one of the first whose work I began to apply about 25 years ago. My book published in Hungary in 2005," The seven secrets of weight loss" included one chapter on Brian Tracy's work, which he gifted to us. He also sent me his book" Success is a journey" as a gift of encouragement. I felt fortunate to meet Brian Tracy on his training seminar in May of 2016, and express my gratitude to him, in person.

this book, we will use these 7 major areas, put the goals through an NLP examination for viability, and draw them on a MindMap®.[3]

Choosing goals without examining your value system and the ecology of your goals may be a waste of time, energy, and finances.

The ecological examination of our goals will ensure that:

- The goal will serve us and everyone around us.
- We invest time and energy into a goal, which has meaning and is ecologically feasible for our environment too.

The ecological examination and the discovery of your value system, needs specific questions to be answered. These questions help you to discover your deep-seated unconscious value system and any leftover blocking beliefs coming from fear. As you have experienced, fears are very deeply rooted. Even

---

[3]   Tony Buzan invented the MindMap® while he researched the efficiency of learning. He has published many books on the science of learning. I learned the MindMap® technology from Tony Buzan in person by attending two of his training seminars in Karachi. I still remember how I was listening to him and had no clue what he was saying. Then after two hours into the course, I realized what it was all about. I was hooked. I use this technology for planning and making my presentations. Drawing Mindmaps awakened the artist in me as well. I used to say I can't draw, Then I spent more than a year producing all sorts of drawings. Attending Tony Buzan's teacher training, I drew a butterfly for him, which he autographed as well.

now, after much cleansing, we have to find them in their hiding places and treat them with loving kindness.

This evaluation process will show you the areas you need to continue working on yourself.

Lastly, our work extends into aligning our inner values and sensations to the goal, so we create the Law of Attraction.

I fused the best to the best, to ensure the success of building a sustainable future.

With this work, you can build a solid foundation, which sets a crystal clear path and smooth sailing ahead of you.

Choosing goals

Let us begin now with the actual planning process.

To complete this exercise, imagine all the money in the world is for your perusal. Everything is possible!

Here are the 7 main categories of your goals. I extended the health category to the practice of your emotional work, which is the practice of new life instructions, values and your rest time. The rest time includes passive rest, sleep, and active rest, which is your meditation.

Now with the complete financial abundance, choose 2-3 specific goals for each category.

1. Personal goals

1.1. Health

- o Nutrition
  - ▪ Food (What, when, how much)
  - ▪ Drinks (What, when, how much)
- o Exercise (What, when and how long)
- o Rest
  - ▪ Sleeping – passive rest – Bedtime and awake time
  - ▪ Meditation – active rest and timing.
- o Emotional work and practicing wisdom.
  - ▪ New life instructions, mindset and beliefs
  - ▪ New value system

Let's look at the subcategories of **Health**. All the small goals you are planning here shall serve your health. Choose such small and specific goals, which are achievable. General goals don't register in the mind. Only specific goals get priority for the mind to make it come true. Write your goals as a list now. Later the goals will be drawn on the MindMap®.

Choose your goals so they will be the source of success. Everything on the MindMap® is achievable.

Goals need to be explicitly worded. Let me give examples of how you need to phrase your goals. Let us see the **Nutrition** sections. Your nutrition means your diet, the way you eat. The following list can make easily achievable goals: Eating 3 fruits, 1 salad or a soup a day. Fried food once a week. Dessert: Cake or ice cream once a week. Drinks: 2.5 liter or 10 cups of water a day. Soft drinks and cokes 1-2 times a year. Choose everything consciously with awareness!

Exercise. Write the minimum activity that you commit yourself to. For example, yoga for 20 minutes on Monday and Wednesday at 7 am. A thirty minute walk on Tuesday, Thursday, and Saturday at 7am. Forty-five minutes of strength training in the gym on Friday afternoon.

Playing with kids makes great goals too for physical activity. Example playing 20 minutes football with the kids 2 times a week after school. Walking the dog for an hour every day is also a great goal.

These are examples only to show you how you need to define your goals. Your mind follows specific instructions and sets your inner clock to remind you to exercise.

Making a shopping list from the MindMap® will remind you to buy enough fruits and vegetables.

Defining your **rest** is an important goal. Your passive rest is your sleep. Set goals for your bedtime and your morning wake up time. If you feel committed to waking up early, your bedtime needs to be early as well. For a 6 or 6:30am wake-up time, you need to sleep at 10pm. An early wake up is necessary if you set your exercise time for 7am.

Choose your daily wake up time even if you don't have any specific work to do. If you don't choose your wake up time, you end up sleeping in and spending time in bed lazing around. Lazing around makes your head drowsy all morning. The drowsy feeling ensures your high coffee intake as well.

Going to bed at 2 am also has a negative effect on your health and well-being. Your body is missing altogether the healthy physical recovery, which begins at 10 pm and ends at 2 am. The psychological and immune system recovery occurs between 2-6 am. This is why the best time to meditate is between 4-6 am. One needs to prepare to make these early meditation times. For example, on the 10-day Vipassana course, the first meditation of the day begins at 4.30 am. If you have to get up at 3 am for an early morning flight, your psychological and immune system recovery will lack. This is the reason you feel your brain can't function in the morning and can catch a cold on the flight.

Plan your morning meditation immediately after you wake up. Set your meditation time for 5 or 10 minutes from 6:45 am on weekdays so you can exercise at 7 am. Plan your meditation for 7:45 am on the weekend. Plan your evening meditation between 8-9 pm. These are examples, so choose your timings consciously to reach your health goals.

Let us see the section of your **emotional work**. The emotional work contains the practice of your new life instructions extracted from the transformation exercise. Read them through and internalize them. Write down the negative behaviors, that you need to stay aware of and practice objective observation. Now write down the antidote vibrations you need to practice. For example, when your anger sensation awakens, apply objective observation. Once you come back to your senses, apply the antidote sensation to anger. The antidote vibrations of anger are calmness, understanding, clarity, and compassion.

If you have an issue with a quick, explosive reaction, then you need to practice objective observation on the sensation, which initially raised causing your outburst. The antidote vibrations to abruptness are patience and acceptance. Practice these two antidote vibrations consciously.

I recommend listing the circumstances where you need to apply these new vibrations and behaviors. An example of circumstance is when your spouse raises his or her voice. Write down the management tools as instructions for yourself. An instruction can look like this: "If my spouse raises his voice, I take a deep breath, look at my husband objectively and I rise above. I wait patiently and see what the event is about. It is possible that my spouse is tired or frustrated by something that happened at work. I practice patience and wait until he finishes talking. Then I give him a hug and ask him to sit down and see how I can help. I continue to help my spouse this way in the future, so he feels loved and taken care of."

The previously mentioned quotation, is a great management tool for elderly parents, teenage kids, or colleagues. Breathing, objective observation, rising above, and applying compassion are excellent management tools in any problematic situation.

Learning to manage stressful situations requires you to be aware of specific difficulties. Choose one difficult situation from your life. A situation that used to cause you to react with your old behaviors. Look at the situation objectively and out of compassion. Write down your management tools, your behaviors in this particular situation. Being aware of the situation and the management tools increases your success rate of staying calm, solving the issue, and handling the situation with compassion. Your emotional work will include the practice of calm, and being compassionate in this case.

1.2. Family goals

o   Parents

o   Spouse or life partner

o   Children

1.3. Friends

Let us see the next categories **Family and Friends**. Choose little goals to maintain a healthy relationship with your family members and friends. A specific goal may be, for example: Calling your parents on the phone once a week if they live far away and you can't visit often. If they live close enough, visiting them every other weekend. Define, which day and time you call or visit. Celebrating together a birthday or seasonal holidays, can also be a goal here.

Create goals with your spouse and children. Create events, trips, or simply spend time together to hang out. It is good to have a meeting with our spouse on a regular basis, to talk over things. This meeting shall be at a mutually agreed time. Your spouse feels loved, taken care of and respected if you asked his or her opinion here.

Find out your spouse's value system to make goals with him or her. See what is important for her or him. If your wife likes flowers, then gifting her flower once a month could be a lovely goal. The flower shows your love, attention, care, and appreciation for her. Therefore, the monthly flower makes a lovely goal for maintaining the relationship. Dinner once a week makes a great goal for strengthening the relationship. Make a date, even at home and let it be about romance and just the two of you. Taking a walk in the park with your spouse and talking over current issues serves your health and relationship goals too.

A loving goal for ladies can be showing support for their husbands. One way to show support is taking part in the husband's hobby. Even if you are not interested, make yourself interested! If you enjoy support from your husband on shopping trips or knitting courses, then you can make yourself interested in fishing too. Imagine what he feels like waiting for you in the mall. So make yourself involved in something he enjoys.

Define a specific goal with each of your children. If your kids are old enough, ask them what they like to do. Spend quality time with your kids to allow them to have different experiences. Spending time together with the entire family is a different goal. Dinner together makes a great daily family goal. Eating dinner together brings the possibility for children too, to talk about their day. Don't allow dinner to be a complaining session, instead, make it a time for expressing gratitude, solving problems, showing support and sharing daily successes.

2. Professional goals

Write 2-3 goals or dreams under the professional branch of your life tree as well. Remember, you have unlimited finances and plenty of time for your professional goals too. These goals shall be your dreams, or something that makes you feel like playing. When something feels like fun, it makes you happy also.

I recommend making one professional goal a business. A business where you are your own boss. Having a small business to take care of you and later your family is a very optimal goal. A small business can be born from a hobby, which can be sewing or making stuffed animals. Any of your hobbies can be turned into a business. Shall your hobby be painting, engraving, pottery or candle making? Promoting your child to build a small business out of the things they like to do is the way today to ensure their livelihood later. Kids are genius and creative. Some do small business at the age of 8 or 10.

If you have a business already and would like to slow down, then a consultant position can be a great goal here. Being a consultant allows more time for your social goals, for example.

3. Goals for owning things

List here the material goals. What do you like to own? House, car, computer, phone, TV, etc. There may be things and objects among these goals, which serve your professional goals too.

Now, let's take a typical example, a house. Your dream house. What does it look like? Draw a picture of the house outside and the floor plan. How will the rooms be distributed? Plan every single little detail down to the tiles, flooring, walls, bathroom, kitchen, bedroom, and furniture. What is the location of your dream house? Is it on a hill, at a lake or in the forest?

Planning in such detail makes you feel energized as you are now working on your dream house already. Planning is part of your dream life. The more details you plan, the more specific things you give to the Universe about your goal. Being particular in the planning helps to make the goal come true in real life exactly what you planned or even better.

4. New Knowledge or skill

Learning keeps us young! Learning and studying stimulate the growth of new brain cells. For best results, exercise your brain every day. Beside daily meditation, learning a language, playing guessing games and puzzles are excellent exercises for brain cells. Completing school or course for your professional goal or hobby come under this list too.

Accept the fact: Life without learning is
actually waiting for death to arrive.

Living your life alive, maintains daily exercise of your brain cells. Commit yourself to the life-long education. Switch yourself on and learn every day! Start Living your Life Alive!

What should you learn? Keep up with the times and stay current. Spend time with children and youngsters. Learning shall be part of your life, just like eating, exercising, and keeping your body clean.

Learning ensures living in constant change. When you
keep learning, the change in life becomes natural.

Personally, I chose something different to study every year. I enjoy learning now through short courses, as well. My Feng Shui advisor course was the last in 2018. This year I am continuing my self-development with gardening, more ceramic work, and baking. I am also interested in wood-work.

My first hobby as a teenager was knitting. I use to wear the sweaters exclusively that I made. I enjoyed being creative and wearing my own designs. I continued sewing my own clothes. I remember sewing my pajama pants and recently designing my dresses. As an adult, I took karate kata, calligraphy, flower design, yoga, NLP, batik, candle making.

I love building sand castles. I would like to take a formal course in making sand sculptures. Thankfully, there are many videos now on this subject too. I enjoy sand castle building so much that while I was living there, we organized 3 sand castle building competitions on the beach of Karachi. My learning continued with attending Tony Buzan and Brian Tracy marketing courses. Last year I participated in a course with our Bullterrier dog, Albert. It was fascinating to learn the Mirror method and communicate with dogs. Besides running together with Albert, I enjoy teaching him as part of spending quality time this way.

Studying languages is also my interest. I studied Russian and German in school. I studied English myself in Hungary and then continued in the USA in an ESL short course. English was an entry requirement for my University studies in the USA. Living in different countries, I learned different accents: American, Australian, Malaysian, and Pakistani versions of English. I also picked up a little Malay, Chinese and Urdu while living in Malaysia and Pakistan. I studied French as a Hobby for a few years.

They say, the more languages you learn, the more culture and people you get to know. Learning languages opens your mind to new things and widens your range of acceptance.

5. Hobby and travel

Write a few things under the hobby section of your life tree. I listed some of my hobbies under learning, as I began those hobbies with learning them first. I still would like to add glass-making for the future.

Whatever you like to do as a hobby list it here. Shall it be drawing, painting, sculpting, bead-work, jewelry making, bird watching, cooking, gardening, pets, sewing, mountain climbing, or anything? Write down how often and for how long you like to do this activity. For example, 2 hours on every other Sunday afternoon.

The traveling section shall include the destination and the attractions you like to do there. Include destinations nationally within your country or internationally. Plan the approximate date as well. Personally, I enjoy traveling to different countries for Vipassana courses. Up to this point, I have gone to 5 different countries with my 8 Vipassana courses. Another personal travel destination is China and visiting The Great Wall. I would like to run, do yoga and meditate there.

6. Spirituality

Under spirituality comes your self-development goals. These goals are about you learning about yourself and supporting your growth as a human being. Spiritual goals may be reading certain books, attending specific courses, or taking trips for soul searching. Pilgrimage, retreats, and daily meditation are also goals for the Spirituality section of your life goals. Studying about different religions, practicing religion, prayers, visiting religious places, or even just reading about religions can be goals for this section too. My spiritual goals are the daily meditations and yearly Vipassana courses for more in-depth inner work.

7. Social contribution

Giving back is great!

> *Giving back brings you the kind of happiness,*
> *which can't be compared to anything else.*

Giving back the universal energy, which constantly flows in us, is necessary for the healthy energy flow. We must keep giving back continuously, so we keep the positive energy current and go with the flow. I have this saying: "When you stop giving back, your life will stagnate, and your health begins to be compromised." Give as much as you can without expecting anything in return. I am not talking about giving money. I am talking about giving your time and effort, kind words, and a smile.

If you feel you are unable to give anything, because giving feels like you are giving from yourself, you have further work with your self-love, acceptance, and abundance.

Some people ask you for favors out of their craving. If you find yourself continually giving and becoming physically and emotionally tired, it is a sign to examine the relationship. Giving should make you feel energized, not worn out. Give as much as you can with a smile. Saying "no" and offering a more sensible solution is also a way to give back while practicing self-respect and self-love. As you grow and clean your past pains out, your ability to give also grows.

Giving back can be doing a favor for someone you know. The most powerful way to give back is to those who you don't know and who can't return your good deed.

The purest and simplest form of social contribution is a smile. A smile expresses acceptance. When you genuinely smile at another person, you show your acceptance. Most people carrying the rejection wound cry or yell for acceptance. So make your smile a social contribution and give people what they perhaps never received up to now. Your smile can be life-saving! Smile at someone you don't know every day.

If smiling at others is difficult, begin smiling at yourself in the morning. If this is going well, then add the social contribution smile to your daily charity list.

Smiling at someone you don't know can be uncomfortable. It is uncomfortable as fear is waking up. Breakthrough the uncomfortable feeling of your fear by focusing on your breathing, using objective observation, and rising above. The awkward feeling shall pass just like all other feelings.

An uncomfortable feeling shows you the place of progress. If you feel uncomfortable, be happy! It is a place of growth! Get over your uncomfortable feelings and start smiling at yourself!

Grow yourself through your genuine smile!

You used to reject people from your life with your sour face. Now start accepting people in your life with your smile.

Make friends with your smile! Reach out to others with your smile!

Stop living a self-rejected lonely life, being a foreigner in your home.

A smile is the simplest way to let a person know that you accept him or her. Create more value by saying, *"Good morning!"* with your smile. Relax, people will quickly get used to you not wanting anything from them! You simply want to give them a smile and wish them a good day.

Be the first who smiles to set a pleasant atmosphere. If you smile and greet others first, you take away the fear of the other person. Your kind tone of voice will make sure that the other person's fear is dissolved. Interrupt people in their comfort zone of sadness and any other negative emotions with your smile. Your good-day wish, stops people in their opposing and rejecting views of you.

Your smile and greeting can be life saving for most people living with their sadness. You never know what others have been through, so be kind.

They say:

"If you can be anything in this world, be kind."

Another social contribution is, giving away your used clothes, visiting children in the hospital or elderly in old homes. Be a loving companion and just talk to them, listen to them, play cards, or read a book. I personally take extra time out to talk to our elderly neighbors in our village. I also cut the grass on the front yard of our next door neighbor. Spending time and listening to them is my contribution because they live alone.

The Life Tree looks like this on the MindMap®.

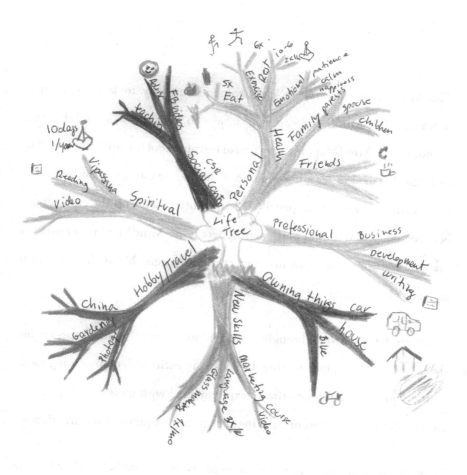

MindMap® is a fantastic learning tool

The MindMap® provides an excellent and fun way to learn if used in education. The MindMap® can help those who were told in school that they are not smart. MindMap® is a very useful learning tool for children. Drawing and coloring makes learning a game. Coloring has an excellent effect on our creativity. Moving the pencil back and forth wakes up the connections between our left and right brain hemisphere. I use MindMap® to prepare my presentations, outline problems, and create solutions. MindMap® makes it easier to plan projects, trips, and holidays.

Learning the MindMap® brought out the hidden "artist" in me. I spent more than a year, drawing and coloring. I filled up an entire wall of my dining room with my pictures. After coloring, I experimented with glass painting. These creations of my drawings or paintings became great presents for my friends.

Drawing and coloring is an excellent preparation exercise before drawing the Life tree. Draw any shape and color it. Draw a rectangle, triangle, or circle. Draw more shapes and color them with different colors. The most important thing in this exercise is to draw and color without any expectation. Color like a child. Get fully involved in your drawing. Be there and make the strokes one by one with full concentration.

Create the picture first in your mind. Then draw the image in your mind onto the paper. Draw line by line. Color line by line.

Coloring is an excellent exercise to practice living in the present moment. Every line you draw is like one task in life. When you pull the first line, you accomplish the first task. Then pull the second line, so you achieve the second task.

Drawing helps you to slow down. Take your time and practice patience. Draw line by line with full concentration. If you are thinking about the second and the third line while you are drawing the first, you are practicing being in the future.

The conditioned mind continuously pulls you out of the now and starts making comments on your drawing. The mind begins judging, questions this drawing exercise, and wants you to stop. Accept the wondering mind without reacting. Bring your concentration back to your drawing smoothly. This exercise makes you aware of your self-criticism. It teaches you to stop criticizing your work and yourself. It teaches you to accept things as they are and find beauty in them. Look for progression. Accept whatever is on the paper, exactly the way it is. Love yourself and your drawing precisely the way it is. Find happiness in creating your picture!

Finding happiness in everything is your free choice.

Running the happiness feeling in your cells is also your free choice!

Practice happiness while you are drawing. Look for the joy in every single line you draw. When you can feel happy for a small line on the paper, you can feel happy for the most minor things in life.

It is **time to draw your Life Tree now**. Even if you are not sure what you want to write on it, just draw the center and the branches. Draw something in the center, which represents you. The center can be a car, a flower, a princess, a sun, or anything. Then draw the branches and color them fully. The branches of the MindMap® are like branches of a tree. The branches are thicker at the trunk and thinned out to the end. Every branch within the same group needs to be the same color. For example, color the personal branches green, the professionals orange and etc.

Write the words on the branch. Choose 1-2 keywords, to remind you of the full goal. The branch should support the words. The words should not hang in the air. Keep the end of the branches open so you can draw further smaller branches out of it later. If you have words or drawings blocking the end, it stops your thinking the subject further. The open-ended branches help your thinking to evolve.

I recommend drawing a draft of the Life Tree first as practice. Don't expect your branches to be perfect. Be happy and just color. Color for the sake of coloring. Whatever your creation is, accept it and be happy! Expecting perfection is still craving and shows a lack of acceptance. Accept your Life tree the way it is. It looks a certain way right now, then it will change as you draw further! Be patient and keep playing while you are coloring! Get into drawing like it's the only thing that exists. I bet you haven't allowed yourself to spend time in such a childish way for a very long time!

Look at your Life tree MindMap®. What does the MindMap® look like?

Don't you think it looks like a neuron, a nerve cell? Moreover, this is the way the brain stores information. The brain makes an association with colors, directions and shapes. We create a memory imprint in our brain, the same way the MindMap® looks.

The brain cells learn via association. We will remember everything and can recall it anytime if we associate it to something. The Life Tree on the MindMap® creates an imprint in the brain and helps us to remember when we have to call our parents, to drink water or rest, etc.

Everything that is on the MindMap® is important and valuable. If you follow the specifics on your MindMap®, you are always working on your goals. Even if you rest, you're working on a goal. The rest is work on your health. Many people have an issue permitting rest to themselves. They believe rest can't make money. As you calm down and realize the value of your health, rest will make sense. If you get used to a hectic lifestyle, resting will take an effort. Reminding yourself that you are working right now on your health, will help you to rest.

What happens when you do something, which is not on the mind map? If it has any meaning and serves you, then put it on your MindMap®. If the activity or behavior doesn't serve you, your mind will question you and make you stop.

The goals on your MindMap® shall be only those which you can accomplish. Whatever is on the MindMap® should serve your success feeling. If you choose exercising 7 days a week and you actually do 4, the MindMap® becomes the source of failure. Choose fewer times of exercise on the MindMap® and do more, to feel even more successful.

Express your goals in the drawing. Instead of writing the words "eating fruit," draw a red or green apple. Draw a stick figure reminding you for walking, running, and yoga. Drawings make deeper associations, and the goal sinks deeper into our brain.

Let go of criticizing yourself for thinking your drawings are childish. It doesn't matter how the apple looks, just draw it. When you hit the spot and can't think of any goal, just keep coloring and beautifying the existing Life tree. The coloring begins to connect the left and right brain, and something all the sudden comes to your mind. You can draw the entire Life Tree before writing goals on it. You will see that all will come by itself if you practice patience!

How does our value system effect our goals?

In this Chapter, you find the answer to:

- How does our value system relate to our goals?

- How deep-seated beliefs show up in our life?

- How can values destroy a goal or make a goal come true?

- What do we have to change in our values to reach our goals?

The belief and values are the direct driving force behind the way we live our lives. I often say: "Look at any one's life and lifestyle and you will see what is vital and essential for that person." Most people's lifestyle shows a lack of importance in their life and health. Most of those who take part in the fitness craze, is for esthetics, to feel more valuable through their muscles and not to be healthy.

After drawing the Life Tree, we will discuss the value system. In this section, you will receive the answer about the necessary changes you have to make in your mind, to make a goal and make it come true.

Before we can call our goal an official goal, we have to examine it. This exercise will reveal our deepest-seated beliefs, which determine our blocking values.

Let us see the values and beliefs through an example:

"I do twenty minutes of yoga or exercise every day at 7am."

What are the **prerequisites to achieve this goal**?

- The first and most important prerequisite is that you must be alive and your health must be the most valuable thing for you. You must have the belief: *"Without my health I have nothing."* It doesn't matter what kind of low fitness level you have, you can do some sort of mild and gentle exercise. If you have issues with your knee or anything else in your body, ask your doctor or physiotherapist, about a suitable physical activity. I am pretty sure you can do some sort of rehab exercises. If your leg has an injury, you can definitely do the upper body and core exercises on the floor. If you have issues with your elbows, you can exercise your lower body and your core.

- Have enough yoga or exercise knowledge so you can complete 20 minutes of exercise safely on your own. If you don't have this knowledge, then ask a professionally certified yoga teacher or personal trainer for a home program. You can find a wide variety of exercise or yoga videos on the internet as well. Make sure the video is from a credible instructor or teacher. You may use Dr. Zsu mini yoga or exercise videos from my fb, vimeo, or youtube channels. I recommend trying out different kinds of yoga exercises. Hatha yoga the most basic, simple, and safe. If you have any joint or muscle issues, please seek professional advice from a medical doctor or a physiotherapist.

- To wake up in the morning on time, you need to sleep on time. Going to bed at 10pm at night will ensure your 6 am awakening.

- Eating dinner and getting into bed early. Attending a party the night before and overeating are limiting factors. Overeating the night before ensures you stay in bed and experience failure for your morning exercise goal. Why? Because you can't get up in the morning! Now your beliefs take over and give you all sorts of justifications: *"It's ok. I'll start to exercise tomorrow! It's ok to skip because I am fat and this one time doesn't count for anything! Why do I need to exercise when I am not in the mood? Why should I exercise, it will be painful? Why should I exercise, others don't exercise either!"*

- Be aware of your old beliefs. If you are not aware, your old beliefs and values talk you out of doing anything for your health. When you note that your mind makes such excuses, immediately start observing these thoughts objectively. Accept your cravings and dislikes. Breathe! Your conditioned thoughts want to talk you out of exercising. Allow these thoughts to be there and observe them objectively. Rise above now and refocus on what you want to do. Apply the same tool to your laziness. Accept it and rise above. Put your laziness aside and focus on exercising and being active. Create a crystal clear vision about getting up and doing what you planned to do. Give the instruction to yourself: *"Get up now! Start your day! Start your exercise!"* Now execute your exercise. Do everything smoothly and effortlessly, discipline yourself, and keep going!

- If your feeling valuable and deserving, you eat dinner early and sleep early. You will wake you up without an alarm. You have a clear vision in your mind about executing your morning exercise, which leaves no room for doubt. Observe every single motion objectively. Observe and feel your muscles going through the motion. Stay grateful for every single movement you do. You are living in the now. The observation practice helps you to stay in the now. You are making a new habit of living in the now. Practice, practice, and practice. Practice makes it easier. This is the way to Live your Life Alive. Living Alive is the only way I feel it makes sense to live!

Real goals and plans originate from inside you. There is
no reason to wrack your brain to come up with goals.

As your meditation brings the blocks to the surface and you manage them, soon your goals hidden inside you will come up too. Daily meditation also turns up the volume on the inner voice of your intuition, so you can notice it. Your inner voice will tell you about your goals, as well.

I believe we all have a reason why we are
here. We are all on a mission.

Our mission was programmed in us at conception or much earlier. Every cell of our body contains information for our mission. We also have the information coded in us, how to achieve this mission.

Every goal, coming from your intuition, comes with
the knowledge and power to make it come true.

In case any information is lacking, you will be prompted where to look or who to ask. People, circumstances, and information will come to you to let you put the necessary knowledge together.

Transforming your blocks and fears opens your
locked up knowledge inside you.

The more blocks you transform to more knowledge will be coming up in you. Your only task is to use your knowledge. Your life is a journey, a process, where the blocks get unplugged step-by-step, and your encoded knowledge regarding your mission comes up to the surface. You reach a point where your inner wisdom takes over your life.

Whatever I write here is an intellectual discussion, until you experience it. Feel the wisdom rippling through your own skin. You need to see and hear this wisdom deep within. Meditation and all the tools you have in this book will take you there.

I am grateful to experience the wisdom within myself. I can't express in words the magic that happens then.

I wish more awareness to all of you, to open more and more locks on your fears. Opening the locks one-by-one brings more and more liberation to you. Opening the locks brings a happy, peaceful, harmonious life, which is abundant in love and the foundation for sustainable wealth.

Why don't we still know what we want in life?

I think there are more of you here reading this book, who still don't know what you want in your life. You are still unable to make any goal. You feel confused, and you can't see from the noise of your life. It is completely ok! So relax. We all need different amounts of time for our journey to clean out the un-serving beliefs. The deeper the beliefs or convictions are the more work you have to do. However, the deeper your convictions are, the greater wisdom is found. So chin up and keep reading.

For a better understanding of the importance of opening the locks on your fears, I will tell you a story.

Once upon a time, in a beautiful home was a wonderful dining room. Imagine the table covered with beautiful tablecloths, set with colorful plates and lovely silverware. It was time for dessert. Can you see the hand-painted delicate plates and the little silver forks and spoons? Look at your plate. Can you imagine a peaked mountain of whipped cream on it? (Hoping everyone likes whipped cream. If you are vegan, believe it is an almond mousse.)

You are wondering: "What could be under the whipped cream? Maybe a slice of chocolate cake or vanilla custard?"

How do you know what is under the whipped cream? Naturally, you have to take eat the whipped cream. You have to remove the whipped cream to see, what is underneath. The whipped cream is fluffy, sweet, and tasty. When the pile of the whipped cream gets lower, the content is visible. Until now, it was only an imagination, now it is visible. Our imagination was built on previous experience, or what other people told us could be there. We had an expectation of what is under the whipped cream.

However, when we finished eating the whipped cream, we find pebbles. Shocking and surprising. We didn't expect stones! What a disappointment! Can you imagine having pebbles under the whipped cream on a dessert plate?

Disappointment makes you dislike the pebbles. The pebbles are heavy and in contrast to the light, fluffy whipped cream. All that heaviness reminds you of the difficulties in your life.

What is the first reaction to experiencing difficulty in life? You want to make it go away and cover it up with whipped cream. Next time we are served a whipped cream covered dessert, we only eat the whipped cream, so the pebbles stay covered. We know now that it is not worth going deeper because it doesn't make sense. It is unimaginable to have something valuable hidden under the pebbles." Why should anyone put a chocolate cake under the stones? It doesn't make sense!" Says the fearful conditioned mind.

The story above is a metaphor for showing you the function of the conditioned mind. The fears work similarly to the pebbles. Some pebbles or fears are frightening, some are heavy, some are sharp, some seem unmovable. The fear or the pebbles wants us to believe that it's not worth it to lift them up. If we lift the pebbles or fears up, we will die. This is the reason we live our lives on the surface and happy to have only whipped cream. Living on the surface makes us believe that whatever is deep down, doesn't bother us. And we gain temporary calmness and think we also enjoy this life. Whatever we don't see, we render non-existent. We pretend that there are no pebbles under the whipped cream. This is our life living in the numbness of our comfort zone. This is a life lived in real poverty.

Do you have an answer now why people eat in excess?

Can you see now why others take drugs?

Can you feel now why some people have sex addiction?

Does it make sense now, why spending money or being aggressive is a hobby for some people?

All the above behaviors are protections because we are unable to stand the emotional poverty and numbness.

Why do we stop at the doorstep of achieving a goal?

Why are we afraid that things will be difficult? Why do we choose mediocrity and say "It is ok for me," while we fight with ourselves every single day?

Do you see why we blame others? Because it is much easier to blame others for those things we are afraid to do.

Let's look at the answers:

- *What are the reasons that we don't know what we want?*
- *What are the reasons our inner knowledge can't come to us?*
- *What are the reasons we are hollow inside?*

Life is about promoting consumerism to accumulate unnecessary things. Look around the world. Look around and note how advertising controls our lives. Can you see how ads promote certain feeling or emotions?

Every sense has a different consciousness and different ability to recognize. Our visual sense, our eyes, tend to be the most influential decision maker for most people. Visual information pictures, influence most of our decisions about buying. **Sixty percent of people will decide to buy something based on what they see.** Images tend to be the most powerful tools to create the "I want it, I buy it right now!" - feeling. Colorful, shiny, sparkling ads using different shapes, curves, and angles that make the product more desirable for a visual person. Seeing a picture turns on the visual consciousness and gets connected to that part of the conditioned mind, which reacts immediately with a craving: "I want it, and you are mine!"

Do you understand the reason behind billboards on the street or electronic screens in store windows, showing pictures or videos to create the "I want it!" feeling?

How many billboards do you see in a day? Hundreds! The "I want it!" feeling becomes a constant feeling, since you travel and see these advertisements. You are bombarded with ads on social media, text messages on the phone, spam emails, TV and radio ads. Then you have leaflets and brochures handed out to you on the street.

When does the craving feeling of "I want it" stops? The feeling may subside for a short while until you execute shopping then and it begins to surface up all over again. Craving is a comfort zone, so it never stops.

What happens when the "I want it" feeling is constant, but you can't buy it. This is the starting point of hatred. This is the driving force to motivate people to break into cars, houses, and shop windows. The desire is so strong in these people that it becomes an obsession, "It has to be mine no matter what." These people driven by craving, take from others at all costs.

The next sense is our hearing. This is the auditory channel, which reacts to sound, voices, and all sorts of auditory information to create the "I want it" feeling. **Twenty percent of people respond to and store information based on what they hear.** They are so-called auditory dominant people. These people learn fast via hearing. They can recall information just by hearing it, remember music and songs very quickly. They don't need to see the product, it is enough if they hear about it. They can imagine the product via what they heard.

A motion picture with a musical background creates a more powerful "I want it" reaction.

The next sensory channel is our skin. Anything we touch, we have kinesthetic information about it. **A kinesthetic person must touch clothes, and they must feel right before he buys them.** Kinesthetic people must try on garments and hold the product in their hands. They need to sit in the car, drive it for the feeling. **Twenty percent of people are motivated to buy their kinesthetic experience.** They need to feel it on their own skin to have the "I want it!" feeling. For a kinesthetic person, the look of the clothes won't count. The clothes have to feel good, have to be soft on their skin before they buy it.

The next two sensory channels are the nose and tongue. The sense of smell and taste are other powerful information for increasing the "I want it!" reaction.

Tasting events are based on occupying all your senses with information. You have the visual picture of the food on a backdrop. The picture is large and very colorful, showing happy people eating the food. The tasting event goes with suitable music. We can hold the food in our hands, smell it and taste it. The pleasant sensation goes through every single cell of the body. Every sense receives information. The reaction creating the "I want it!" feeling, is being generated with full power. If you don't have the metalevel filter above the senses telling you "It doesn't make sense," then you will buy the product.

No wonder why shopping centers and restaurants have such visual stimulation. The bright fruits and vegetables, the colorful clothes and candy. The purpose of the display is to create an emotion. The meat stands and the cold cuts being lightened up in such color to brighten the meat color. Displays and light are increasing the visual reaction of "I want it!"

Take a look at the clothes in the stores. How do shop owners get women's attention? The clothes in the store window are on mannequins, or TV screens that show models wearing the dress. The purpose is to demonstrate a message visually: *"If you put this dress on, you will look like her. You will have the same confidence, and you will be valued!"* The shops are not selling dresses and products, they are selling an emotion through those items.

Look at car ads. Minimally dressed, sexy, curvy ladies that are hugging or laying on top of the car. They wear high heels and extensive makeup. If these are real car show events, the ladies wear strong perfume to create a stronger "I want it" feeling for men.

Cleaning products are promoted to ladies by muscular guys.

Sweets, candies, and toys are advertised for children by using cute animated figures.

Look at our lives today. Most people are living in noisy cities, filled with billboards, where even public transportation is filled with ads. People sell stuff to you even while you are standing at a red light. The information overload continues at home with TV and the internet. You can't run away from being exposed to multiple stimulation. We are bombarded by information saying, "Buy me!" This information overload is the reason my husband and I live in the countryside away from the noise and visual information of the city. After getting used to the silence and nature, spending a day in the city makes my head and body so tired, I feel like I ran a marathon.

Wake up and see the aim of the advertising profession consciously. Ads want to prevent you from hearing, seeing and feeling what is inside you. Can you see the powerful control of advertisement in your life? Advertising perfectly suppresses our intuition! Ads keep our focus outside. Ads create constant illusions and keep us craving. The giant information flow coming from ads and the continuous chat conversations on social media, keep our head in noise all day long. Being in noise all day long makes you afraid to be quiet and silent. Noise is the comfort zone and doesn't allow time and space to sink into ourselves. Noise interrupting you to move the pebbles and see what is underneath.

Noise is the number one reason you can't
reach your knowledge deep within.

Only in silence can you reach your knowledge,
which defines your goals.

Too many pictures, too much noise and too much to experience all at once, keeps your inner knowledge locked up.

Living in the information overload makes the road disappear under your feet. It is like trying to walk through a walkway covered with a foot of snow.

You must clean the snow off the walkway to see where the road is. You must clean out the information under your feet, so you know where to put your feet.

How does your conditioned mind react when you want to take the first step? Your conditioned mind wants you to believe it will be worse than before. Taking the first step, therefore, uncovering the snow is most fearful. Fear wants to creep back and take control over you. Fear wants to keep you in the noisy comfort zone. Fear wants to keep you deaf, blind, and numb.

It is possible still for fear to creep back, so breathe. Stay aware of your fear and look at it objectively. Rise above and take one step at a time. Take one step in any direction, so you move out of stagnation. The first step is the beginning of cleaning yourself. Besides cleaning yourself, clean your home. Dust off the furniture so the color of the wood is visible.

It doesn't matter where you start working on yourself. When you step on the road of living with awareness, your inner voice becomes louder, and you will hear what your next step should be. Trust your intuition! Your inner voice shows you the way.

And yes, you have to do what you are afraid of. Meditate, and you will have every step visible for how to solve all those things you used to be afraid of.

When you can manage your emotions, you can manage your life. Remember your tools for managing yourself are, your breath, your ability to observe objectively. You are aware of your senses through your senses and aware of your reactions. Accept and rise above your feelings as they come and go. Everything is always changing.

If we don't quiet down, we don't give ourselves a chance to look inside. When you remove the incoming information, you have an opportunity to reach into the information, the knowledge laying under your fears inside you.

Until we are brave enough to do this deep work, we will use all sorts of magic tricks. We don't watch billboards, but instead, we look at a Buddha statue or candlelight. We may use relaxation music and expect the music will calm us down. Some choose 5 scoops of ice cream or mountains of cakes, chocolates, and sweets, to get you out of the unbearable feeling of your fears.

We eat to suppress unwanted feelings. We eat until our stomachs burst. We eat until we are in a sugar coma, so we don't feel our fears.

Treating the root cause of fear brings a permanent solution. If you don't address the root cause, but are involved in extroversions, fear comes back all over again. Fear will keep coming back until it screams so loud that we either die or do something to change!

The question is:

- *What would you like to happen in your life?*
- *Do you give yourself a chance to look inside and get to know who lives there?*

The foundation of a meaningful life

The foundation of a meaningful life begins in with your belief that you are good enough. When you genuinely accept that you are good enough the way you are, and you are in abundance, you can live in a state of completely letting go. The state of letting go helps to create a future, which is profitable for you and the entire society. A future, which serves everyone. When the "I" disappears and is replaced by "we."

If you still have doubts about your future, I recommend you meditate shortly then come back and read on.

Your empowering future begins with transforming your past. Apologies for repeating myself about the transformation work, however, it is vital that you actually do the job and not just read about it. To achieve and sustain your goals, you need to clean out the accumulated pain inside of you.

The new future has to be built on a solid foundation. You can't make a new home on an old, rotting, corroded, shaky foundation. You build a new house on a new stable and solid foundation. Be patient, stay calm, and your time invested will be worth it. (Craving and impatience will come up from time to time, to remind you to practice patience and calmness.)

What are the reasons you should stay patient and calm? Because you deserve to experience life in happiness, staying relaxed and peace while working for your goals. You deserve to experience how life is when your mind is not pulling you left and right and you can stay focused in the center.

The foundation of your future is practicing
the wisdom taken out of your past.
Take your wisdom list, keep reading, and internalize
it over and over again. This is how simple it is.

The essence of transformation work to reach new life instructions, which can drive our new behaviors, makes our new life.

Expecting a new life without practicing

new behaviors is merely silly.

Remember:

> *Your life events around you will suit the behavior skills you*
> *have. Change your behavior skills then your life will change!*
> *New behavior needs practice until it becomes a habit.*
> *You used to practice your old behavior as well.*

Your changed behavior may be strange for your immediate environment at first. However, your family and friends will get used to it as their life will be better as well.

III

Evaluating your beliefs and values behind your goals

Beliefs define our lives. What we believe to be true defines what is important and valuable for us. What we believe to be important, defines our attitude towards life, and determine our behavior. What you beleive, projects the quality and the achievability of the goals you set. Therefore, the way you live your life represents your beliefs.

Your journey brings further stations to face your deep-seated limiting beliefs about your self-importance and self woth. You will need to manage these fear-crumbs surfacing up, again and again, to make sure your goals will be reached.

Evaluating your value system makes sure you catch all other hidden blocking beliefs and fears. If you haven't done it up to now, the time is now.

Evaluating your values

Exercise 1.

Write a vertical list of things, which are essential for you now. This can be work, family, safety, self-development, excitement, learning, sports, eating, riding a motorbike, boating, partying, meeting people, being alone, social contribution, buying a new car, bike, etc. Please take a few minutes and write down what is important for you today.

Write at least 5 things. Now put them in a hierarchy. Number 1 is the most important, and number 5 is the least. If you wrote 10 things, then number them 1 to 10.

If you are done, leave this list here and go to the next exercise.

Exercise 2.

- *What would you do if you had an infinite amount of money?*
- *What would you do that seems like playing since you have the financial backing for it?*

- *What would make you excited every day?*
- *What can you hardly wait to do, when you wake up in the morning?*

Meditate shortly, observe your breath, and you will have an answer.

It is completely alright not having an answer now. Practice patience! Do something useful around the house, go for a walk or a run. Do some yoga or dance for a few minutes. Let the question sink in for a few days. Let go wanting to have an answer! Meditate and observe your breathing without expecting anything from the meditation. Meditation only works without expectation. Meditation works in the state of complete let go. This is the state of let go you need to practice in your life too. Do your things, and the answer will come on its own due time.

Once you have a list, take a look. Reflect on this list and your life. Can you see how your values affect your goals?

Can you see how your values or the order of them needs to change to make your goals come true?

How do you think your values and beliefs need to change, so they will allow you to have positive goals?

We discuss the change of values and beleifs in detail in chapter V. Until then let me show you the picture creation exercise, which further helps you with your goals. The visual practice of your goals prepares you for the ecological evaluation of the goal.

IV

Your goal in picture

In this Chapter, you find the answer to:

- What are the reasons I have to create a picture of my goal?
- How do I create my goal in a picture so it will come true?

If you were able to come up with one goal, then proceed to the **Picture-creating exercise:**

- *See your goal in front of your mind's eye. Imagine your goal! How will it look in the very moment when it comes true?*
- *What picture will you see that tells you that your goal came true?*
- *Look at this picture through your own eyes.*
- *What does the image look like? If it is black and white, color it.*
- *How is color quality? If the color is too dull brighten it up.*

- *How big is the size of your picture? If it is small like a photo on your desk, then enlarge it to life-size. Make the image so large, that people and objects are life size.*

- *How lively is the picture? How much energy do you feel in the picture? If the energy level is too low, turn up the volume on it. Put more life and energy into the picture. Make the picture into a movie. See people moving and doing things with high energy.*

- *How is the sound level of your film? If it is silent, add sounds and voices appropriate for that scenario. Hear what needs to be heard here.*

- *Now step into the movie and talk to the people. Make yourself part of the film.*

- *How do you feel about being in the movie? Feel all your emotions celebrating your goal! Your goal has just come true!*

- *Now draw a colorful picture of your goal on paper.*

How did it go?

Were you able to create a picture?

Are there any others things holding you back?

If there are any blocks or doubts, you need to work with them and transform them. This picture creating exercise helps you to dig out even deeper fears. You need to be empty of doubts and filled with courage, diligence and willingess to work to create a picture of your goal. Keep working on those and repeat the picture creating exercise.

If you are succesful with the picture creation
and feel energized; Congratulations!
Your dream has come true, and it is working!

Yes, it has come true!

The more detail the brain sees, the more intense the
experience of the goal will be. The higher the intensity of
the experience, the greater the belief for the brain.

If it's real in your mind, then you will believe that your goal is done.
It only takes time, until the goal becomes visible in physical life too. Until then, you have some planning, working, and evaluation to do. Then you have replanning, restrategizing and more work to do. The present moment will bring what you have to do. Stay aware and work consciously for your goal.

V

The ecological evaluation of your goal

In this Chapter, you find the answer to:

- How do I know that a goal is achievable and it wasn't craving?

- What do I have to do to make my goal achievable?

- What behaviors serve my goal?

- How does my goal affect me, my life and my environment?

Creating a picture of your goal is a very powerful exercise preparing the ecological evaluation. To make sure we filter out very deep-seated blocks, we need to evaluate this picture for its ecology.

The ecological evaluation of your goal looks into the achievability of your goal. This assessment shows also what you have to change in yourself for the goal to come true. This evaluation filters out all the possible cravings from your goal.

The evaluation extends beyond reaching the goal and evaluates its consequences. A goal can bring you certain gains and losses. Are you aware of these?

A goal not only brings financial gain but can also adversely affect your personal life, your relationships. We must evaluate our goal for these consequences.

Let us begin the ecological evaluation of your goal. **The first step is to draw the limit line or success point for the goal.** Pick one point that is necessary to reach, a point that you verified the goal is real. This creates a checkmark for this goal. The goal is done. You may have the checkmark as the picture you just created in the previous chapter. Now evaluate: Is the image or film is suitable for the limit line?

The limit line or success point needs to be a point that we reach as soon as possible. Therefore, the picture you chose for your goal, maybe a point further away. How long will it take you to reach this goal? Would there be an earlier point that you can choose as a success line?

The success line of your goal is the first point, that makes you believe that your goal is visible in the physical world. The purpose of reaching this success point as early as possible, is so your motivation and inspiration stay high. You will need this inspiration to continue working diligently.

Beginning to work on your goal without setting a success point, might cause you to invest a lot of time, effort, and money but won't see the fruit of your work. Of course, there will be the fruit of your results, but you won't count these as partial fulfillment in the long-term outcome. You can pour your energy by the bucket into achieving the goal but you will never be satisfied.

We never know what we have reached, if we
don't set a success line and a finish line.

Thankfully, we know today, how to create an effective process for achieving a goal. To create an effective method, we need to use our head.

Invest energy into something that leads to something!

Lots of you like to have your own company and to work for yourself. I promote working for yourself very much. The common issue with a goal working for yourself, is that the success point is too far out. One of my young clients made a goal of having a large office building with 50 employees. This is a brilliant goal. However, this should not be the success point for the goal. This can be the finish line of the goal. The final goal, in this case, has to be broken down to a success line and to partial goals. We must work backward from the goal and break it down to smaller ones. The partial goals have to be broken down to smaller ones. Working backward helps you to find your first success-line.

If the success line is too far away, it can make your goal an undigestable bite. Choosing the large office with 50 employees your limit line or success point, can dim your inspiration. If you are at zero now, it will take a long time to reach this goal. You need to have super high perseverance and diligence to achieve this point. Lots of you say you know how to persevere but will give up working on the goal when the success point or limit line is too far away.

I recommend breaking down your final goal to smaller, more digestible parts, that can be achieved earlier. Make the earliest point your success point. Reaching any success point calls for a celebration for reaching the goal. Celebrate reaching each small step.

What if you could accept working for yourself, as a registered entrepreneur, as a success-point? You work full-time from home in your office. You have enough orders or clients to make 10% more than your previous salary. Reaching this point is much easier to reach than the large office building. Take this as a success point and plan from here.

Celebrating each small step makes us acknowledge and appreciate ourselves and feel a little proud of ourselves.

Have success in your life every single day. Observing your breath and being grateful for it daily is the first practice for success. If you are grateful for each breath and feel successful just by breathing everything, else in your life is a bonus.

Extend your success feeling beyond your breath to small accomplishments. For example, celebrate your success for accomplishing your morning walk, run, or exercise. Walking or running 100 yards longer in your run today, is another success. This success counts toward your health goal. But it's still a success after all.

Celebrate small goals every single day beyond exercise. Eating 3 fruits a day is also another goal, which counts as a success. Smiling at another person you don't know is reaching another goal. These small steps are part of building the overall success feeling in yourself and achieving the larger goal.

> *Reaching small steps, is what life is about. A*
> *journey of a lifetime is made of small steps.*

How many small steps do you need to take for covering 1000 miles?

Evaluation of your current behaviors is the next exercise. Evaluating your behavior can further help you find any hidden blocking beliefs and values. Evaluating your behavior shows if you are really conscious about your behavior in reference to your goals.

Here are the questions to assess your behaviors:

- *What kind of thinking, behavior or attitude is necessary to practice making your goal a physical reality?*
- *What is the kind of thinking, behavior or attitude is necessary to destroy your goal of a physical reality?*

The answer to these questions makes you aware of your current behavior.

Can you see your behavior right now?

Is the outcome of your current negative behavior clear to you?

Can you recognize that your current behavior is actually destroying your goal?

Whatever doesn't bring you forward is holding you back.

You must develop enough awareness to catch your destructive thoughts, words, and behavior; breathe and become proactive. Proactive thoughts, words, and behavior take you forward.

Compare the proactive behaviors with life instruction from your transformation exercise.

Can you see the proactive behaviors making your goals come true, are the same as your new life instructions?

Can you see now why you might not have been able to reach goals in your life? Only because you are practicing destructive behavior. You have been practicing the only behavior you ever knew.

Be conscious about your arising doubts. Your doubts are only ensuring that you need to practice your new life instructions. Observe your doubts. Your doubts may call your attention to some detail what you have not paid attention to. So be grateful for your doubts to bring you new information and then let them go. Do you see how fantastic your built-in wisdom is? You only have to reach down for your inner wisdom.

The role of your doubts are to plug up your intuition channel, to make you stressed and talk you out of doing anything then make you regret not doing it.

Evaluate your character

The next part of the evaluation makes you aware of the changes, reaching a goal can make in your life.

- *How is reaching the goal affect your environment and those who are important for you?*
- *How will your goal affect your family and personal relationships?*

You must stay aware of the changes in your life and the changes in your relationships due to your goal. If your relationships are important and the goal coming true negatively affect your relationships, the goal is not ecological. You can lose a lot more, losing your personal relationships, than the money you gained with the goal coming true. Take care of your relationships in advance or modify your goal, so it serves your relationships too. You may need to bring one of your family members in the business or replace your family member as the load grows too large. Have an honest conversation with the family member and find out what you have to do to save the relationship.

Be aware of the irrational fears of your family. Their fears can be a blocking factor for your goal. You need to manage their worry and know the amount of information you can disclose to them. If they are habitually worried and don't want to work on their fears, you need to keep them under control. Ensure them regularly that all is well. If your parents are obsessive about expressing their fears they can't be your emotional support. You may find emotional support from friends then.

> *The most powerful support to make your goal come true is within you. You must learn to reach for strength, diligence, perseverance and patience within yourself. This is the reason why we meditate.*

Breath observation and then vipassana meditation keeps you continuously connected to the universal power, via your intuition channel. There is no higher power in emotional support than what you can receive from the Universe. Don't expect this support from anyone else.

> *The source of your inner strength is your intuition!*

An emotionally supportive home environment is a bonus for your goals. When you initially work from home, you may be less available for family matters. You need to make sure it is ok with your spouse to take on more responsibility and load. It is essential to bring resolution to this issue and lay down your roles at home. Come to an agreement with your spouse about taking care of your valuable relationships, while you are working from home.

Evaluating the gains

The next evaluation is about the gains that the goal can bring in your life.

- *What do you gain by having your goal come true?*

- *What do you lose by having your goal come true?*

- *What do you gain by not having your goal come true?*

- *What do you lose by not having your goal come true?*

These tricky questions are specifically designed for your subconscious mind, to dig out some leftover negative beliefs. Sink into yourself and answer each question.

If you have anything to gain by not having your goal come true then you will continue to crave, wish, or dream. These blocks and fears behind these cravings must be addressed. Apply the transformation exercise on these fears and blocks too. These fears are even more profound than previously discovered. Going through the previous activities outlined in this book allow you to reach this depth.

Meditate, meditate, meditate and you will know what to do!

> *The best time to meditate is when your mind is the most confused.*

> *The most appropriate time to meditate is when your mind wants to talk you out of meditating because you are too stressed.*

What other changes can your goal bring you as person?

- *Can you imagine what the goal coming true will make you?*

- *How will the goal coming true change you as a person?*

- *What kind of person will you become?*

- *What will happen to your value system?*

- *What will be important for you once your goal comes true?*

- *Where will you put the money that this new business will bring you?*

- *What will be the next goal that you use this gain or money for?*

Take your time please and answer the above questions honestly.

Aligning your values to your goals

We arrived at another essential station on your new journey.

It is time to take out the importance list you wrote earlier in chapter III. Take a look at the list.

- *What do you need to change in your list, since you went through your evaluation exercises?*

- *Did your values remain the same or changed? If any of them changed, how did they change?*

Zsuzsanna Fajcsak-Simon

- *Look at the order of your values. How do the order of your values support your goal?*
- *Do you have to change something in the order of your values to make your goal come true?*

Let me explain what I mean here:

If money is the first, second is family and third is your health on your value list, then making money will take a toll on your health. If you feel guilty working on your health, transform your guilt feeling. Let the guilt feeling go to the Universe! Let the deserving feeling take its place.

Continue to work on the order of your values until you realize that your health has to be at the top of the list. Without your health, there is no work, no money, no family, and no friends. No hobbies, no cars, no travels, no learning either!

If the excitement of driving cars is on the top of your list, what happens to your health and personal relationships at home, when you are always on the road.

If you put your relationship first followed by work then your health, you will compromise your health and work for your relationship. Take a little time and consider the above.

Planning one specific goal consciously

In this Chapter, you find the answer to:

- How do I start from zero?
- What are the specific steps I need to take?

The previous exercises prepared you to build a new and solid foundation of your values and beliefs. Now let's make the walls of your new house. Choose the bricks then lay them down one by one.

Let us make a professional goal, for example. The first step to making this goal come true is looking into who has done it before.

- *Is there been anyone else who built such a house or did this business that you want to do?*

- *If yes, who succeeded among them?*

- *What were the reasons for this person's success?*

- *What did this person do? Look this person up if he or she is alive. Check out the person on social media, read his articles, and watch his videos. What can you learn from this person?*

- *If the person was not successful earlier, what were the reasons? What can you learn from this person?*

- *If nobody did anything precisely that you are planning, then was there anyone who did anything similar?*

- *What forums can be helpful to learn from regarding your goal?*

- *If you are the first, you are the pioneer in the field. You must start somewhere, so start. What is the first step you can take?*

- *Who can you call?*

- *What do you have to look up?*

- *What are the prerequisites for your goal?*

- *What do you already have in the prerequisites?*

- *How much knowledge and finance do you have to start?*

- *What do you have to learn to start your work?*

- *Who can you ask for help?*

- *Who do you have to get to know?*

- *What is the very first step you can do in this very moment?*

- *What do you have to look up on the internet?*

- *Who can you call?*

- *Do this first step right now!*

Now continue planning your steps here.

Emotional support for your goal

My first advice regarding the publicity of your goal is to talk about your goal only to those who can support you emotionally or keep it to yourself. Later on, as you are on your journey, emotional support will come from all unexpected places. Be patient and do your thing.

Handling negative criticism

There are many nay-sayers who want to talk you out of your goal. They are talking from their fear. They are like a disturbing thought coming up from the conditioned mind, so manage them. Breathe, observe objectively, rise above. It shall pass. Learn from their opinion and keep your goals to yourself.

It is possible to find something positive in a negative criticism too. A criticizing person may actually give positive advise, without even knowing it. Observe the criticism objectively and evaluate it. This criticism may bring you an issue to your attention, that you haven't come across. So stay grateful for the criticism, it was for your own good. Even a criticizing person can deliver help if you have the mindset to look from a different point of view. Everything happens for you!

The first step and the next steps reaching your goal

If you are really passionate about your goal, then the first step will be apparent to you in a short time. The Universe will bring a circumstance, a person, or a piece of information to define your first step. All the following steps will come one-by-one.

Be patient and concentrate on the step you are taking right now. Take that step to the best of your ability because achieving this step will make the next step visible.

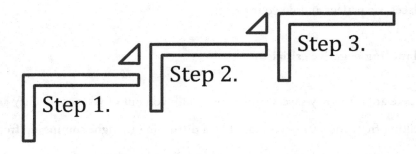

Are you thinking about the 3rd step when taking the first?

It is entirely normal, as impatience and craving come from deep down. Craving and impatience can disturb your focus and drive you crazy. Most mistakes happen this way. Craving and impatience make you miss information on the map for example and you end up getting lost. Craving and impatience make you run the red light and have all sorts of consequences.

Stay at the first step you are taking right now! Once step one is completed, take the second step. While your craving and impatience want you to think about the 3rd step, you may just complete the goal at step 2. You have been thinking about step 3, but there will be no step 3! So practice patience!

The racing mind needs to be accepted and observed. Do the coloring exercise. Draw shapes and color them line-by-line.

Draw each line with full concentration. These two exercises can greatly help you regain your focus and keep yourself in the present moment. Right now, you practiced patience and calm out of your new life instructions.

Practicing all your new life instructions
will make your goals come true.

Write this above sentence on a paper and stick it on the wall. Place it somewhere you see it daily. Remind yourself to breathe, observe objectively, rise above, practice patience, and calm. These are your main tools to keep yourself in a favorable physiological state and in the present moment.

The Now is the source of your intuition.

Awareness is the roof of your new house. Awareness protects you from the rain, snow, and storms. Awareness keeps you safe, keeps you dry and warm. Awareness brings answers in due time.

If you have not completed the evaluation exercise for your goal, please go back and complete it. Learn the steps or the questions of the evaluation and use it when a new idea comes to you. Now you can even do the evaluation in your head and decide faster about the idea.

VIII

Building an empowering lifespan

In this Chapter, you find the answer to:

- How do I build a lifespan out of my goals?

- What are the tools for building an empowering lifespan?

Congratulations on reaching this chapter! Congratulations on taking such a huge step towards your future! It is time now to open our mind wider so your goals will become even more meaningful.

The lifespan-walk is the next exercise to bring further wisdom and add more meaning to your goals.

The Lifespan-walk

Chose a 25-30 yard long, straight path. This path shall be smooth, level, without any objects blocking the way. This can be a walkway, part of the sidewalk, a path in the park or a grassy field.

An indoor corridor can suit if nothing else is available.

Attention, please! The Lifespan exercise is a powerful experience!
Ask your close friend to assist you in asking the questions during the exercise.

Make a note of your starting point. This point is the "Now." The Now is the exact date and time, where you are standing at this moment. In front of you is your entire life. The end of this path is the point where our soul leaves our body.

Now take as many steps forward to cover the next 5 years. Take these steps now! Stop at this point and look down on yourself.

+ 5 years in steps

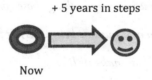

Now

Congratulate yourself on making these 5 years!

Look back and look down on your path covering the past 5 years.

Answer the following questions (have a friend ask you these questions):

- *What is the date 5 years from now?*

- *How old are you?*

- *What do you look like?*

- *How do you feel?*

- *What did you do for your health to look and feel like this?*

- *How is your personal life?*

- *What did you accomplish from the goals placed on the Lifetree?*

- *What else has happened during this time?*

- *How are you professionally?*

- *What skills did you learn?*

- *What hobbies did you take on?*

- *Where did you travel?*

- *How is your spiritual life?*

- *What have you done for your social contribution?*

- *Take a look at your 5 year path and note the point of your actions for your goals. What did you learn by making those goals come true?*

- *How did you grow as a human being during this time?*

- *What progress did you make in life?*

Congratulate yourself again.

You can record your answers with a voice recorder, or your friend can make notes.

Great!

Now turn towards the future and take again enough steps to cover 5 years.

+ 5 years in steps

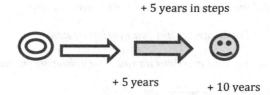

+ 5 years   + 10 years

Congratulate yourself on these 10 years! What is the date now, 10 years later?

Answer all the questions that you answered at the end of year 5.

Now walk enough steps again, to cover another 5 years. Stand there and repeat the question and answer evaluation at this point too.

+ 5 years in steps

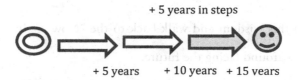

+ 5 years   + 10 years   + 15 years

Now cover again 5 more years in steps. Congratulate yourself and repeat the question and answer evaluation.

+ 5 years in steps

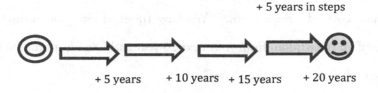

+ 5 years   + 10 years   + 15 years   + 20 years

Go through all the questions and answer them honestly.

Now summarize the past 20 years:

- *What did you have to do to keep your health the way it is, 20 years later?*
- *What kind of behaviors did you develop by now?*
- *What feelings and emotions do you have vibrating in you?*
- *How differently do you see the world?*
- *Who did you become?*
- *What is important now in your life?*
- *How do you spend your days?*

Congratulate and appreciate yourself now! Acknowledge all the values that you learned on this journey. Acknowledge all the new behaviors, which are part of you now.

Now take all this wisdom and walk back to the "Now" point. Stop in the Now and turn around facing the future.

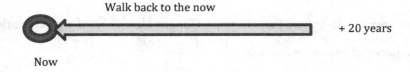

Walk back to the now

+ 20 years

Now

You have covered a huge journey! You have travelled into your future! You collected all the wisdom from your next 20 year path! You just brought back all the tools you need in the "Now."

You developed new values, human characters and they are in you right now!

Write all your new values, beliefs, behaviors, and characters down.

- *How do these new beliefs, values, behaviors make your life look like now?*
- *What will you change in your life in the very next moment?*
- *How did your goals change due to new values and beliefs?*
- *What other goals can you draw on your Life Tree?*
- *Did you realize just how much time you have to practice patience and living in the "Now"?*
- *Did you realize the amount of time you have for your relationships?*
- *Did you realize that you deserve to take care of your relationships because you live in true abundance?*

Meditate over the above questions and sink into yourself. Re-draw your Life Tree, if necessary. Re-draw it as many times as you like. Place your Life Tree on the wall where you can see it. Visit your Life Tree often, to ensure yourself about your daily personal health activities. Check if you are following everything on the Life Tree.

Give all your long term and large goals to the Universe. Allow the Universe to take over and carry on your daily tasks.

Update your Life Tree every 6 months. Place a checkmark next to the goals, which are done and add more goals. Make your Life Tree full, so your life will always be full of valuable and meaningful things, which bring maximum joy.

Step into the now and enjoy all the wonders that the moment brings you. It is your choice to stress about something or have a good laugh. This is how simple it is if you "Live your Life Alive!"

Realize:
It's up to you how you choose to live the
events that life brings you.

It is also up to you what life events mean to you!

Dear Reader,

Thank you for allowing me to bring you an experience with this book. Congratulations on completing it!

I wish you to walk on this beautiful path with awareness to experience more love, happiness, joy, freedom, harmony, peace, and success!

May you be happy and healthy because you deserve to Live your Life Alive!

With all my love,

Dr. Zsu

Biography

Zsuzsanna Fajcsak-Simon

Dr. Zsu

Ph.D., M.A., M.A., M.Sc., C.N.S.

Dr. Zsu is an Integrated Health Expert, a Performance Coach, the founder of Alive – an integrated Mind and Lifestyle Education program to "Live your Life Alive."

Dr. Zsu is schooled in Physical Education, Exercise Physiology, Clinical Nutrition, Certified Nutrition Specialist, Functional Diagnostic Medicine, NLP, and Timeline Therapy. She is a Yoga master trainer, who is committed to making a difference to optimize performance through mindset and lifestyle.

Her Ph.D. study was a pioneer in the field of blood sugar regulation diet in Hungary. Her research was based on the Glycemic Index diet and exercise for childhood obesity.

Dr. Zsu is known for establishing the Gluten-free diet in Hungary in 2002. Dr. Zsu pioneered in establishing Fitness aerobics in Hungary in 1991. She co-authored the nationally used Aerobics instructor trainer book. Her book teaching gluten-free and glycemic controlled diet was published in Hungary in 2005.

Dr. Zsu spent 4.5 years working with elite athletes as part of her consultancy at the Malaysian National Sport Institute Sport Nutrition Center.

Dr. Zsu spent 5.5 years in Pakistan working on education reform and health, bringing physical fitness and yoga into a lifestyle. She has voluntarily taken part in many social causes as a trainer, educator, and motivational speaker inspiring youth for a healthy, meaningful life in Pakistan.

The 11 years spent in Asia were a milestone in her personal development as well.

Dr. Zsu, has over 25 years of experience and delivers her sessions world-wide inspiring people to transform their fears, experience change by utilizing skills to become self managing individuals to become the entrepreneurs of their own lives.

Dr. Zsu and her enlightening teaching for a happier healthier lifestyle are widely enjoyed on social media as well.

Dr. Zsu's special projects include building healthy balanced youth in universities. She has been taking part in youth programs, training doctors for adding alternative and preventative care to traditional treatment, training school teachers for more effective teaching. Dr. Zsu has been helping corporations build healthy, happy, productive employees.

Assisting athletes (amateur or professional) to optimize their performance is a special interest to Dr. Zsu.

As an Advocate of physical health, she has been leading many public walks, yoga, and exercise sessions.

———∽∾∿∽———

Dr. Zsu's "Recharge your life" residential retreats, and online programs are powerful life changing experiences for anyone ready to break through the past and Live their Lives Alive.

Printed in the United States
By Bookmasters